English Language Teaching as a Second Career

CAL SERIES ON LANGUAGE EDUCATION

Series Editors: **Terrence G. Wiley, M. Beatriz Arias** and **Joy K. Peyton**, *Center for Applied Linguistics, Washington, DC, USA.*

Current and aspiring education professionals need accessible, high-quality, research-based resources on language learning, instruction, and assessment. This series provides such resources, serving to inform teachers' classroom practice, enhance teacher education, and build the background knowledge of undergraduate and graduate students in applied linguistics and other language-related fields.

The books in this series explore a broad range of issues in applied linguistics and language education and are written in a style that is accessible to a broad audience, including those who are new to the field. Each book addresses a topic of relevance to those who are studying or working in the fields of language learning, language instruction, and language assessment, whether in English as a second language or other world languages. Topic areas include approaches to language instruction and assessment; approaches to content instruction and assessment for language learners; professional development for educators working with language learners; principles of second language acquisition for educators; and connections between language policy and educational practice.

Full details of all the books in this series and of all our other publications can be found on http://www.multilingual-matters.com, or by writing to Multilingual Matters, St Nicholas House, 31-34 High Street, Bristol BS1 2AW, UK.

CAL SERIES ON LANGUAGE EDUCATION: 1

English Language Teaching as a Second Career

Sarah J. Shin

MULTILINGUAL MATTERS
Bristol • Blue Ridge Summit

Library of Congress Cataloging in Publication Data
A catalog record for this book is available from the Library of Congress.
Shin, Sarah J., 1970-
English Language Teaching as a Second Career/Sarah J. Shin.
Description: Bristol: Multilingual Matters, [2016] |
Series: CAL Series on Language Education: 1 |
Includes bibliographical references and index.
Identifiers: LCCN 2016031379| ISBN 9781783096930 (hbk : alk. paper) | ISBN
9781783096923 (pbk : alk. paper) | ISBN 9781783096961 (kindle)
Subjects: LCSH: English language–Study and teaching–Foreign speakers. |
English teachers--Training of.
Classification: LCC PE1128.A2 S5123 2016 | DDC 428.0071–dc23 LC record available
at https://lccn.loc.gov/2016031379

British Library Cataloguing in Publication Data
A catalogue entry for this book is available from the British Library.

ISBN-13: 978-1-78309-693-0 (hbk)
ISBN-13: 978-1-78309-692-3 (pbk)

Multilingual Matters
UK: St Nicholas House, 31-34 High Street, Bristol BS1 2AW, UK.
USA: NBN, Blue Ridge Summit, PA, USA.

Website: www.multilingual-matters.com
Twitter: Multi_Ling_Mat
Facebook: https://www.facebook.com/multilingualmatters
Blog: www.channelviewpublications.wordpress.com

The Center for Applied Linguistics is a private, nonprofit organization promoting access, equity and mutual understanding for linguistically and culturally diverse people around the world.

www.cal.org

The policy of Multilingual Matters/Channel View Publications is to use papers that are natural, renewable and recyclable products, made from wood grown in sustainable forests. In the manufacturing process of our books, and to further support our policy, preference is given to printers that have FSC and PEFC Chain of Custody certification. The FSC and/or PEFC logos will appear on those books where full certification has been granted to the printer concerned.

Typeset by Deanta Global Publishing Services Limited.
Printed and bound in the UK by the CPI Books Group Ltd.
Printed and bound in the US by Edwards Brothers Malloy, Inc.

To the memory of
my colleague and friend,
John E. Nelson, 1943-2016

Contents

Acknowledgments

I want to thank Joy Peyton and Jeannie Rennie, my editors at the Center for Applied Linguistics (CAL), for their enthusiastic support of this project and their critical feedback during the various stages of preparing the manuscript. Thanks also go to the external reviewer for Multilingual Matters; to the reviewers at CAL; and to the following people who spent many hours reading and commenting on the book: Liz England, John Nelson, Judah Ronch, Liz Steenrod, G. Richard Tucker and Charlene Uhl. I also wish to thank May Chung for compiling the indexes for this book.

I very gratefully acknowledge my debt to the 30 men and women whose stories are featured in this book. They kindly gave me their time to talk about their experiences and helped me understand the importance of continuous development and lifelong learning.

Finally, my deepest thanks go to my husband, Yoon Ki Shin, who gave so generously of his love and encouragement, and our sons, Isaac and Joshua, who are my biggest cheerleaders.

Sarah J. Shin

Introduction

Dramatic increases in immigrant and refugee populations in the United States have produced a pressing need for well-trained English as a second language (ESL) teachers in both K-12 and adult education. A record 40.4 million foreign-born persons lived in the United States in 2011, an increase of 9.3 million since 2000 (Pew Hispanic Center, 2013). One in five US residents – 63.2 million Americans – age 5 and over speak a language other than English at home (Camarota & Ziegler, 2015). Although school districts and communities throughout the country have been striving to hire sufficient numbers of teachers who understand the language acquisition process and are able to work with students and families from diverse cultural backgrounds, the supply of ESL teachers has not kept up with the demand (Diaz & Mahadevan, 2011). A great number of English learners are being served by teachers who lack training in teaching linguistically diverse students. Nationwide, only about a quarter of the teachers who work with these students have received any substantive preparation in ESL teaching strategies and language acquisition theory (Zeichner, 2003).

Fortunately, the nation's shortage of qualified ESL teachers is being addressed in part by a growing number of well-educated Americans with valuable work experience in other careers. Being civic-minded and passionate about service, these individuals find a sense of purpose and personal fulfillment in helping students learn English. They enjoy connecting with people from different cultures and draw a great deal of satisfaction from their work in K-12 schools, community colleges and literacy organizations. Many of them say that teaching English learners provides them with opportunities for meaningful social interaction and creative thinking, which contribute to their overall mental and physical well-being.

This book tells the stories of adults who pursue opportunities to teach ESL as a second, third or fourth career. Thanks to extraordinary medical and technological advances in the modern world, people are staying healthier and living longer than ever before. With significantly increased life expectancy, adult lives now frequently outlast initial careers, and it has become quite ordinary for people to change jobs multiple times during their lifetime. More and more adults – by choice, necessity or some combination of the two – are working well into what used to be known as the 'retirement' years (Freedman, 2007). Indeed, we are living in an age when traditional retirement increasingly marks the beginning of a new phase of work (Vacarr, 2014). In contemplating a transition to a new career, many Americans say that they are interested in entering professions that help improve the quality of life in their communities, such as education, social services and health care (MetLife Foundation/Civic Ventures, 2005). While money is an important reason for looking for work in later life, what many people want more than anything else is to be able to work with a purpose and be useful to others (AARP, 2014).

As an ESL teacher trainer at a university, I interact with a growing number of people in their forties, fifties and sixties, who find satisfaction in helping students learn English. Having had a wide range of work and life experiences, these individuals infuse considerable insights and diversity into our teacher training program. Some come to our program looking to switch to a full-time career in teaching English to speakers of other languages (TESOL), while others just want to teach part-time. Many are actively involved in tutoring and volunteer work with literacy organizations in their communities, where they interact with immigrants and refugees from around the world. Most find this work to be immensely rewarding and plan to continue doing some form of teaching during their retirement. These individuals are moving beyond midlife careers in search of a calling in the second half of life, and many consider TESOL to be that calling. Given the growing need for well-qualified ESL teachers across the United States on the one hand, and people's desire to do work that makes a social impact on the other, the trend that we see today of adults returning to school to be prepared for a career in TESOL is likely to intensify in the coming years.

However, there is currently no book-length description of what is on the minds of these adults, what they are looking for in their work with English learners and what their experiences are like as they return to school to be trained for a career in education alongside people in their twenties and thirties. Drawing from in-depth interviews and observations of 30 current and former students (ages 45–73) in our Master of Arts (MA) in TESOL program, I provide portraits of these individuals as they develop as teachers. I discuss their job histories and how teaching ESL figures into their life trajectories. I describe the processes they go through to launch their teaching careers, the successes and challenges that they face and the evolving significance of their work in their overall life goals and achievements. I also discuss the value of intergenerational cooperation and the benefits of school staffing models that allow expert and novice teachers across the lifespan to work in collaborative learning communities.

This book has immediate relevance to the following people. For teacher trainers, it shows how adults with a variety of work and life experiences develop as teachers and what can be done to support them during coursework, student teaching and the first years of teaching. For school administrators, it provides insights into how to recruit, supervise and support an increasingly age-diverse teaching workforce. For teachers, education researchers and policymakers interested in education issues, it will foster a greater understanding of individuals entering the teaching profession as a second or third career and of ways to capitalize on the strengths of educators of diverse backgrounds for the benefit of all students.

In the following paragraphs, I describe the organization of the book.

Chapter 1: Wanted: Well-Trained ESL Teachers

The United States is currently undergoing two major demographic shifts. On the one hand, the country is becoming more racially diverse, much of which is driven by immigration and higher birth rates among some groups. On the other hand, the country is getting considerably older as the massive baby boom generation moves into retirement. This introductory chapter describes the growing need for well-trained ESL teachers in both K-12 and adult classrooms and how mid- and late-career adults with work experience in various fields are poised to meet this demand.

Chapter 2: Adulthood II

This chapter reviews the research on life stages. I describe Erik Erikson's (1963) groundbreaking model of eight life stages and explain how it has been developed by other scholars to accommodate extended life expectancy and improved health in today's society. Both Gail Sheehy and Mary Catherine Bateson, for example, break down Erikson's Stage 7 (Adulthood) into two stages: Adulthood I (ages 30–45) and Adulthood II (ages 45–85+). I describe defining features of Adulthood II by using specific examples from my study participants' various life trajectories.

Chapter 3: Cognitive and Social Benefits of Teaching ESL

In this chapter, I discuss what the participants in my study find attractive about teaching ESL. Research shows that the human brain remains capable of growth throughout life and that mental activity keeps the brain healthy. Through specific examples from the participants' teaching episodes, I show how finding new ways to present information to students stimulates the brain and satisfies people's need to be creative. I also discuss the social benefits of connecting with people from different cultures and how this type of shared experience promotes mental and physical health.

Chapter 4: The Role of Prior Work Experiences in Choosing TESOL

Not many children grow up thinking that they will become an ESL teacher (a teacher, yes; but not an ESL teacher). Instead, many ESL teachers discover the profession by volunteering as literacy tutors in the community, helping neighbors who speak little English or working or traveling abroad. Consequently, TESOL attracts professionals with experiences in other fields. In this chapter, I briefly review entry requirements to MA TESOL programs and describe the diverse backgrounds and job histories of the participants in my program. I show how these prior experiences shape their new learning in the teacher training program.

Chapter 5: Constructing a New Professional Identity

Learning to become a teacher is fundamentally a social process that involves increasing participation in a new community of practice and constructing a different professional identity. In this chapter, I examine how the study participants see themselves as teachers of English learners and reconcile the various professional identities they have constructed in other careers. I describe their reactions to ESL materials and concepts covered in the teacher training program and explore the challenges they face in negotiating different communities of practice.

Chapter 6: Learning to Teach

For those who are new to teaching, standing in front of a classroom full of students can be a frightening experience. Learning to teach is a complex, long-term process that requires careful training and reflection. This chapter describes the participants' experiences as classroom teachers and the lessons they have learned from working with their students and colleagues. It describes their strategies for coping with stage fright, tackling classroom management issues and planning and delivering lessons. It addresses questions such as: What do the study participants know about teaching and learning, and what do they learn as they gain classroom experience? What motivates them to teach the way they do? What kind of support do they need in order to overcome difficulties?

Chapter 7: Launching a Career in TESOL

In this chapter, I describe the post-program activities of the study participants. I discuss how they are faring as teachers in K-12 schools, community colleges and literacy organizations, and the level of job satisfaction in each setting. I first describe the state of the ESL job market and the occupational outlook for ESL educators in the United States. I then discuss some of the difficulties that the participants experience related to instruction, complying with educational laws and policies and developing professionally. I also consider the circumstances of those who are biding their time and currently not teaching for a variety of reasons. I discuss what they are doing to keep engaged with TESOL and continue to grow as professionals.

Chapter 8: A Vision for Lifelong Learning

The pattern that we see today of adults returning to school to be trained for a different career will only intensify in the coming years. In this final chapter, I discuss lessons that I have learned from working with a diverse pool of teacher candidates and what teacher training programs and institutions of higher education can do to better meet their needs. I also describe the need for rethinking teacher staffing models at schools to allow expert and novice teachers across the age spectrum to work in teams. I make a case for creating a shared vision for lifelong learning that encourages individuals to experiment with new ideas and different types of work, regardless of where they are in the life cycle.

1 Wanted: Well-Trained ESL Teachers

The United States is in the midst of two profound demographic shifts. On the one hand, the US population is becoming more ethnically and racially diverse, a transformation driven mostly by immigration and higher birth rates among some groups. On the other hand, the US population is getting considerably older as the massive baby boom generation moves into retirement. In this chapter, I explore the social and educational implications of these demographic changes. In particular, I describe the growing need for well-trained English as a second language (ESL) teachers in both K-12 and adult classrooms and how mid- and late-career adults with work experience in various fields are poised to meet this demand.

Increasing Racial and Ethnic Diversity in the United States

The United States is a more ethnically and racially diverse nation today than it was in the past. According to the 2010 US census, the total population of the United States was 309 million, a 9.7% increase from 281 million in 2000. The population increase during the 2000s arose mainly from the so-called *new minorities* – Hispanic and Asian populations – which grew faster than any other major race or ethnic group (Frey, 2011a, 2011b; Humes *et al.*, 2011). Constituting 16.3% of the total US population, Hispanics are now the largest minority group in the United States. The Asian population had the fastest rate of growth – 43.4% – of all ethnic and racial groups between 2000 and 2010.

Population projections forecast that in the coming decades the United States will become a 'plurality nation', where the white population remains the largest single group, but no group is in the majority (US Census Bureau, 2012a). Much of this is fueled by higher birth rates among non-white groups. Although the census projections predict that the country will become a 'majority-minority' nation in 2042, the shift will come much earlier for younger age groups – 2018 for children under age 18 (Frey, 2012a). Already, non-white babies comprise more than half of all births in the United States; as of July 1, 2011, 50.4% of the nation's population under age 1 was non-white (US Census Bureau, 2012b). School systems across the United States are at the forefront of demographic change as the school-age population (ages 5–17) is expected to become majority-minority in 2020 (Frey, 2012a). Figure 1.1 shows

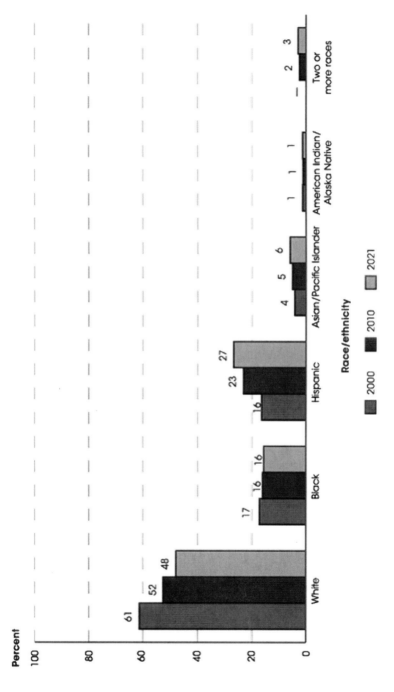

Figure 1.1 Percentage distribution of US public school students enrolled in prekindergarten through 12th grade, by race/ethnicity: Selected years, fall 2000–fall 2021 (Source: US Department of Education, National Center for Education Statistics, Projections of Education Statistics to 2021; Common Core of Data (CCD), 'State Nonfiscal Survey of Public Elementary and Secondary Education', selected years, 2000–2001 through 2010–2011)

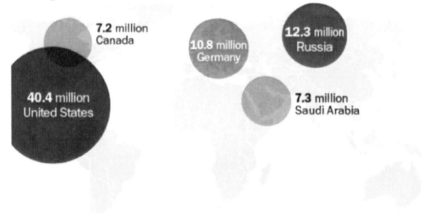

2011 American Community Survey (1% IPUMS) for U.S. and 2010 World Bank estimates for all others.

Figure 1.2 The United States as the #1 destination for immigrants in the world (Reproduced by permission of Pew Research Center)

that white students' share of pre-K through 12th grade enrollment decreased from 61% to 52% between 2000 and 2010 and is projected to drop further, to 48%, by 2021. In contrast, the percentage of Hispanic students increased from 16% to 23% between 2000 and 2010 and is projected to reach 27% by 2021.

In addition to higher birth rates among non-white populations, immigration is contributing to increased racial and ethnic diversity. In 2011, a record 40.4 million foreign-born persons lived in the United States, an increase of 9.3 million since 2000 (Pew Hispanic Center, 2013). Figure 1.2 shows that the United States is the most popular destination in the world for immigrants (Pew Hispanic Center, 2013). However, international migration is also a global phenomenon that contributes to population diversity in most West European countries and other English-speaking countries such as Australia, Canada and New Zealand (Coleman, 2015). Many countries in the developed world have low birth rates, whose effects are partly offset by the addition of immigrants from abroad.

America's Aging Population

The other major demographic change that is taking place in the United States has to do with a rapidly aging population. Over the coming decades, people age 65 and over will make up an increasingly larger share of the US population. The 65+ population is expected to more than double between

2012 and 2060, from 43 million to 92 million (US Census Bureau, 2012a). This means that while one in seven people in the United States today is 65 or over, the 65+ population will represent over one in five US residents by 2060.

Much of the aging of the US population can be attributed to the baby boom generation – the cohort of Americans born between 1946 and 1964. Numbering 77 million, baby boomers today represent a quarter of the total US population (Ewing, 2012). In contrast to an increasingly non-white population of young people in the United States, the baby boom generation is overwhelmingly white. Whites account for 82.2% of all baby boomers; the black population, at 11.6%, is the largest minority group within the baby boom generation (Hellmich, 2010).

The aging of the US population is fueled by increased life expectancy, and lower overall birth rates (National Research Council, 2012). Due to improved nutrition, sanitation and medicine, people are living longer than in the past. Average life expectancy at birth in the United States was only 47.3 years in 1900, but it had increased to 78.5 years by 2009 (Arias, 2014). At the same time, overall birth rates have been falling. American couples are having fewer children and having them later in life than previous generations. Whereas in 1957 – at the height of the post-World War II baby boom – the fertility rate was 3.7 births per woman, the average rate for 2006–2010 was less than the replacement level of 2.1 births per woman (National Research Council, 2012). Replacement level refers to the total fertility rate at which a population exactly replaces itself from one generation to the next, without migration. A natural outcome of fewer children being born and more adults living longer is an aging population.

Population aging is actually a global phenomenon. While there were 810 million people age 60 or over in the world in 2012, accounting for 11.5% of the total world population, the over-60 population is projected to reach 2 billion by 2050, or 22% of the global population (United Nations Population Fund, 2012). Population aging is progressing fastest in developing countries. Whereas two out of three people age 60 or over live in developing countries today, nearly four in five people age 60 or over will live in the developing world by 2050. Recent declines in fertility rates in developing countries such as India, Mexico, Brazil and China are contributing to population aging in these countries and signal slower population growth in the coming years (Jacobsen et al., 2011). While the country with the oldest population in the world today is Japan, where more than 30% of the population is age 60 or over, there will be 64 countries where older people make up more than 30% of their population by 2050 (United Nations Population Fund, 2012).

One of the reasons that the population of the United States is not aging as rapidly as other countries is the infusion of new immigrants.

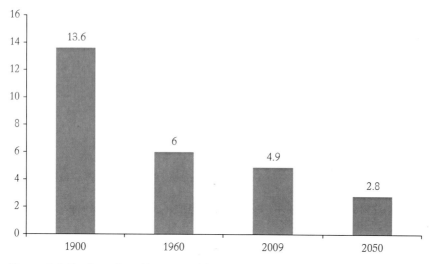

Figure 1.3 Number of working-age adults per retiree, 1900–2050 (Source: Jacobsen *et al.*, 2011)

Because immigrants tend to be younger and have higher rates of labor force participation than native-born Americans, they lessen the impact of aging among the native-born population and workforce (Myers, 2007). However, current levels of immigration and birth rates are not enough to completely offset the effects of baby boomers' retirement (Ewing, 2012). The over-65 population is projected to grow far more quickly than the working-age population over the coming decades, placing an enormous economic burden on taxpayers and workers. As can be seen in Figure 1.3, the elderly support ratio – the number of working-age adults (ages 18–64) per retiree (ages 65 or over) – decreased from 13.6 in 1900 to 6 in 1960, then to 4.9 in 2009; it is expected to drop further to 2.8 by 2050 (Jacobsen *et al.*, 2011). This presents immense challenges to government programs such as Social Security[1] and Medicare[2], which help support older persons. In the coming decades, the United States will face an increasing need for new taxpayers to help fund these programs.

Government expenditures on Social Security and Medicare are projected to reach almost 15% of US gross domestic product (GDP) by 2050, which is up from 4% in 1970 (Ewing, 2012). In addition, driven by the rising cost of health-care services, as well as the sharp increase in the number of people receiving benefits, expenditures for Medicare are projected to exceed those for Social Security by 2030 (Jacobsen *et al.*, 2011).

Researchers generally agree that increases in immigration will improve the financial status of Social Security and Medicare by a modest amount. Although immigration cannot fully compensate for the funding deficits of these government programs, it can make those shortfalls less severe

(Van de Water, 2008). Because supporting the rapidly increasing number of retirees is expected to place immense strain on the budgets of federal and state governments, larger contributions will be required from a new corps of taxpayers, many of whom will be immigrants and their children (Myers, 2007). Today, the children of immigrants are the fastest growing demographic group within the US population. In 2009, nearly a quarter of all people age 17 and under in the United States had at least one immigrant parent (Tienda & Haskins, 2011). As these children come of age and join the workforce, the taxes they pay will help to sustain Social Security and Medicare for decades to come (Ewing, 2012).

However, the contributions that young people make to society are contingent on the opportunities that they receive, mainly through education (Frey, 2012b). Non-white youth in the United States face many barriers to academic and social success. They are more likely than white youth to attend segregated, underfunded schools with high student–teacher ratios, overcrowding and many students living in poverty (Fry, 2008). They are also much more likely than white youth to drop out of high school. Currently, high school dropout rates for Hispanics are more than twice as high as those of non-Hispanic whites (Aud et al., 2013). Failing to finish high school hurts not only the dropouts but also the overall economy. A single high school dropout costs the nation approximately $260,000 in lost earnings, taxes and productivity over the course of his or her lifetime (Amos, 2008). In addition, more than a third of Hispanic and black children live in poverty (Lopez & Velasco, 2011). Childhood poverty is linked with a range of negative adult socioeconomic outcomes, from poor school achievement and behavioral problems to lower earnings in the labor market (Tienda & Haskins, 2011).

Many analysts warn that if the United States does not improve academic performance among Hispanic and black children, the nation will have difficulty producing sufficient numbers of high-paying jobs to generate the tax revenue to maintain a robust retirement safety net (Brownstein, 2010). Helping young people advance into middle-class jobs through better educational opportunities is directly linked to the social and economic well-being of future retirees. It is a necessary investment in a society where the ratio of senior citizens to working-age adults continues to increase. Such investment requires strengthening early education, improving language education for young people and reducing financial and non-financial barriers to college (Tienda & Haskins, 2011). However, public spending greatly favors the older population over children; the US federal government currently spends $7 per elderly person for every $1 it spends per child (Isaacs, 2009). The rapid growth in public spending on retirement and health benefits for the elderly will place an increasingly heavy tax burden on today's children, who will grow up to be working-age adults in the coming decades.

Generational Gap between the Gray and the Brown

Some observers point out that a significant generational gap is emerging between a heavily non-white population of young people and an overwhelmingly white population of older people in the United States (Frey, 2012b). In a *National Journal* cover story, Ronald Brownstein (2010) discusses the contrast in attitudes and desires between the mostly white older generation and the increasingly non-white younger population, or, what he calls 'the gray' and 'the brown'. He argues that the two groups are 'on a collision course that could rattle American politics for decades'. Comparing these two groups to tectonic plates, he notes that the two 'slow-moving, but irreversible forces may generate enormous turbulence as they grind against each other in the years ahead'. Specifically, Brownstein refers to a growing tension between an older population that is increasingly resistant to taxes and public spending, and a younger population that views government education, health and social welfare programs as their avenues to upward mobility.

Significant racial differences by age exist in many parts of the United States, especially in states with growing Hispanic populations such as Arizona, Nevada, California, Texas, New Mexico and Florida (Frey, 2011a). Whereas whites compose a majority of the senior population in every state except Hawaii, non-whites compose a majority of the youth population in seven states and at least one-third of young people in 17 more (Brownstein, 2010). The largest race–age gap is found in Arizona, where less than 40% of the state's children are white, compared with more than 80% of its seniors (Frey *et al.*, 2011).

There are clear generational gaps in Americans' attitudes toward immigration. While older people are more likely to voice a negative opinion about immigrants, young people are more likely to emphasize the benefits of new immigrants for American society (Cave, 2010). A survey conducted by the Pew Research Center found that only 23% of baby boomers regard the country's growing population of immigrants as a change for the better, whereas 43% saw it as a change for the worse (Pew Research Center, 2011). Almost half of the baby boomers surveyed thought that the growing number of newcomers from other countries represented a threat to traditional US customs and values. In contrast, the survey found that young people were much more favorably disposed toward newcomers. Only 27% of the millennial generation (defined in this study as people born between 1981 and 1993) felt that newcomers threaten traditional American customs and values; more than two-thirds of the millennials believed that immigrants strengthen American society.

The Pew Research Center survey also found that there are deep generational divides in Americans' opinions about government. More baby boomers (54%) prefer a smaller government that provides fewer social services than a bigger government that provides more services (35%), while millennials prefer a bigger government (56%) over a smaller government (35%). That baby boomers tend to favor a smaller government with fewer services is intriguing, given that they grew up benefiting from a wide range of government programs. Baby boomers were born to parents whose upward mobility was boosted by far-reaching public programs such as the GI Bill, which provides educational assistance to servicemen, veterans and their dependents (Frey, 2012b). In fact, baby boomers were more supportive of big government in their twenties and thirties (Pew Research Center, 2011). In recent years, however, more baby boomers have come to call themselves conservatives and have become critical of government performance. About three-quarters of baby boomers say that when something is run by the government, it is usually inefficient and wasteful (Pew Research Center, 2011).

In terms of how public money is spent, younger people tend to support funding for schools, affordable housing and health care for their children, while the older population tends to favor maintaining income during retirement and protecting programs for seniors. These contrasting attitudes in turn surface in sharp divisions between political candidates and parties that advocate for different amounts of government support for programs helping the young, such as education or affordable housing, and those benefiting seniors, such as Social Security or Medicare (Brownstein, 2010). Debates on how to close budget deficits often fall along racial boundaries, which are increasingly delineated by age. Whereas Republican legislators and governors – most of whom rely primarily on the votes of older white people – prefer to close budget gaps mainly by cutting spending, Democrats – who rely more heavily on the votes of minorities – typically prefer tax increases (Brownstein, 2010).

What explains the negative attitudes of many baby boomers toward immigrants? Part of the reason why baby boomers are not very accepting of the increasing racial diversity in the United States is that they grew up in an era when the country was much more homogeneous. From 1946 to 1964, the share of immigrants was at its lowest level in the 20th century, and most of the immigrants were white Europeans (Frey, 2012b). Baby boomers generally had minimal involvement with people from other countries and grew up in largely white suburbs or segregated neighborhoods. In contrast, today's young people are living in a much more multiracial country and have more opportunities to interact with immigrants and minority populations through college or by moving into urban areas (Cave, 2010).

Although older Americans may feel uneasy about the changing face of America, their future is intimately tied to the success of the younger, multiethnic population. In his book, *Immigrants and Boomers: Forging a New Social Contract for the Future of America*, demographer Dowell Myers (2007) uses the example of California to make a case for investing in the education and integration of immigrants into American society. He explains that the surge in immigration after the passage of the Immigration and Naturalization Act of 1965 was concentrated at first in California, where the foreign-born share of the population jumped from 8.8% to 21.7% between 1970 and 1990 before beginning to grow more slowly. Meanwhile, the foreign-born share of the rest of the United States remained at 7.9% in 1990, only accelerating thereafter. Myers thus believes that California provides a window on the future of the United States by showing the changes experienced by long-settled immigrants and their fellow citizens. Myers points out that in California today, the central question in the immigration debate has shifted from blocking illegal immigration and controlling the border – issues that are currently at the forefront of the national immigration debate – to questions such as 'What is to be done about the challenges posed by the state's increasingly large population of settled immigrants? Is California doomed to rising poverty, deskilling of its workforce, and social decline?' (Myers, 2007: 4).

Myers states that in California, a substantial electoral gap has opened up as the state's demographic change has raced ahead of political participation. Although the white population has fallen below 45% of California's residents, it retains a two-thirds majority at the polls. He predicts that this electoral imbalance will continue for many years, at least until 2024 or 2031. He worries that the outgoing majority is unlikely to vote for future-oriented investments such as education and infrastructure that would require higher taxes today if they do not feel that they are benefiting personally from these investments. He believes that a majority of today's voters do not recognize the urgent need to invest in the next generation, even though there are serious doubts about the readiness of the younger generation to take the place of outgoing white workers in a knowledge-based economy. He argues:

> We must immediately begin to address the needs of this younger generation, not only for its own sake, or to avoid conflict, but because of self-interest rightly understood by the older generation. If we invest in the younger generation now, there is a substantial added payoff promised to the older generation, as well as to the state of California and the whole of the nation. That payoff will come in the form of future skilled workers to replace the retirees, new middle-class taxpayers to support retirement benefits and other services, and future home buyers who can afford to pay a good price to seniors. This payoff will be a response to a collective need, and investing for that payoff is a collective responsibility. (Myers, 2007: 195)

What does investing in the younger generation look like? What challenges do children from immigrant families face, and what can be done to help them overcome barriers to success?

Challenges Facing Children From Immigrant Families

Many children from immigrant families experience serious problems with schooling, physical and mental health and poverty (Tienda & Haskins, 2011). On most social indicators, children of immigrant parents fare significantly worse than children of non-immigrant parents. For instance, children in immigrant families are much more likely to be poor than children in native-born families (Hernandez, 2004). Poverty often translates to lack of access to adequate nutrition, health care and education resources, which can lead to negative health and school outcomes. Because poverty affects a greater proportion of non-white children, it accentuates racial disparities in children's health (Edelman & Jones, 2004). In addition, children of immigrant families are far more likely than children of US-born families to have parents who have not graduated from high school (Shields & Behrman, 2004). Poorly educated parents are less able to help their children with their schoolwork and less able to negotiate educational and other institutions to promote their children's academic success.

Language is another challenge facing immigrant children. More than a quarter of children of immigrants live in homes where no one over the age of 14 has a strong command of the English language (Shields & Behrman, 2004). If no one in the home speaks English well, the family is likely to experience problems finding well-paying jobs and accessing health care and other social services. In fact, immigrants are overrepresented among workers who are paid the least and are more likely than US-born workers to have only part-time work with no benefits (Shields & Behrman, 2004). In recent decades, the shift in the American economy from manufacturing to services and technology has resulted in a larger wage gap between those with high levels of education and skills and those without (Nightingale & Fix, 2004). While immigrants in earlier times could labor on farms, work in factories and build railroads without speaking much English, today's knowledge-based economy requires English ability for all but the lowest-paying jobs. English acquisition is critical to the social and economic success of new immigrants as well as for their participation in civic life. However, a Pew Hispanic Center report shows that 55% of immigrants eligible to naturalize and 67% of immigrants soon to be eligible have limited English proficiency (Passel, 2007).

In addition, racism and negative societal attitudes toward minorities are a significant barrier to immigrant children's success. Schools serving primarily minority children tend to have fewer resources, lower teacher expectations and condescending attitudes toward students of non-mainstream backgrounds. When students who speak languages other than English enter school, they are often labeled as deficient in the language of school (e.g. 'limited English proficient') and are identified for what they cannot do rather than what they can, which leads to feelings of disempowerment and academic failure. Schools, as a dominant group institution, often require students from non-dominant language and cultural backgrounds to abandon their cultural identity and language as a necessary condition for success in the mainstream society (Cummins, 2000). This process of cultural assimilation can have negative consequences for children's health and well-being, especially among immigrant families with few economic resources. Although children from immigrant backgrounds may enter school with positive attitudes toward education, many become disillusioned by adolescence, and their attitudes toward teachers and academic achievement can turn negative, leading to academic failure and risky social behaviors (Coll & Szalacha, 2004).

About 10% of the school-age population in the United States – 4.7 million students from age 5 through 17 – are not fully proficient in English (Aud *et al.*, 2013). These students are most at risk for academic failure; on practically every educational measure, English learners perform at lower levels than almost any other category of students (Gándara & Hopkins, 2010). Figures 1.4 and 1.5 show the average National Assessment of Educational Progress (NAEP) reading scores for fourth- and eighth-grade students, respectively. Notice how the scores of English learners are consistently and significantly lower than those of other students in all assessment years between 2002 and 2011.

Many English learners are fluent in the conversational English needed for everyday interaction but have considerable difficulty in navigating the dense, decontextualized language of academic English (Scarcella, 2002). While many make fairly rapid progress from beginning to intermediate levels of proficiency in English, few progress beyond the intermediate level to achieve the high levels of English literacy that are required to meet grade-level standards in content areas (August & Shanahan, 2006).

Aside from lack of English and school-based literacy skills, numerous non-linguistic factors contribute to the poor academic performance of English learners. A Pew Hispanic Center analysis of the academic performance of English learners in five states that educate 70% of the nation's English learners (Arizona, California, Florida, New York and Texas) shows that these students tend to go to schools that have low standardized test scores (Fry, 2008). The report explains that these low levels of academic performance are not solely attributable to poor achievement by English learners. These same schools report poor achievement by other groups as well and have a set of characteristics associated with poor school performance, such as high student–teacher ratios, overcrowding and many students living in poverty. The report found that when English learners are not isolated in these low-achieving schools, the gap in test score results is considerably narrower. It also found that in each of the five states, about 90% of the English learners who took the state assessments were educated in public schools in which English learners make up either a majority or a substantial minority of the

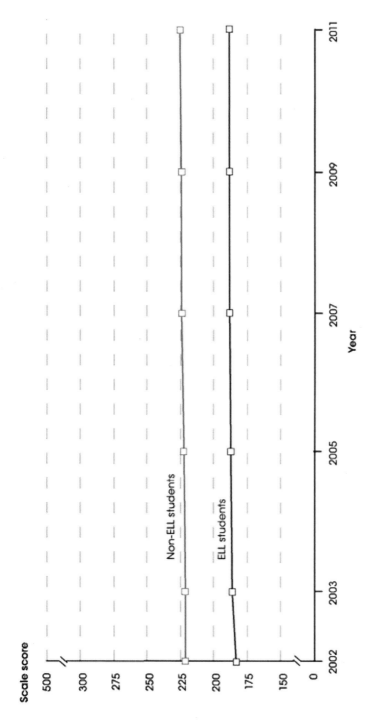

Figure 1.4 Average reading scores of fourth-grade students, by English language learner (ELL) status: Selected years, 2002–2011 (Source: US Department of Education, National Center for Education Statistics, National Assessment of Educational Progress (NAEP), selected years, 2002–2011 Reading Assessments, NAEP Data Explorer)

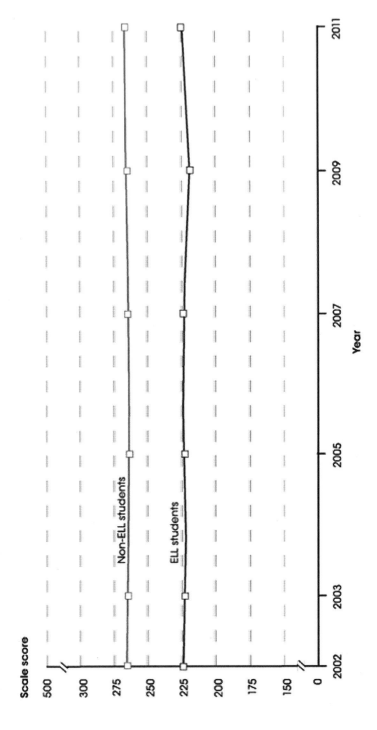

Figure 1.5 Average reading scores of eighth-grade students, by English language learner (ELL) status: Selected years, 2002–2011 (Source: US Department of Education, National Center for Education Statistics, National Assessment of Educational Progress (NAEP), selected years, 2002–2011 Reading Assessments, NAEP Data Explorer)

student population. In these schools, English learners have limited access to native English input and must learn English from other English learners.

What Should Be Done to Help English Learners Succeed?

Although there are no quick, easy solutions to the problem of poor academic performance, what schools can do is find ways to end the isolation of English learners and help them develop academic English. Teachers need to know the specific linguistic challenges faced by English learners in different subject matter classes, including textbook difficulty, the demands made by classroom interactions and the characteristics of the language challenges present in standardized tests (Valdés, 2001). Teachers need to be trained to teach the structural aspects of academic English explicitly to students, and the students need to concentrate on language form, in addition to engaging in communicative language use (Shin, 2013).

More broadly, schools should view English learners as emergent bilinguals, with the potential to succeed academically and socially, and not as failed attempts at assimilation into mainstream culture (Bartlett & García, 2011). All students should be encouraged to become bilingual. English learners should be supported to maintain their native languages while learning English, and native English speakers should be supported to learn a language other than English well enough to develop functional competence. Schools serving English learners must work simultaneously on student assessments, school structures and leadership, the professional development of teachers, the integration of language and content instruction and parent and family involvement (Calderón *et al.*, 2011). The students' ethnic communities should be encouraged to participate as partners in their education and to contribute the 'funds of knowledge' that exist in their communities to this educational partnership (González *et al.*, 2005).

Furthermore, the developmental needs of English learners, especially those who are at greatest risk of failure, should be addressed. While participation in preschool and early education programs has been shown to have substantial short-term and long-term benefits, children from immigrant families have lower rates of participation in these programs than other children (Brandon, 2004). Many immigrant families face structural barriers such as affordability, availability and access, as well as language barriers and bureaucratic complexity, which prevent them from taking advantage of early education programs (Karoly & Gonzalez, 2011). Federal, state and local education agencies should reduce these barriers and strengthen outreach efforts to encourage more children of immigrants to attend preschool and early education programs (Shields & Behrman, 2004).

Obstacles to obtaining post-secondary education should also be reduced. The federal DREAM Act (Development, Relief and Education for Alien Minors Act), which has been introduced numerous times in Congress but never enacted, would make post-secondary education or military service a viable path toward citizenship for undocumented children of immigrants. As of February 2014, 15 states had passed their own versions of the DREAM Act, permitting undocumented immigrant students to become eligible for in-state tuition if they graduate from state high schools, have two to three years of residence in the state and apply to a state college or university (Morse, 2014). However, students from immigrant families often lack information about how to finance college costs and are less likely than other students to apply for student loans (Zarate & Pachon, 2006). Because more immigrant students attend community colleges than any other type of post-secondary institution, community colleges in particular could offer outreach programs that help students navigate the financial aid system (Teranishi et al., 2011). In addition, hiring additional qualified ESL instructors would enhance instructional offerings at post-secondary institutions and help prepare immigrant students for academic work in different disciplines.

To ensure English learners' access to high-quality English language programs, appropriations for ESL infrastructure by local and state governments should be increased (Chrisman & Crandall, 2007). Free or low-cost ESL classes usually fill up quickly and often have long waiting lists. In 2009, only 921,548 of the 38.5 million foreign-born residents in the United States were enrolled in federally funded, state-administered ESL programs (US Department of Education, Office of Vocational and Adult Education, 2011). In addition to federally funded programs, ESL instruction is offered by volunteer and faith-based organizations, museums, libraries and other community centers, private language schools and academic institutions (Center for Applied Linguistics, 2010). However, even with these programs, the demand for low-cost ESL classes far outstrips supply. Many immigrants wait months or even years to enroll in government-financed English classes, which are often overcrowded and lack textbooks (Santos, 2007). Thus, greater support for ESL learners is needed from local, state and federal agencies as well as community organizations. Strengthening ESL education at both pre-K-12 and adult levels is a necessary investment in a society that is increasingly dependent on the success of students from immigrant families.

Toward a Future of Intergenerational Cooperation

The popular press often portrays the older generation as a group of self-centered, self-serving people who use their votes to push their own interest to the forefront with little regard for future generations. For example, in a *Newsweek* article titled, 'How We Need to Learn to Say No to the Elderly', David Frum (2012) criticizes those who 'unabashedly vote their interests as a demographic group... shift[ing] the costs of an aging society onto other groups'. He complains that 'in politics, as in economics... it is the old who are too often driving any way they like—and the young who are scrambling to get out of the way'. Seniors are depicted as single-handedly offloading the burden of financing entitlement programs such as Social Security and Medicare on the young while they spend several decades of their retirement on government-subsidized vacations. The younger generation, meanwhile, struggles to make ends meet with greatly diminished economic resources and staggering government debt.

However, when we look more closely at what many Americans do at individual and community levels, among them we see a strong set of adults who are ready to do more than spend decades of leisure-oriented retirement. They are a highly educated group actively engaged in purpose-driven work in their communities. The idealism that many boomers grew up with is very much alive in their desire to volunteer in their communities and make a positive contribution to society. In fact, baby boomers volunteer today at higher rates than previous generations did at around the same age (Corporation for National and Community Service, 2007). In addition, whether for financial need or for enjoyment, most boomers say that they plan on working past the traditional retirement age of 65. According to an AARP survey, 7 in 10 experienced workers aged 45–74 reported that they plan to work during retirement, including 29% who expect to work part-time for enjoyment and 23% who expect to work part-time for the income (AARP, 2014). The AARP survey explains that while money is certainly an important reason for looking for work, what many people want is to be able to work with a purpose and to remain productive and useful.

In his book, *Encore: Finding Work That Matters in the Second Half of Life*, Marc Freedman (2007) points out that throughout the United States, a leading edge of baby boomers is breaking fresh ground in the search for purpose and contribution in the second half of life. He explains that this group recognizes that adult lives now frequently outlast initial careers and is taking this emerging reality to redefine retirement:

> Instead of the freedom *from* work, they are searching for the freedom *to* work; instead of saving for a 'secure retirement', they are underwriting an encore career. Instead of accepting the notion of a career as an arc that rises in youth, peaks in midlife, and declines into retirement, they are charting a new trajectory—one that for many will reach its apex of meaning and impact when others in past generations headed for the sidelines. (Freedman, 2007: 12)

Freedman calls attention to the fact that this group of Americans is especially interested in careers of service. A MetLife Foundation/Civic Ventures (2005) survey of 1000 adults aged 50–70 found that half of the respondents were interested in taking jobs to help improve the quality of life in their communities. Of those aged 50–59, 60% said it is important that work in retirement serve the community and those in need. The survey found that

- 78% of those who may work in retirement are interested in working to help the poor, the elderly and other people in need.
- 56% are interested in dealing with health issues, whether working in a hospital or with an organization fighting a particular disease.
- 55% are interested in a teaching or other educational position.
- 45% are interested in working in a youth program.

These findings highlight the broad interest among Americans in giving back to their communities and contradict the self-absorbed, self-serving image of the elderly portrayed in the media. Millions of people are already volunteering their talents and time to address society's most pressing problems.

Likewise, this book makes a case for taking a multi-age perspective when thinking about society, social advancement and work. Novelli and Goyer (2004) argue that the United States must respond to growing racial diversity and aging in its population through a paradigm of intergenerational cooperation. They believe that it is a mistake to view the graying and browning of the American population as a precursor to inevitable generational and cultural conflict. Rather, they point out that the American society has the capacity to invest in children and support older persons at the same time. Many important social issues are shared across generations, and adults play a critical role in caring for and mentoring children. Thus, rather than setting the older generation in opposition to the young as if these two groups have nothing to do with one another, they propose incorporating a life cycle perspective that views today's children as tomorrow's parents, and today's parents as tomorrow's grandparents (I explore the human life cycle in greater detail in Chapter 2). Considered in this way, investing in children's health makes sense, as health and well-being in later life are linked to good nutrition and healthy habits formed earlier. Poverty is also a cross-generational issue, since over half of those who live in poverty in the United States are either under 18 or over 65, and more than 2.4 million grandparents are responsible for the basic needs of grandchildren living with them, though 20% of these grandparents live in poverty (Novelli & Goyer, 2004). All generations stand to gain from policies and services that take an intergenerational approach.

Baby Boomers as ESL Teachers: A Win–Win Situation

Given the sweeping demographic shifts, the education and integration of immigrants into American society is an urgent social issue that requires an intergenerational approach. We have seen in this chapter that had it not been for immigration, the negative impact of an aging population on the US economy would be more pronounced. That people from all over the world want to live and work in the United States constitutes a considerable advantage and potential resource for the nation. However, how the United States works with all students will largely determine whether it stays globally competitive over the coming decades. Today's youth represent tomorrow's workforce, who will not only pay the payroll taxes that will be required to fund Social Security and Medicare benefits for the baby boomers, but also serve as the backbone of an increasingly knowledge-based economy. Baby boomers have a critical role to play in how well these young people are prepared to enter the workforce.

Specifically, my argument in this book is that baby boomers – with their high levels of education and passion for careers in service – make ideal ESL teachers, and that they should be supported to develop as professionals. The participants in my study are at the leading edge of society, forging a constructive path for the future of America. While racial and cultural differences are often discussed as challenges and impediments to forming cross-generational partnerships, cultural diversity is what draws these adults to their work with English learners. They are thrilled to learn about students' lives in their home countries and sympathize with their often arduous journey to the United States. They are drawn to their students' respect for the elderly. They find enormous satisfaction in helping people in need and are gratified to learn that their service is wanted and appreciated.

There is a great deal of give and take between the teachers and their students in the ESL classroom. Many teachers find a sense of purpose and personal fulfillment in providing students with the kind of help that they desperately need. In addition to the intellectual stimulation of preparing and teaching lessons, the teachers also benefit socially from interacting with people from different backgrounds and develop a greater understanding of other cultures. The students, in turn, get from their teachers practical support for navigating life in the United States, a native English-speaking model and language coach, and an advocate. In many ways, the ESL classroom represents a microcosm of the kind of society that promotes mutual understanding rather than cultural clashes, and fosters cross-generational dialogue and cooperation that help improve the quality of life for everyone in the community. A beautiful synergy is created when boomers and their students come together and learn from one another.

Teaching and advocating for English learners is very much aligned with the civic-minded spirit of many boomers who want to make a lasting contribution to their communities. As we saw earlier in this chapter, the need for English classes for both adults and children is enormous. At the same time, the boomers' desire to work with purpose, direction and a sense of fulfillment is also very significant. Given this, boomers serving as teachers of English learners is a win–win for both groups. Each has something to offer the other, and while the immediate goals of the two groups may be different, this kind of intergenerational cooperation could be a catalyst for social change, directly addressing one of the most urgent problems facing society.

A Note About the Methodology

In the following chapters, I show what is on the minds of the adults who work with English learners and what their experiences are like as they enter the field of teaching. Drawing from the interviews of 30 students in the Master of Arts in Teaching English to Speakers of Other Languages (MA TESOL) program at the University of Maryland Baltimore County, I provide portraits of these individuals as they develop as teachers. The 30 participants are between 45 and 73 years of age and have worked in a variety of jobs in different fields, from corporate to nonprofit sectors, from salaried positions to self-owned businesses, from blue-collar to white-collar jobs, from part-time to full-time work (the educational backgrounds and job histories of the participants are discussed in detail in Chapter 4). In selecting the participants, I sought to achieve a sample that reflected a broad range of experiences and viewpoints. To understand how people develop both during and after teacher preparation, I interviewed 14 participants who were taking courses in the TESOL program and 16 who had graduated from the program. All 30 participants have taken one or more courses that I teach in the TESOL program.

To generate the work histories and perspectives of the participants, I conducted in-depth, semi-structured interviews adapting an expressive autobiographical interview approach (Wallace, 2001). The expressive autobiographical interview blends an autobiography technique with a structured expressive interview method to draw out the participant's view of reality as it relates to a desired topic. The interviewer develops questions around the topic and directs these questions to the participants during crucial points of the participant's narrative account. The questions were related to each person's reasons for teaching ESL, educational background and work history, experiences in the TESOL program and development of teaching skills. The individual interviews lasted between 30 minutes and 2 hours and were audio-recorded and transcribed. In addition to the 30 individual interviews, I conducted follow-up interviews with 3 participants and observed their classroom teaching.

The interview transcripts were reviewed, coded and thematically analyzed following grounded theory protocol (Glaser, 2002). In the analysis, descriptive labels were given to topics emerging from the data, and related concepts thus obtained were classified into categories through constant comparison of data (Corbin & Strauss, 2008). From this analysis, several categories presented themselves: (a) motivations for choosing TESOL, (b) TESOL as a new community of practice, (c) classroom experiences and

(d) continuing personal and professional development. These categories were then related to what the participants hoped to accomplish in their new careers and interpreted through the conceptual lenses of teacher learning and development.

Throughout the book, I explore the factors shaping the participants' view of themselves and attitudes toward their work with English learners. I also examine how they position themselves relative to other members of the ESL teaching community and how their instructional decisions are linked to their personal and professional identities. In this analysis, statements that they made about teaching ESL – using descriptors such as *rewarding, exciting, grounding* and *a ton of work* and phrases such as 'in order to make the class fun, you really have to be sensitive to where people are coming from' – provided discursive resources for making sense of their decisions and actions. These statements reveal not only what they choose to do but also how they explain these decisions and their goals of making a positive impact in the classroom and beyond.

Notes

(1) Social Security is a federal insurance program in the United States that provides benefits to retired people and those who are unemployed or disabled.
(2) Medicare is a federal health insurance program in the United States for people who are 65 or older and certain younger people with disabilities.

2   Adulthood II

Consider the following statistics: A 45-year-old American woman who remains free of heart disease and cancer can expect to see her 92nd birthday; a 45-year-old man in similar condition, his 88th birthday (Arias, 2014; Mensah & Brown, 2007). This means that today's 45-year-olds who maintain reasonably good health can look forward to living another half of their lives. Throughout much of human history, 40 was regarded as a fairly ripe old age. Life expectancy at birth in the United States in 1880 was only 39.4 years (Jaminet & Jaminet, 2012). But with extraordinary advances in biomedicine in the last century, longevity has become a global reality. A profound shift has taken place in the human condition, and a new developmental stage – a second stage of adulthood – has been added to the life cycle (Bateson, 2010). 'Imagine the day you turn 45 as the infancy of another life', writes Gail Sheehy (1995), author of *New Passages: Mapping Your Life Across Time*. Millions of people in their forties, fifties and sixties today, Sheehy notes, are able to make dramatic changes in their lives and habits, and look forward to living decades more in relatively good health. She asserts that the traditional boundaries of adulthood, beginning at 21 and ending at 65, are completely out of date and in need of revision.

Many contemporary scholars of adult development agree. They point out that the stage between the end of young adulthood and the beginning of true old age – which these days amounts to a period that can last a half century – is a time for new possibilities and discoveries, when people's personalities and brains are still pliable and open to change (Cohen, 2005). The decades after age 45 are motivating more and more people to 'stretch their independence, learn new skills, return to school, plunge into new careers, rediscover the creativity and adventurousness of their youths, and, at last, to listen to their own needs' (Sheehy, 1995: 140). No longer constrained by the everyday responsibilities of childrearing, full-time jobs and career building, and boosted by the luxuries of better health and longevity, millions of men and women are embracing the second stage of their adulthood to seek out new opportunities for personal and professional growth. In this chapter, I show how the participants in my study experience their second adulthood and how a career in TESOL fits into their overall life goals.

I first review Erik Erikson's (1963) theory of psychosocial development, which has become the basis for many subsequent studies on aging. Erikson was one of the first scholars to chart the sequence of life stages from birth to death and to describe adult development as an opportunity for growth rather than an inevitable decline in physical and mental capacity. He was also among the first developmental psychologists to recognize that human learning and identities are not developed in a vacuum but are shaped by the cultural and historical settings in which people live. He argued that people born during different historical periods will have different world views, and the experiences of one generation may not be the same as those of another. Despite the groundbreaking nature of his work, however, Erikson gave only limited attention to older age. I discuss how the study of adulthood has further developed through the contributions of contemporary scholars such as Gail Sheehy, Mary Catherine Bateson and Gene Cohen, and how human development is increasingly viewed as a lifelong process. I describe the defining features of later adulthood by way of the experiences and perceptions of the participants in my study and show how they are deriving personal fulfillment through their work with people who are learning English as a second language.

Erikson's Eight Stages of Psychosocial Development

Erikson (1963) outlined eight stages of psychosocial development across the human lifespan and characterized each stage in terms of an issue or crisis that must be resolved (see Table 2.1). He argued that the way in which each developmental crisis is resolved will determine whether the individual will experience happiness or discontent, and that each stage builds on the successful resolution of challenges faced by the individual in preceding stages. In Erikson's Stage 1, newborn babies are utterly dependent on their parents or caregivers to provide for their most basic needs - food, comfort and affection. If infants receive consistent and responsive care, they will develop a sense of trust, which they will carry to other relationships in the future. But if the care is inconsistent or harsh, they will develop a sense of mistrust, anxiety and insecurity. Erikson argued that success in Stage 1 leads to the virtue (or strength) of hope. By developing trust, infants can

Table 2.1 Erikson's eight stages of psychosocial development

Stage	Psychosocial crisis	Basic virtue
1. Infancy	Basic trust vs. basic mistrust	Hope
2. Early childhood	Autonomy vs. shame, doubt	Will
3. Play age	Initiative vs. guilt	Purpose
4. School age	Industry vs. inferiority	Competence
5. Adolescence	Identity vs. role confusion	Fidelity
6. Young adulthood	Intimacy vs. isolation	Love
7. Adulthood	Generativity vs. stagnation	Care
8. Mature age	Ego integrity vs. despair	Wisdom

hope that as new crises arise in the future, they can count on the support of other people.

Once children reach the toddler stage (Stage 2), they strive for autonomy as they learn to walk, talk, feed themselves and use the toilet. If caregivers are encouraging and reassuring of the children's initiative to do things for themselves during this stage, they will develop confidence in their ability to survive in the world. Success in Stage 2 will lead to the strength of will. If however, caregivers are overprotective or disapproving of children's acts of independence, they may begin to feel ashamed of their behavior and doubt their ability to manage in the world on their own terms.

In Stage 3, children become more assertive and independent as their motor skills develop. Play is a central aspect of Stage 3, as it provides children with regular opportunities to interact socially with others and take initiative in creating games. If, however, children's actions are discouraged through criticism or excessive parental control, they may develop a sense of guilt. It is important for parents to be encouraging of children's initiatives but consistent in discipline so that they can learn to accept, without a sense of guilt, that certain things are not allowed. Successful resolution of the challenges in Stage 3 will lead to strength of purpose.

In Stage 4, school is the most important event as children learn to read and write, do mathematics and acquire specific skills that are valued by society. It is essential for children at this stage to discover the joys of being productive, which leads to competence; otherwise they will develop a sense of inferiority.

In Stage 5, adolescence, the main challenge is identity versus role confusion. It is during this stage that adolescents will examine their identity and try to find out who they are. To successfully resolve the conflict of identity, Erikson suggests that adolescents must integrate the healthy resolution of all earlier conflicts - trust, autonomy, fidelity and industry.

In Stage 6, young adults explore love relationships that may lead to longer-term commitments. Successful completion of this stage can lead to intimacy and a sense of security in a relationship. On the other hand, individuals who avoid intimacy and fear commitment may feel isolated, lonely and depressed.

Stage 7, adulthood, is the main focus of this book. According to Erikson, the most important challenge of adulthood is 'generativity', which refers to one's ability to look outside oneself and contribute to caring for others through such activities as parenting, work and service to the community. If this stage is not resolved productively, people will experience 'stagnation' and 'often begin to indulge themselves as if they were their one and only child' (Erikson, 1963: 267). This self-indulgence inhibits people's continuous development in the later stages of their lives and leads to feelings of emptiness.

The life course concludes with mature age (Stage 8), a time for reflecting on one's life and contemplating one's accomplishments. Erikson contends that individuals who accept responsibility for their own lives and have a sense of fulfillment can accept the inevitability of death with a sense of integrity and dignity. Whereas success at Stage 8 will lead to the strength of wisdom, individuals who see their lives as unproductive and are unable to achieve satisfaction will despair and fear death.

Psychosocial Development in Adulthood

Erikson argued that people pass through each of the eight stages one at a time, one after another, and that the challenges of each stage must be mastered before one can move to the next stage. But Gene Cohen, one of Erikson's former students and a renowned scholar on aging, believes that it is a mistake to view development as a straight-line process, in which failure to succeed at one developmental step necessarily blocks progress in other developmental stages. Cohen (2005) contends that the human brain is much more flexible and adaptable than Erikson's theory suggests and argues that a theoretical framework that does not require a lockstep view of human development is necessary to understand how older adults continue to grow and develop. Many other contemporary scholars of aging agree with Cohen. Mary Catherine Bateson argues that the dangers that Erikson described for Stages 5, 6 and 7 – role confusion, isolation and stagnation – are familiar problems in later life and that the resolutions in each of these stages need to be *reworked* as aging progresses. She maintains that longevity creates the need for the growth involved in readdressing these issues, especially the continuous re-examination and reaffirmation of identity. For Bateson (2010: 90), the new issue posed for identity in old age is: Am I *still* the person I have spent a lifetime becoming, and do I still want to be that person? How can I affirm that identity and yet accept the knowledge that I will die?

Figure 2.1 summarizes how adult life stages are theorized by several prominent scholars of aging. Notice that the last two stages in Erikson's model – Adulthood and Mature Age – are divided into smaller segments by Bateson, Sheehy and Cohen. Both Bateson (2010) and Sheehy (1995) divide Erikson's Stage 7 (Adulthood) into two stages: Adulthood I (ages 30–45) and Adulthood II (ages 45–85+). Sheehy further breaks down Adulthood II into Age of Mastery (ages 45–64), when people become more certain about the values they stand for and less concerned about performing and pleasing others, and Age of Integrity (ages 65–85+), when all that has been lived and learned comes together to provide for a time of grace and generosity. Cohen conceptualizes adulthood somewhat differently as four overlapping phases: Midlife reevaluation (ages 40–65), Liberation (from the late fifties into the seventies), Summing up (from the late sixties through the eighties), and Encore (ages 80+). In the following, I discuss these more recent frameworks on adult development with examples from interviews of the participants in my study.

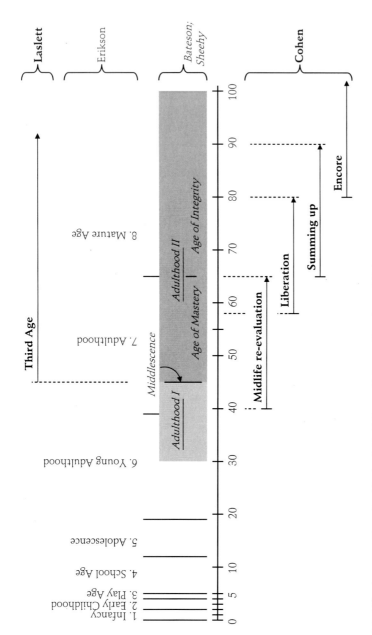

Figure 2.1 Life stages, as theorized by Laslett, Erikson, Bateson, Sheehy and Cohen
(Source: Sarah J. Shin)

Adulthood II

Adulthood I for most people is the primary childrearing and career building period. It is a busy time of work and parenting responsibilities, marked by major life events such as first job, marriage, childbirth and so on. Then, as people pass 45 or so, they transition into another adult lifetime – 30, 40, even 50 years of Adulthood II. According to Sheehy (1995), Adulthood II does not mean a period of decline and decrepitude but rather represents the stage of the greatest well-being in the lives of most healthy people. It is a time when the wisdom gathered from life lived thus far is combined with the energy that comes from a new freedom from day-to-day responsibility to produce what Bateson (2010: 19) calls *active wisdom*, which gives older adults 'the potential for altering the shape of public and family life in America'. Bateson argues that those in Adulthood II – who have the time and the perspective for reflection and the willingness to acquire new skills – are best equipped to advocate for future generations through their creativity and greater engagement in civic life. For the participants in my study, *active wisdom* partly manifests itself in the way that they contribute to improving the lives of English learners through their teaching, advocacy and service in the community.

Bateson (2010: 79) contends that Adulthood II replicates earlier life stages in relation to identity and that the physiological changes during adolescence that trigger a search for a sense of identity are mirrored by the physiological changes of aging. Therefore, just as it was 'confusing in adolescence to be flooded with hormones', it is 'confusing again as they dwindle'; just as it was 'confusing in adolescence to discover zits on one's face', it is 'confusing again to deal with wrinkles'. Bateson (2010: 19) describes the passage from Adulthood I to Adulthood II as a time when 'you reflect that you have done much of what you hoped to do in life but it is not too late to do something more or different'. Sheehy (1995) calls the transition leading into Adulthood II 'middlescence' – a time when people experience the death of first adulthood and pass into the beginning of second adulthood. She observes that people in middlescence are in flux and often act as foolishly and capriciously as adolescents:

> The striving, competing, proving, and besting of rivals that lent a furious intensity to our young adulthood, forming the basis of our ego identities, now feel more like a dull repetition of duty: *Why do I have to work so hard? What is it all for?* There is also the inevitable anger and frustration at physical changes in the body. A mourning period usually sets in. *Am I ready to accept the ebbing of my physical prowess? Losing the unfair advantage of youthful beauty? Giving up the magic of fertility?* Disillusion and ennui are just as natural to this passage as mood swings are to adolescence. (Sheehy, 1995: 145–146)

One of my study participants, 53-year-old Elaine, fits the bill of someone who may be undergoing middlescence. For more than 20 years, she has worked as a part-time chiropractor in a private office she shared with her husband, who is also a chiropractor. She describes her husband as a workaholic, for whom 'It's just work, work, work, work, work. Work is his life'. But for Elaine, her part-time schedule in a family-owned practice has enabled her to spend most of her time taking care of their three daughters and work as little as a couple of mornings a week. As the years passed, Elaine was able to gradually add more hours at the office though her children always remained a higher priority. When I asked her what prompted her to pursue TESOL training, she said that her youngest child is in her last year in high school and about to leave for college:

> With the prospect of the kids leaving and my entering a new chapter, I was thinking of just changing everything, just kind of being different. While the kids were at home, so much of my focus was on the kids. I worked on the side but my life was really the kids. Once they were old enough to be more independent, the office became a little more dominant, but for me, the kids were the main thing. And so, feeling like that part of me is leaving, I'm kind of thinking of shaking things up a little bit and trying something totally different. I didn't have time and energy to do all the stuff with the kids, plus do the office, the house, the husband, and have time for the greater people outside that realm. It just was too hard. I didn't have time to develop that piece, so I feel like it's time to open up that piece and develop that more. (Elaine)

Elaine's entry into 'a new chapter' in her life is set in motion by 'the kids leaving', an event of enormous significance for someone for whom 'the kids were the main thing' for more than two decades. Faced with the prospect of an empty nest and the conclusion of a major chapter in her life, Elaine very much feels like 'changing everything', 'shaking things up a little bit' and trying 'something totally different'. These phrases clearly indicate someone who is in transition, searching for a way to make sense of the changes in her life. With her youngest child about to leave the house, Elaine is compelled to re-examine her life to find a different purpose to which she can devote her newly freed time and energies. Her decision to pursue training to become an ESL teacher was a way of rechanneling the energy she used to reserve for her family to benefit 'the greater people outside that realm'.

In addition to the emotional upheaval and grief associated with the empty nest, Elaine's decision was motivated by physical changes in her body. She reported that an illness a few years ago prompted her to look into a different kind of job that did not require her to treat patients all day:

One of the things that made me start thinking about options was a couple of years ago, I wasn't feeling well. I was starting to think, how am I going to stand over people and work on them all day if I don't feel well? I had some energy problems and a bunch of stuff going on. I didn't feel good. And I thought, I can't do this when I'm 60. It's hard work. It's physical labor. So I was trying to think of other things I could do that wouldn't be so physically taxing. (Elaine)

Elaine's condition did improve eventually, but her struggle with this illness was a wake-up call. She needed to have a plan for a time when she could no longer function adequately as a chiropractor. In this way, Elaine's decision to pursue training to become an ESL teacher was not only a way to recreate herself and be of service to the greater public but also a form of personal insurance for the future.

Third Age, Third Quarter, Third Chapter: What's in a Name?

In the literature on aging, Adulthood II has been referred to by a variety of other names. Peter Laslett, a British historian and sociologist, calls this stage 'Third Age', a term that is widely used in Britain. Laslett's (1991) theory postulates a framework for describing the stages of the life course, consisting of four periods or ages: the First Age of dependence and childhood, the Second Age of adulthood and work life, the Third Age of fulfillment and the Fourth Age of dependency and frailty. He argued that the difference in contemporary society is the emergence of the Third Age, a new period between the end of work responsibilities and parenting duties and the beginning of dependent old age. According to Laslett, life has its culmination in the Third Age, the age of personal achievement and fulfillment, not in the Second Age, nor in the Fourth. One of Laslett's biggest contributions to the study of aging is his clarification that the aging population is made up of a large group of people in the Third Age and a much smaller group in the Fourth Age. Thus, what Laslett envisions is several decades of Third Age, when people are able to contribute their skills meaningfully to society, followed by a relatively short Fourth Age and death.

The term *Third Age* came from the Université du Troisième Age (University of the Third Age), lifelong learning academies which flourished in France in the 1970s and 1980s. Rather than having set starting and ending ages, Third Age refers to an approximately defined segment of the life course characterized by the pursuit of voluntary and meaningful activities, following retirement from work and childrearing responsibilities, and preceding the period of true old age. Therefore, the starting age and duration of the Third Age can vary widely depending on the life circumstances and health status of each individual. Some people may arrive at their Third Age in their early fifties (or even earlier) and remain in this stage beyond their 80th birthday. Since the Third Age is identified as the period during which the peak of personal life is achieved, anyone who reaches the goal of a successful career brought to a peak of attainment could be said to live in the Third Age. Therefore, many athletes who attain their peak during the First Age could be said to live part of the Third Age while they are still in their First Age.

Laslett's notion of the Third Age bears some resemblance to Alan Pifer's concept of the 'Third Quarter' of life (age 50–75) and to Sara Lawrence-Lightfoot's 'Third Chapter', both of which divide the life course in a way that regards the years after retirement as a time of personal fulfillment and achievement rather than as a period of meaninglessness and decline (Lawrence-Lightfoot, 2009; Pifer & Bronte, 1986). Marc Freedman (2011), a social entrepreneur, calls this period the 'encore years'. Third Age can also be likened to Bernice Neugarten's (1996) concept of the 'young-old', a group composed of people who are approximately 55–75 and are distinguished from the 'old-old', who are 75 and over. Neugarten points out that while the young-old often overlap with the middle-aged, the young-old are distinguishable from the middle-aged by the fact that they are retired and are, for the most part, freed from the responsibilities of full-time work.

Although individuals in the Third Age are largely free of the active parenting and work duties associated with the Second Age, Laslett believes that personal achievement and emotional fulfillment can be had when individuals in the Third Age accept social responsibility. Laslett (1991: 196) contends, 'Growing older does not absolve a person from responsibility, certainly not responsibility for the social future'. He goes on to write that older people 'owe less to their own individual futures—now comparatively short—and more to the future of others—all others.... The elderly of any society can be said to be *trustees* for the future'. Laslett's vision is echoed in Erikson's concept of 'generativity' and Bateson's notion of 'active wisdom' in that it is outward-looking – it focuses on individuals making contributions to the well-being and prosperity of others rather than just those of themselves. It is also reflected in Lawrence-Lightfoot's (2009: xi) description of older adults, in which she writes, 'After years of striving to climb the ladder of success and to make their individual mark, their impulse is now to "give forward" to the next generations, to leave a legacy, to be of service. Their forced sacrifices turn into altruism'. Thus, by 'giving forward', older adults can work to promote a brighter future for everyone, even those who are not yet born. This is a very positive view of later life, one that recognizes the potential contributions that older adults can continue to make to benefit the world around them.

Cohen's Model of Adult Development

Similarly, Cohen (2000) presents a view of adulthood that is fundamentally optimistic about the human potential for lifelong growth, creativity and fulfillment. Based on his studies of more than 3,000 older adults, Cohen identified four distinct developmental phases of late life: (1) midlife re-evaluation, (2) liberation, (3) summing up and (4) encore (see Figure 2.1). Like Laslett's loosely defined ages, Cohen's concept of phases is more fluid and dynamic than Erikson's eight stages and allows for more individual variation. He acknowledges that people may experience the four phases in different ways and sometimes in a slightly different sequence:

(1) Midlife re-evaluation phase (ages 40–65): This phase is a time for exploration and transition. Cohen contends that this is not the same thing as a midlife crisis, which he claims is a cultural myth. Of the more than 3,000 older adults that he studied, he found that only 10% had a true midlife crisis. What he has seen is rather a re-evaluation, which he claims people experience not as a crisis but as an honest appraisal of where they have been and where they are going. Cohen (2005: 62–63) shows that midlife re-evaluation often leads to a series of realizations that can produce the following positive qualities in older adults:

- Less impulsive responses to situations and people in daily life.
- A more thoughtful perspective on work.
- Openness to new ideas or complexity in life.
- Greater respect for intuitive feelings.

Cohen observes that most people experience midlife re-evaluation as a quest – a desire to break new ground, answer deep questions and search for what is true and meaningful in their lives.

(2) Liberation phase (from late fifties into seventies): This is a time when people feel a desire to experiment, innovate and free themselves from earlier inhibitions or limitations. Cohen states that this desire often overlaps with midlife re-evaluation and increases in its intensity throughout the late fifties and sixties and into the seventies. People in this phase often express the sense of 'If not now, when?' People tend to feel comfortable about themselves by this time, and retirement often provides a new feeling of finally having free time to try something new.

(3) Summing-up phase (from late sixties through eighties): This phase, usually occurring in one's late sixties through the seventies and eighties, is a time of recapitulation and review. Cohen states that people in this phase have the desire to find larger meaning in the story of their lives and to share the wisdom they have accrued in their lifetime through personal storytelling, community activism and volunteerism.

(4) Encore phase (age 80+): This final phase, which typically occurs in people in their eighties and above, is the time of advancing age. During this time, Cohen notes that creative expression is shaped by the desire to make strong, lasting contributions on a personal or community level, to affirm life, to take care of unfinished business and to celebrate one's own contributions to the world.

A series of personal reflections by the participants in my study reflect Cohen's adult life phases and the common experience of continued growth in different ways. Sometimes the comments offer a clear indication of a single phase; other times they signal a transition or overlapping of the phases. What I found from the interviews was that often the decision to seek TESOL training during second adulthood is not based on a single factor but is motivated by a host of personal, familial and professional reasons. For some, the decision was relatively straightforward and did not require much thinking. For others, it was significantly more complicated, requiring some soul-searching and difficult conversations.

Andrea: Out of the office and into the community

One of the participants in my study, 57-year-old Andrea, could be said to be in the liberation phase. Foreign languages have always been an integral part of Andrea's life. A daughter of a diplomat, Andrea grew up in a number of foreign countries and was exposed to a variety of languages and cultures. Learning new languages came naturally for Andrea, and she graduated college with a major in French and a minor in German. Shortly thereafter, she was hired by the US federal government to learn Russian so that she could work as a Russian language analyst. She said, 'This was the late 70s. I was paid to go to class 8 hours a day, 5 days a week for 56 weeks to learn Russian'. Upon completion of her language training, Andrea worked for two years as a Russian language analyst and later did some work involving French and German. She has had 9 different jobs in 31 years, all language related, with the same organization. For some time, Andrea had been looking for ways to be intellectually stimulated outside of her work. 'The language department that I work in has a lot of non-native speakers of English in it', she explained, 'So I found that I was always helping other people with resumes and things like that. And I started thinking about how much I really knew about my own language'. Finally, when her son, whom she raised as a single mother, left home for college, she felt it was time for her to go to graduate school:

> My son moved out on a Monday and I said, Great! I have free time on my hands now. So, let's go to grad school! Literally. So I applied two days later. There were several goals. One, get out of the office because it was getting stultifying and I needed some sort of intellectual stimulation. [A colleague of mine at work] had spoken highly about

several of the classes that she'd taken [at UMBC] and I was curious about that. I had the time to do it because my son, who was 19, had moved out. So I didn't feel any obligation to be here and fix dinner every night for him. (Andrea)

Andrea's newly found sense of freedom is contrasted here with her earlier feeling of being tethered down with work and mothering responsibilities. By drawing a distinction between the 'stultifying' office and parental obligations on the one hand, and 'free time' and her need for 'intellectual stimulation' on the other, Andrea creates a new context for experimentation and innovation as she embarks on the next chapter of her life.

When I asked her why she chose to do a graduate degree in TESOL, Andrea talked about a volunteer teaching experience she had a year ago at a local literacy council, which she enjoyed very much:

They gave me who they thought was a tough student—a 45-year-old, Nicaraguan-born immigrant. When she moved here, she went to an American high school but she didn't graduate. And her goal was to eventually get her GED. I said it's a good goal. She said she wanted to do it in 3 months. I said, give yourself 3 years, you will make it. I was very upfront with her. I think it's the most rewarding when in two months, you see someone go from writing two or three simple sentences to actually writing five paragraphs. In two months! Compared to what I do at [my current job], this is infinitely more rewarding. She really opened up and was really willing to work hard on things. I loved the fact that she took it very seriously. This was something she was very motivated to do. It's extraordinarily satisfying to work with someone like that. It's probably the best teaching experience I've ever had. (Andrea)

Andrea shared that after retiring, she would like to continue working as a tutor for one of the local literacy councils. She believes that her TESOL training will be useful in her work with immigrant adults and perhaps even training literacy tutors.

Paula: Helping to empower people

Paula, 54, could be said to be in both the midlife re-evaluation and the liberation phases. A highly accomplished neuroscientist with a PhD in biology, Paula told me that when she was an undergraduate student, receiving the course catalogue was like getting a Christmas present. She loved reading the course descriptions and was fascinated by what people studied in different disciplines. Although she was interested in many different subjects ranging from the natural sciences to the humanities and the arts, she eventually chose to major in biology because she enjoyed helping people and thought that a background in biology would prepare her well for a career in health care. She said that she was particularly drawn to nursing and even worked as a nursing assistant for a few semesters. But when the time came for her to apply to graduate school, many of the nurses who worked with her talked her out of nursing, saying that nurses are underpaid, overworked and underappreciated. They encouraged her to go to medical school and become a doctor instead.

Paula listened to the nurses' advice, and applied for and was accepted into one of the top medical schools in the United States. After two years of coursework however, she developed a severe depression. Paula had previously been diagnosed with bipolar disorder but the disease had been in remission. A lack of sleep in medical school, however, aggravated her symptoms to the point where she became extremely ill and unable to function normally. She took a leave of absence for one year to recover from her depression but when she came back to resume her studies, the symptoms returned. After floundering for a while, she eventually gave up medicine to pursue a PhD in biology instead, thinking she could transfer some of her medical school coursework into it. When I asked her whether the PhD program worked out better for her than medical school, she explained:

> I finished the Ph.D. but from the beginning I didn't like the research. What had attracted me to medicine was to work with people. But I thought, well, there are other sides to science, it's not just research. I kept hoping I would find a niche. And the long and the short of it is, after 15 years, I never did find a niche. I did some postdoctoral training. I did a lot of research and published extensively in refereed journals. But I was never happy. (Paula)

After spending 15 years as a laboratory researcher and never liking research, Paula had a powerful desire to break free from her inhibitions and start anew. At the time of my interview with her, Paula had resigned from her tenure-track assistant professor position at a major research university, an enviable job for any aspiring academic. She had been in that position for four years and was well on her way to achieving promotion and tenure at her university. But she was not happy and was resolved to leave the job. Since her resignation, Paula has been teaching ESL as a part-time instructor at community colleges. When I asked her if she missed her former job, she explained:

> I was publishing and I had grants. But I was miserable. I didn't want the job. I was killing rats daily. In order to make my research succeed better, I probably would have been killing cats daily. The research that had been most productive for me had been with cats. And I finally swore I wasn't going to do any more of it. I was doing some gruesome procedures on rats that were out. They were not conscious, but even so, it was just so ugly, icky, gross... It's fascinating to read and think about

research on neuroscience, but I couldn't stomach it. As you know, you don't succeed in a tenure-track position without the research. I hated it. I hated it with a passion. But I always loved the teaching. (Paula)

As a university professor, I sympathized with Paula's dilemma. Academics spend a good part of their youth, energy, time and money training to be researchers. But upon completion of their degrees, not everyone is able to secure full-time jobs. Tenure-track jobs in major research universities are especially in short supply, and compared to the number of people graduating with new PhD's each year, there are far fewer openings for new full-time hires. Many newly minted PhD's end up settling for less. Some make do with several part-time teaching positions in different colleges; others switch out of their chosen fields altogether. Knowing well how fierce competition can be for a tenure-track position, I knew Paula's decision to voluntarily give up her job was not an easy one. In spite of that, Paula was truly miserable in her job and 'hated it with a passion':

What finally clinched in my mind was the saying that you don't throw good money after bad. If it's not something that's working, why put more on it? If I was starting over, I'd teach ESL. Then I said to myself, why not? Why not do it? I don't have children. I'm not tied down in the way some people are. I could afford to go to school. I have a husband who's supportive. I could afford to do it. So, why not? (Paula)

In making her decision, Paula was motivated by a quest to find what is meaningful in her life and what made her truly happy. After 15 years of constantly suppressing her aversion to laboratory research and failing to find another side to science that she could be drawn to, Paula finally walked away from her job. Before she submitted her resignation, however, Paula finished her MA in TESOL by taking classes in the evening. She admits that taking two or three classes a semester while holding a full-time job was pretty difficult, but she was determined to obtain the degree that would finally free her to do what she wanted. The conversations she had with her husband that led up to her resignation, however, were painful at times. I was able to interview Paula's husband, Mark, who confessed:

Paula's really been very kind in saying that I was supportive. But the truth is I was really very conflicted a lot of the time when this was coming up. After all this time you spent doing this just to walk away? But then the other part of it was, she was doing volunteer teaching at [a community center], and she would come home and would be beaming. She would be smiling. There were many hard conversations. I thought, I don't know where this is going, but this is obviously the right choice. (Mark, Paula's husband)

Both Paula and Mark now realize that as difficult as the decision to leave her former job was, staying with it would have made her life unbearable. But the inner conflict that Mark had about supporting Paula to do what made her truly happy while wondering whether she was making the biggest mistake of her life was obviously significant. He knew that what mattered most to Paula at this stage in her life was to be finally free from her earlier inhibitions and follow her heart. He knew she should not have to stay in a job she loathed just to have the appearance of a successful academic in the eyes of other people. When I asked Paula what she finds attractive about teaching English as a second language, she explained:

> It's very practical. It gives people a power that almost no other teaching can give. The power to communicate, you know. Without the ability to speak English in a country that's English-speaking, people are incredibly handicapped. I think that the ability to help in that way is so empowering. I always wanted to teach something very practical and very helpful. I couldn't think of anything more helpful or more practical than teaching the language that a person needs to go to the grocery store, to go to the bank, to get a degree, to get a better job, to do the things they need to do in order to succeed in the country where they live. (Paula)

Paula told me that years ago when she had just quit medical school, she volunteered as an ESL teacher teaching Hispanic adults at a local church. 'It was just something to help out in the community', she said, but it turned out to be a life-changing experience. She said that for years when she was working as a neuroscientist, she would come home after a long day at the lab and say to Mark, 'I'm going to be an ESL teacher'. While at that time, Paula said this as a joke and was not serious about it, she now realizes that working with adult immigrants is what she has wanted to do all along.

Anna: 'It's time to give back'

Anna, 61, could be said to be somewhere between the Liberation and the Summing-up phases. She retired after 34 years of working for the US federal government as a foreign language specialist. She got married eight months ago to a 72-year-old man who has an adult son from his previous marriage, but this was Anna's first marriage. Anna described herself as a late bloomer: 'It took me a long time to find the right guy but I finally did'. The eldest of six children, Anna said that she was given a lot of responsibility at a young age. 'I wasn't really in a hurry to have children of my own, because I felt I had already raised one bunch of kids before I even became an adult. I did all that [parenting] stuff already. I don't have to repeat it'. Anna took a special liking to foreign languages and cultures from when she was young and eventually majored in Spanish both as an undergraduate and as a graduate student. However, when she finished graduate school, she couldn't find a job teaching Spanish. Fortunately, she was offered a job as a foreign language specialist with the US federal government and was able to put her Spanish training to good use.

Although getting married recently and taking care of her sick mother who lives in another state have been keeping her quite busy, Anna shared that when she was still working full-time, her greatest fear about retiring was not having something useful to do. 'I didn't want to just sit around the house and feel like there's nothing left for me to do with the rest of my life'. After thinking about what to do that would be useful, she decided that teaching English to adults was something she could do well, given her expertise in languages:

> The job I had with the government was interesting but I didn't always see the immediate benefits of what I was doing. I guess you could say it was a more abstract kind of contribution to the world. But I wanted something that had more obvious impact on somebody else. Right now I'm looking for something where I can help people in a very practical, concrete way. I feel like it's time for me to give back. Where can I do the most good? Where can I be effective and do something that's truly worthwhile? Somewhere between 45 and 50, I started feeling like I've been so blessed in life. I had a stable home life growing up. I had parents who really valued education and made sacrifices so I could get a really good education. I got an excellent job offer and worked in a field that I was interested in, and for all those years, I have a secure retirement. I've been healthy most of my life. I've had a lot of blessings. I've kind of grown up with the philosophy that you don't just take all of that. You also give back. (Anna)

Anna's desire to 'help people in a very practical, concrete way' is similar to what Andrea and Paula described as their motivations for working with adult English learners. But with Anna, there is an additional sense of urgency to sum up her life's work and discoveries and to share them with other people, to leave a legacy. By recounting all the blessings she has had in her life – parents who valued education and made sacrifices for her, a good job and a secure retirement, physical health – Anna expresses a profound desire to 'give back' after receiving much in life.

David: 'I feel like I have a lot to say, and I want to say it'

Compared to Anna, who is summing up her life after retirement, 63-year-old David is in a rather different situation. After several years of part-time teaching jobs and numerous private tutoring arrangements,

David finally landed a full-time position last year as an academic coordinator of an undergraduate student learning support center. In this role, he coordinates an International Teaching Assistants (ITA) program and teaches advanced diction to improve ITAs' speaking and teaching skills. He also runs a retention program for undergraduate students who are on the suspension trail and teaches them strategies for developing good study habits. His workshops on time management and overcoming test anxiety have helped many struggling students to turn their academic careers around and graduate from college. In many ways, David is well positioned to help struggling students, because he himself had difficulty finishing school – he did not graduate from college until he was in his late forties:

> I dropped out of college to go to Vietnam. My major was education. I wanted to be an English teacher. That was back in 1963. But I was so messed up as a human being. I had so many personal problems. I didn't know who I was. I was immature and wasn't ready for college at all. I dropped out, joined the military, and went off to Vietnam. (David)

When he returned from Vietnam, David said he was in business for himself for about 20 years, doing many different kinds of work in unrelated fields:

> I was in family business. I was buying and selling used steel drums, 55 gallon drums. It was my father's business, and when he retired, I took it over. Before that, I'd worked with the handicapped and mentally retarded. I worked in electronics for a little while for the telephone company, and I couldn't hold onto the job very long. I was bored by it. I sold exotic birds, and had my own business painting houses, and did a lot of work with the United Cerebral Palsy and the mentally retarded in section 8 housing as a counselor and things like that. I've done all kinds of things in my life. You couldn't pin me down. (David)

A heart attack in his early forties, however, forced David to give up his business and consider going back to school. He tutored his way through college and eventually received his bachelor's degree in English at the age of 49. He then waited a year and did his graduate work in TESOL while working as a graduate student writing advisor at the same university. Throughout his years tutoring students, David said he was particularly drawn to students who were having difficulties, not the ones who were doing well. So, when the academic coordinator position at the student learning support center came up, he knew he wanted the job. When I asked him how long he plans to work, he said:

I'll probably retire when I'm about 70. I have a 7-year plan, but it depends. One of the things I want to do is finish my book of poetry. I want to do some writing because I enjoy it so much. I have a rich inner life. I feel like I have a lot to say, and I want to say it. I want to explore that creative part of myself. It's something I started really getting serious about later in life. I'm working on it, but the thing of it is, I have to make a living. Most of my life I've been struggling to make a living and I've never been financially successful. And now that I'm in a more comfortable situation, I just feel this calling, this craving to fulfill that part of myself. (David)

David's work on poetry is motivated by his desire to find a larger meaning in the story of his life and to share the wisdom he has accrued. His poetry serves as an autobiography and personal storytelling, a way to share the lessons and fortunes of a lifetime. David's need to explore the creative part of himself is an intense longing, a desire that is echoed in the narratives of many people in the Summing-up phase (Cohen, 2000).

Turning Crises into Opportunities

Whether it was deciding what to do with a newly found freedom from parenting or work responsibilities, or facing one's own mortality or breaking free from earlier limitations or inhibitions, the individuals in my study have arrived at their decision to pursue TESOL training in later life in myriad ways. What we saw in the previous section is that there was really no clear age-based pattern for determining what phase each person may be in. The liberation once associated with retirement at age 65 occurred across a wider range of ages among participants in my study, and delayed marriage/childbearing and unconventional career trajectories made it difficult to apply any strict age-based categorization. Some of them came to TESOL having been laid off from their previous jobs, while others came to TESOL leaving work that they found unsatisfactory. Several sought to make a full-time career out of ESL teaching while others looked to teach ESL on a part-time basis during their retirement. While TESOL figured differently in the lives of each of the participants, what I found over and over in their stories was the way in which life's challenges were turned into opportunities for growth and learning. In fact, decisions to pursue TESOL training were often made when the participants were faced with a crisis.

Henry: Downsized but not defeated

Henry, aged 45, worked as an engineer for the US Navy for nine years before his department was downsized and he was let go:

When I first started with [the Navy] in '89, that was about the time when we won the Cold War and the Department of Defense started downsizing. Finally, 9 years later, the downsizing got to the headquarters where I worked, and all the engineers in my department were offered a financial incentive to leave. For me, [what they offered me] was enough for me to think, wow, this could pay for a good part of grad school! And I'd been thinking of teaching for many years. So I thought I'd kick myself if I don't take this opportunity to get into teaching and try it out. So I took the incentive and ran. I took the money and went full-time into the TESOL program. (Henry)

In the TESOL program, Henry took four courses each semester and finished his master's degree in just a year and a half. Upon graduation, he was hired as a full-time ESL teacher at a large high school with several hundred ESL students. When asked how he knew he wanted a master's in TESOL, he said that while he was working as an engineer for the Navy, he had done some volunteer work in the evenings teaching adult immigrants. That and several other volunteer teaching opportunities in the local community had convinced him that if given the chance, he would enjoy teaching full-time. His termination from the Navy and the financial incentive he was offered provided him with the perfect opportunity to develop a second career. A son of first-generation Greek immigrants, Henry said immigrants have always been an integral part of his life growing up. And now, as an ESL teacher, he draws a great deal of satisfaction from helping immigrant students meet their life goals. He said that the best part of teaching is 'seeing the light bulb go off and seeing the "aha!" moments'.

Julia: Forging a new life after losing her husband

Transitions in midlife are sometimes triggered by involuntary losses, such as a death or serious illness of a family member, which can act as a catalyst for voluntary changes in the way people live their lives (Sheehy, 1995). Julia, aged 54, who has built a successful career in social work, decided to become an ESL teacher after her husband passed away, leaving her with their two daughters, 10 and 13 years old:

For me, the main reason I chose ESL is because my husband died. I have 28 years in social work, and most of that was with the state. If my husband was still living, I would have stayed so that I could have collected my pension after 30 years. But the nature of the job being sometimes emergency work was making it difficult for me, because I didn't have plans for my children for those hours. When my husband was working as a firefighter, I could work my hours somewhat around his. But after he died, I was left alone to take care of the kids. I would have made it work somehow if I had to, but I did have the privilege of having his pension. So that gave me a big cushion as far as being able to do something else. When I've had situations in my life like this that were traumatic, I've tried to find something positive in the situation. I thought to myself, well, this is an opportunity for me to recreate myself. (Julia)

Julia explained that her husband's death was not the first traumatic event that she had to deal with in her life. Years ago, when she was working in hospice home care, Julia had lost two of her brothers in succession and was struggling in her marriage to her first husband. She said that the losses in her family and her difficult marriage had prompted her to leave the hospice job even though she found the work 'very rewarding and very interesting'. Changing jobs within the state government was relatively easy and offered Julia a means to cope with the challenging circumstances in her personal life. She went to work for the Department of Social Services in the foster care program but found the job very stressful because 'the foster care system was a mess'. Within a year, she ended up changing jobs again, this time to work for adult protective services, a job which she liked much better and has kept for most of her career as a social worker. Her choice of TESOL now is again a way for her to 'find something positive' in a crisis and turn it into an opportunity to recreate herself.

Joni: Regaining confidence after divorce

For some participants in my study, divorce acted as a catalyst for change in second adulthood. Sheehy (1995) notes that while divorce is always painful, the forced assertion of self and the educational pursuits that many people, especially women, resume after getting divorced open up a new range of possibilities for growth in second adulthood. Joni, aged 47, had graduated from college with a degree in English and worked as a paralegal for several years before she met her husband. Once she got married, she moved frequently to follow her husband, whose job required him to relocate every few years. During this time, she mostly cared for their two children and worked in a couple of part-time jobs to supplement the family income. Joni said she knew she wanted to pursue a career in teaching eventually, perhaps when the children grew up. However, it wasn't until she was separated from her husband that she was forced to think seriously about going back to school to become a teacher:

TESOL didn't come in until after 2003, when I started getting serious. Up until then, I was pretty much staying home, raising kids, and working part-time. I had had a couple of part-time jobs in schools to know that I wanted to do something in teaching, but I didn't really know what subject I wanted to teach. What precipitated going back to school was getting divorced. One of the reasons I never went back to school was I didn't have the confidence that I could do it. (Joni)

Like many married women with children, Joni's primary focus for many years was caring for her family. When she did work outside the home, it was always on a part-time basis mainly to supplement her husband's income. But as a newly divorced single mother, she needed to find a way to support herself and her children, and while lack of confidence had prevented her from pursuing graduate education for years, she now had to overcome her fears and chart a new path on her own. Gathering her courage, she did research on graduate programs in the area, talked to people she knew and decided to pursue a degree in TESOL. Once admitted into the TESOL program, Joni needed a great deal of encouragement and reassurance from program faculty, but she managed to finish her MA in TESOL with excellent grades, received her state teaching license and was hired as a full-time ESL teacher at an elementary school.

Conclusion

Increasing longevity – through improved nutrition, sanitation, medicine, education and economic well-being – is one of humanity's great achievements (United Nations Populations Fund, 2012). Throughout the world, people are living longer and staying healthier than they used to in the past. While only 4 in 10 people in the United States lived to the age of 65 in 1900, well over 8 in 10 people today live past their 65th birthday (Arias, 2014). The fact that most middle-aged Americans today have a living parent is an extraordinary occurrence with no precedent in human history (Sheehy, 1995). With the survival of many grandparents to become great-grandparents and the improved health conditions of older adults, we now have the first four-generation society in history (Bateson, 2010).

As a result of dramatically increased life expectancy, a new developmental stage has emerged in the life cycle. Call it Second Adulthood, Adulthood II, Third Age, Third Quarter, Third Chapter, Encore years or young-old, the period between the end of young adulthood and the onset of true old age can easily cover a span of four or five decades. What are people doing with this new stage of life? How does it change our concept of the life cycle, of adulthood, of work, of finding meaning and personal fulfillment in later life? An important consequence of increased life expectancy is that people need to be able to support themselves financially for more years. A 62-year-old American today could easily require 30 or more years of retirement income, which motivates him or her to work beyond the traditional retirement age of 65. More and more people are working into older ages, and while just over one-fifth of men and about one-sixth of women ages 65 and over were in the labor force in 2009, these figures are projected to increase to 27% for men and 19% for women by 2018 (Jacobsen *et al.*, 2011). Four out of five baby boomers expect to work well into what used to be known as the retirement years (Freedman, 2007).

What sets apart this new generation of adults in terms of work is that they are moving beyond midlife careers in search of a calling in the second half of life (Freedman, 2007). They focus on what matters most and are no longer satisfied to work simply to bring home the paycheck. While younger adults may be preoccupied with establishing their careers and attaining status and prestige, those in Adulthood II are much less occupied with these concerns. They look for deeper meaning in what they do and are more interested in having an impact on the world around them. Having the wisdom from life lived thus far, they want to see their work count for something greater than themselves and make a difference in the world, thus their constant refrain of wanting to see 'concrete and practical' results of their work. Driven by a sense of 'If not now, when?', they are able to break away from their former limitations and break new ground on the kind of work they choose to do.

This is where TESOL comes into their lives. It acts as a channel for them to engage with people who are very much in need of and could benefit from their service. The participants in my study found personal fulfillment in directing their energies toward helping their students become proficient in English, a skill they considered indispensable for life in the United States. A common theme that surfaced over and over in my interviews was the desire among the men and women in my study to use their expertise to 'give back' and 'be useful to the broader community'. They were no longer interested in measuring success in terms of making it to the top of the career ladder and achieving status for personal reasons only. Instead, they were in search of ways to use their knowledge, skills and training for the benefit of the larger community, to help people in need in concrete ways. By returning to school to be trained as ESL teachers, they took active steps to work not only toward their own future but also the futures of others. They did not choose teaching blindly, rather their decisions were informed by their experiences volunteering as teachers of English in their communities. They were not content to sit by the sidelines and let Second Adulthood happen to them without their active involvement. In this way, they are very much at the forefront of change, actively planning and charting a new path in their lives.

3   Cognitive and Social Benefits of Teaching ESL

In this chapter, I explore what the participants in my study find attractive about teaching ESL. In particular, I describe how working with English learners provides cognitive and social benefits to aging boomers. Research shows that the human brain remains capable of growth throughout life and that vigorous mental activity keeps the brain healthy. I explain here how teaching ESL provides adults with opportunities for intellectual and creative thinking. I illustrate, using examples from the study participants' teaching episodes, how finding new ways to present information to students stimulates the brain and fulfills people's desire to be creative. I also discuss the social benefits of interacting with people from different cultures and how this type of shared experience promotes mental and physical health in later life.

The Power of the Aging Brain

How is the adult brain different from a child's brain? We often think of a child's brain as a sponge, soaking up information around it. It seems as though children have an infinite capacity to learn new things. They seem to acquire new vocabulary with ease and only need to hear a word once to be able to remember it. In contrast, older people often complain about memory loss and seem less adept at developing new skills and abilities than younger people. The popular saying, 'You can't teach an old dog new tricks', captures the common view that the older brain is set in its ways and cannot be changed. However, psychiatrist Gene Cohen (2005: xv) argues that 'not only can old dogs learn well, they are actually better at many types of intellectual tasks than young dogs'. In his book, *The Mature Mind: The Positive Power of the Aging Brain*, Cohen (2005: 4) describes four key attributes of the brain that bolster an optimistic view of human potential in later adulthood:

- The brain continually resculpts itself in response to experience and learning.
- New brain cells *do* form throughout life.
- The brain's emotional circuitry matures and becomes more balanced with age.
- The brain's two hemispheres are more equally used by older adults.

Research in recent decades has shown that the human brain is far more flexible and adaptable than once thought (Taylor & Lamoreaux, 2008). Throughout one's life, the brain grows and rewires itself in response to stimulation and learning, and there is strong evidence that the adult human brain is remarkably plastic and capable of new accomplishments even during the last chapter of life (Lustig et al., 2009). A large body of research has shown that new experiences, skill acquisition and training in various areas of life result in physical, chemical and functional remodeling of the brain (e.g. Bezzola et al., 2011; Smith et al., 2009).

There are fundamental differences between neurons and other cells in the human body. Whereas normal body cells grow, divide and die, neurons do not divide; only a relatively small percentage of neurons die as people age, and the vast majority of the neurons that people were born with still work in their old age (Cohen, 2005). As people age, the brain not only retains its capacity to make new connections between neurons, but it can also grow entirely new neurons. Among the many different types of cells found in the human body, neurons hold special potential, because the effects of aging present new opportunities for intellectual growth and creativity.

Despite the brain's potential for lifelong learning and accomplishments, the literature on cognitive aging has tended to focus on the problems of older age. As recently as the 1970s, many experts viewed older age as a 'disease' and believed that the mind and body 'naturally fell apart, like a car after many years of use' (Cohen, 2005: xxii). Aging was often written off as a bad thing, an inevitable decline that humans must face before they die. In his book, *Major Issues in Cognitive Aging*, psychologist Timothy Salthouse (2010: 4) writes, 'Perhaps more than in many other areas of scientific research, assertions about cognitive aging may be influenced as much by the authors' preconceptions and attitudes as by systematic evaluations of empirical research'. He states that claims researchers have made about mental decline in older adults are sometimes based on personal impressions rather than on robust and replicated research findings.

Much research has reported, for example, that people's performance on many psychometric tests deteriorates as they age. Compared to younger adults, older adults tend to be slower in solving complicated math problems, have longer reaction times and have less efficient short-term memory storage. These results have been widely taken to mean that cognitive information processing capacities decline across adulthood. But a recent study by Michael Ramscar and his colleagues at the University of Tübingen suggests that the poorer performance of older adults on psychometric tests does not signal a weakening of mental capacities but rather reflects increased demands on memory search, which increases with aging (Ramscar et al., 2014). The researchers argue that the older brain works more slowly than the younger brain because it has stored more information over a longer lifetime, which takes more time to process. Much as a computer struggles as the hard drive fills up with data, so do humans take longer to process the increasingly larger amounts of data that are stored in the brain as time passes. In other words, the older brain is slower than the younger brain, because it has to sift through a greater amount of information in recalling facts and making decisions, not because it has experienced cognitive decline.

Studies like this have become increasingly common in recent decades, as perceptions about aging have changed. Boosted by health and longevity, many adults retain sound mental and emotional faculties even as their physical resources gradually deteriorate. Researchers are now more aware that much of the weakening in mental abilities often associated with aging is caused by specific diseases such as micro-strokes and Alzheimer's disease and mental illnesses such as depression. In fact, healthy older brains are often as good as or better than younger brains in a wide variety of tasks (Cohen, 2005).

What Exactly Can the Healthy Older Brain Do?

The emerging picture of the aging brain is that it is not any less capable of mental processing than the younger brain. In fact, having accumulated more knowledge over a longer lifespan, the older brain has a number of distinct advantages in problem-solving, social relationships and creative thinking. Below, I discuss three areas in which the older brain may show superior performance to that of the younger brain: developmental intelligence, regulating emotions and creativity.

Developmental intelligence

According to Cohen (2005), developmental intelligence is the degree to which a person has manifested his or her unique neurological, emotional, intellectual and psychological capacities. It represents the growing interaction of cognition, emotional intelligence, judgment, social skills, life experience and consciousness. Advanced developmental intelligence is sometimes called 'post-formal operations', because it is developed later than 'formal operations' – the general capacity for higher-order reasoning and abstract thinking that develops during adolescence (Cohen, 2005). Post-formal operations are characterized by three types of thinking: (1) relativistic thinking – recognizing that knowledge may be relative and not absolute; (2) dualistic thinking – the ability to resolve contradictions in opposing and seemingly incompatible views; and (3) systematic thinking – being able to see the larger picture, to distinguish between the forest and the trees (Cohen, 2005: xx).

Cohen (2005) contends that these three types of thinking are advanced because they do not come naturally in youth; it takes time, experience and effort to develop more flexible and subtle thinking:

Many aspects of life are simply too complicated and subtle to learn quickly, which is why experience counts in so many spheres of life. Human relationships, for example, are notoriously complicated, and it can take decades to acquire the deep knowledge and understanding it takes to be a truly effective therapist, pastor, manager, or politician. There is simply no substitute for acquired learning in such fields as editing, law, medicine, coaching, and many areas of science. In these and many other fields, age generally trumps youth. Of course, age alone is no guarantee of excellence, but excellence in many fields can be achieved only after many years of hard work and experience. (Cohen, 2005: 5)

An excellent example of older adults' greater capacity for adaptability and flexible thinking can be seen in the way that one participant, Lesley, taught reading skills to a young student.

Lesley: Seeing the big picture

Prior to coming to TESOL, Lesley had worked for nearly 20 years as a customer service agent for a major airline company. Before that, she was a software engineer/corporate trainer/project manager in the communications industry. For one of the assignments in my reading and writing methods course in our TESOL program, I ask teacher candidates to teach a preliterate child using the Language Experience Approach (LEA) and reflect on the experience. The LEA is a powerful teaching technique used widely in beginning literacy classrooms to help young readers make the connection between speech and print. Upon the teacher's prompt, the student tells a story orally, which the teacher writes down verbatim on the board. The written text comprising the student's own words is then used for lessons on reading, writing, word analysis and grammar. Lesley did this activity with her 5-year-old granddaughter and assesses the experience:

The activity went pretty well. When Angela saw her story written out on the tablet, her first reaction was 'I said that much!' I asked her if she wanted to read her story to me. She was hesitant. I could sense she was trying to remember exactly what she had said and was unsure. I began to read the story to her, pointing to the words as I read. However, her mother had been watching us and came over and insisted that Angela try to read the text. This did not go very well. I sensed a lot of tension between them and quickly interrupted and read the story back to Angela. We spent some time talking about her drawing. I read her the story one more time, pointing to each word, and then ended the activity. It was obvious that Angela made the connection between the words she used to tell me the story and the words I recorded. I think that the second part of the activity, where we tried to read her story, would have been more successful if her mother had not insisted she try to read the words. (Lesley)

Lesley brings many positive qualities to this one-on-one teaching situation. She first tries to determine if Angela can recognize any of the words in the text by asking her if she wants to read her story. Upon noticing Angela's hesitation, Lesley begins to read the story to her, pointing to each word as she reads. However, Angela's mother insists that Angela try to read the text on her own. It is not difficult to see why Angela's mother is so intent on having Angela read the text despite her lack of ability and willingness to do so at this time. She knows full well that reading is the basis of all school-based work and is crucial for her daughter's academic success. She has high expectations for Angela and may even feel that it is her job as a 'good' parent to push her academically. But her insistence only leads to tension, which Lesley tries to dissipate by reading the story back to Angela and continuing with the rest of the lesson. Lesley exhibits more patience and flexibility than does Angela's mother. No doubt drawing from her own experience as a parent and her many years of work as an airline customer service agent dealing with passengers complaining about lost baggage, canceled flights and other problems, Lesley is able to take a step back and see the big picture. She is able to observe the child for the slightest signs of excitement, reluctance, distraction and anxiety, and makes decisions about when to push her and when to pull back.

By engaging Angela in a meaningful conversation about her story and drawing, Lesley attempts to instill confidence in her ability as a budding reader and promote a positive view of literacy. We see Lesley drawing on post-formal thinking and looking at this teaching situation with accumulated life experience and wisdom. Whereas Angela's mother is more concerned with ensuring the child's rapid progress as a reader, Lesley knows that it is more important for young learners to develop a positive appreciation for reading and to take smaller steps to mastery. Because Lesley knows that too much expectation for quick progress could stifle the child's interest in learning to read, she tries to provide a less rigid, more student-centered lesson that would sustain the child's attention and curiosity while at the same time keeping her eyes focused on the ultimate goal of literacy. This more balanced view of learning is in fact what most literacy educators advocate.

Regulating emotions

Aside from their capacity for post-formal thinking, older adults show social and emotional functioning that is often superior to that of younger adults. A large body of research suggests that emotional well-being improves as people age. In a recent study, a group of researchers examined the developmental course of emotional experience in a representative sample of adults spanning early to very late adulthood (Carstensen *et al.*, 2011). The participants reported their emotional states at five randomly selected times each day for a one-week period. The researchers repeated the procedure with the same participants five years later, and then five years after that. The study found that the participants reported more positive overall emotional well-being as they aged, with greater emotional stability over time.

Older adults experience lower levels of negative emotion, anxiety, anger and major depressive disorder than younger adults (Blazer, 2003; Carstensen *et al.*, 2000; Charles & Carstensen, 2009). On reports of overall affective well-being, people who are 60 and 70 years of age report lower levels of negative affect and higher levels of satisfaction than do people in their twenties and thirties (Charles *et al.*, 2001). There are age differences in how people perceive and remember emotional material. Compared to younger adults, older adults pay more attention to positive emotional stimuli and are less likely to remember negative emotional experiences (Charles & Carstensen, 2008; Isaacowitz *et al.*, 2006; Mather & Carstensen, 2003). In a study where younger and older adults listened to negative comments directed toward them and were asked to talk about their responses to these comments, Charles and Carstensen (2008) found that younger adults were more likely to react to these negative comments by making disparaging remarks toward the people speaking and reflecting on what they had just heard. In contrast, older adults made few comments about what they had heard and instead made comments that were less negative and focused less on the criticisms. Older adults also made fewer requests for more information about the motives of the people speaking and seemed to be less engaged in the conflict.

Older adults also describe negative situations in their own lives less negatively than do younger adults. In one study, Charles and Almeida (2007) found that when evaluating relatively minor but negative daily stressors that they had experienced across the week, older adults tended to perceive these events as less severe than younger adults did. Older people view their worlds as more benign and defuse tense social situations more effectively by negotiating their environments in such a way as to minimize potential stressors. Another study showed that whereas young adults and older adults did not differ in terms of acceptance and awareness of emotional responses, younger adults experienced greater difficulties with regulating their emotions (Orgeta, 2009). Older adults, on the other hand, were better at engaging in goal-directed behavior and refraining from impulsive emotional responses. In general, increasing age was associated with greater access to emotion regulation strategies and greater clarity of emotions.

The age differences in emotional functioning may be partly due to changes in how the brain – in particular, the emotion-processing center known as the amygdala – responds to positive and negative events (Cohen, 2005). The amygdala intercepts sensory information flowing in from our eyes, ears and nose and sends off impulses that change our behavior. Research using functional magnetic resonance imaging (fMRI) has shown that activity in the amygdala decreases with age, specifically in response to negative emotions such as fear, anger and hatred. In one study, the brains of younger and older participants were scanned as they looked at cheerful, distressing and neutral photographs (Mather *et al.*, 2004). The researchers found that both the younger subjects (ages 18–29) and the older subjects (ages between 70 and 90) showed greater activation in the amygdala for emotional pictures than for neutral pictures. However, for older adults, seeing positive pictures led to greater activation of amygdalae than seeing negative pictures, whereas this was not the case for younger adults.

In sum, when it comes to emotional well-being, aging provides clear advantages. We are able to focus more on the positive aspects of life and stay calmer in the face of life's challenges as we grow older. While younger adults tend to use more outwardly aggressive strategies when dealing with conflict, a tendency that reflects their generally lower levels of impulse control and self-awareness, older adults are able to modulate their emotional responses and react with more care and greater awareness of both themselves and others (Cohen, 2005). These positive aspects of aging are the result not only of experience and learning but also of basic changes in brain function as people age.

Patricia: Achieving peace of mind through self-awareness

Older adults' capacity to practice patience and refrain from impulsive emotional responses makes them ideally suited to work with diverse groups of students and colleagues in schools. A case in point is Patricia, who received her master's degree in TESOL and has been working as a full-time ESL teacher at a middle school. When she was in her early twenties, Patricia had dropped out of college to get married and start a family. After she had her three children, she went back to school in her forties to finish her bachelor's degree in English. She initially became interested in TESOL through tutoring English learners at a local community college. When asked what the best part of being an ESL teacher is, she enthusiastically replied that it's her students:

> I just like the kids. I love being with the kids. The year I started teaching in the middle school was the year my youngest got out of middle school. My youngest started high school and people teased me about that, because I just had to permanently plant myself in middle school.... From

the beginning, I liked working with [immigrant] students. They were the underdog, for one thing. They had so many things stacked against them, but they were still determined to succeed. And they would work so hard and were so grateful for any help I would give them that I thought, 'Why would I work with these nasty little American children, when I could work with [the ESL] kids?' You know, it was a no brainer. (Patricia)

Patricia talked at length about how much she has enjoyed working with children, especially those who come from disadvantaged backgrounds. She attributed this interest to her mother, who was a kindergarten teacher. Patricia's mother had always shown special interest in underprivileged children and frequently volunteered to teach in Head Start programs and lead Girl Scout troops, where she would take in 'all the kids no one else would take'. Since Patricia was always in her mother's troop, she naturally had plenty of opportunities to interact with children of diverse backgrounds while growing up.

Now in her fifties, Patricia sees herself following in her mother's footsteps and championing the cause of the 'underdog'. She finds her work with English learners enormously gratifying and prefers it to teaching students who may not face the same challenges. In articulating her choice of ESL students, she exhibits a high degree of self-awareness and a clear sense of direction, which she may not have had to the same extent when she was younger. Having realized that she derives the most amount of satisfaction from working with ESL students, who are 'so grateful for any help I would give them', she has chosen to devote much of her energies to meeting the needs of newcomer students. For example, she created a new program at her school called 'Welcome Everybody' in which Spanish-speaking and Korean-speaking eighth-grade students are paired with incoming sixth-grade newcomer ESL students to help them navigate middle school and American culture. The idea for this program came to her as she observed that some of her more successful students were those who had access to a strong peer group. Her program won kudos from her principal and has become a model for other ESL programs in the district.

Although Patricia draws a lot of satisfaction from interacting with her students, she has had some difficulty in her relationships with some of the teachers at the school, many of whom are in their twenties.

There are a lot of twenty somethings at our school who are very cliquish. They've decided that they like each other, but they don't really want to include anybody else. And when you have to plan with those people or work closely with them for some reason or other, it's a little difficult sometimes. But I just laugh it off, because I don't really want to get involved in that. You can only do so much. And you have to keep a sense of humor. (Patricia)

Patricia has developed a strategy for dealing with the social exclusion of her younger colleagues; she infuses humor into uncomfortable interpersonal situations. No matter what she does or how hard she tries, Patricia thinks that the younger teachers are not likely to accept her into their inner circles. But instead of letting her colleagues' offhand comments and behavior upset her, she simply shrugs them off. By having a strong self-awareness and being realistic about her relationships with people, Patricia exhibits a high degree of emotional intelligence. And while she remains cordial with everyone and strives to be cooperative with other teachers, she does not sacrifice her sense of self to be included in these social groups. Instead, she focuses her energies on what makes her truly happy and is able to achieve peace of mind and a sense of fulfillment in an otherwise stressful social environment.

Creativity

In addition to keeping emotions in balance, older adults may have an advantage over younger people in the area of creativity. There is mounting evidence that the aging brain can innovate, create and contribute to society in extraordinary ways. Contrary to the popular assumption that creativity is the sole purview of youth, Gene Cohen (2000) argues in his book, *The Creative Age*, that creativity is a strength at *all ages* and can deepen and become richer as people get older. He also argues that *everyone* has what it takes to be creative, contradicting the common belief that creative people are either born with inherited talent or raised in a special environment.

What is creativity? Traditional definitions of creativity comprise two parts: (1) originality and (2) functionality. People are considered creative when they produce an idea or product that has not existed before, and the idea or product is sufficiently functional to meet some criteria of usefulness (Kersting, 2003). Psychologists often make a distinction between 'Big C' creativity and 'little c' creativity (Simonton, 2010). While 'Big C' creativity applies to the extraordinary accomplishments of great scientists, artists and inventors (e.g. Einstein's theory of relativity, Picasso's invention of cubism and Edison's electrical inventions), creativity with a 'little c' is grounded in the diversity of everyday activities and accomplishments (Cohen, 2000).

Cohen explains that every person has certain areas in which he or she has a special interest – be it writing memos or teaching a lesson or selling something – and that after working for a while, each person can get to be as good as anybody they know in their immediate world. In other words, creativity is not just for geniuses; everyone can develop creativity with a 'little c'. 'Little c' creativity applies to individuals who set small challenges for themselves in everyday life, like preparing a meal a little differently, creating a new floral arrangement or approaching a problem at work from a new angle. While 'little c' creativity may never reach a level of public awareness or broader impact that changes the world, it enhances the life of the creator and provides satisfaction for the creator and for others.

Creative thinking often extends beyond the individual mind and involves social interaction. In her book, *Notebooks of the Mind*, Vera John-Steiner (1997) shows that many of the opportunities for creativity that we encounter in life are social in nature. She argues that creativity is not a personality trait but rather a dynamic, interactive system, for which shared experience is crucial. Her approach is based on a Vygotskyan, sociocultural theory of the mind, which views interaction with caregivers, peers, teachers and the material world as the basis for learning and intellectual development. Other researchers support John-Steiner's social view of creativity (e.g. Csikszentmihalyi, 2013; Gardner, 1983, 1993; Wallace & Gruber, 1989). Csikszentmihalyi (2013: 1) argues that a creative idea or product is an outcome of the synergy of many sources, including the people and conditions in the environment. He shows that, contrary to the popular image of the lone genius toiling away in solitude, creative people need a culture and community of experts that can foster and validate one another's work. Creativity is fueled by meaningful social interaction.

Research shows that the aging brain resembles the creative brain in important ways. In a recent study, psychologist Sunghan Kim and his colleagues found that older adults (ages 61–74) were generally more distractible than younger adults (ages 18–23). However, the researchers also found that older adults were better able to use the distracting information to solve problems presented later in the study (Kim *et al.*, 2007). The authors point out that the older adults' propensity for distractibility is also found in highly creative individuals who resort to a broader rather than narrower focus in solving problems. Having a wider view (i.e. being more distractible) allows the individual to combine seemingly disparate and unrelated bits of information into new and original ideas. For older adults, having access to an increasing warehouse of knowledge gained over a lifetime of learning and experience, combined with their tendency to zoom out and see the bigger picture, provides fertile ground for creativity (Carson, 2009).

Creative activity is linked to substantial health benefits, including mental clarity, increased awareness, improved emotional states and physical healing (Perlstein, 2006; Schmidt, 2006; Sherman, 2006). Creativity is a 'central source of meaning in our lives' (Csikszentmihalyi, 2013: 1), and older adults can experience personal growth and transcend the immediacy of the physical problems associated with aging through creative activity (Flood & Phillips, 2007). Participating in creative work leads to lower blood pressure, stabilized heart rate and hormone levels and the release of endorphins, improving the function of the immune system (Lane, 2005). Creativity interventions such as art-related therapy (e.g. music therapy, poetry therapy, drama therapy, dance and movement therapy) promote overall mental and physical health, improve the quality of life for those who are ill and reduce the risk factors in people needing long-term care (Cohen, 2006; Hanna, 2006).

Social interaction, a key ingredient in creative activity, is also associated with better health. People with strong social networks and high levels of social activity are less likely than their more socially disengaged peers to experience declines in cognitive functioning (e.g. Barnes *et al.*, 2004; Glei *et al.*, 2005). In a study that followed more than 1,200 older adults who were tested over a three-year period, epidemiologist Laura Fratiglioni and her colleagues found that participants with strong and positive social networks were 60% less likely to show signs of dementia three years later (Fratiglioni *et al.*, 2000). People who engage in volunteer activities that are either socially or mentally demanding also perform better in cognitive tasks than do those engaged in solitary activities with low cognitive demands (Singh-Manoux *et al.*, 2003). In addition to fending off decline, strong social networks help individuals regain cognitive functioning after a stroke (Glymour *et al.*, 2008). People who report strong social networks are also at lower risk for illness and mortality (Berkman *et al.*, 2000; Ryff & Singer, 2001).

Anna: Keeping Alzheimer's at bay by activating the brain

In Chapter 2, I introduced Anna, a 61-year-old retiree who decided to pursue a second career in TESOL after more than 30 years of working for the federal government as a foreign language specialist. Anna summarized the cognitive benefits of teaching ESL as follows:

> [Teaching ESL] keeps your mind active. When you're working with people from other cultures, they're always telling you surprising things and giving you something thought-provoking. It keeps the wheels turning inside your head. My worst nightmare is having Alzheimer's, because you lose the essence of who you are. I hope that by keeping myself involved in what's going on around me and challenging my way of thinking and doing things, I can keep my mind going. It really activates my brain to plan what I'm going to teach students and think about how to explain various aspects of English. When I come up with a new idea about how to teach something, I get a lot of satisfaction out of that. It's kind of fulfilling a need that I have to be creative. (Anna)

As someone who fears getting Alzheimer's disease more than anything else, Anna is well versed in the literature on mental health and aging. While she knows that there is no proven way to prevent Alzheimer's, she believes that she can do certain things to reduce her risk of developing the disease. In addition to leading a healthy lifestyle with regular physical exercise and a nutritious diet, she tries to maintain strong social connections and keep her mind active. She finds her interactions with her ESL students especially energizing, because they provide her with novel insights and show her different ways of thinking about things. While planning lessons takes a considerable amount of energy and gives her brain a 'workout', she enjoys the creative process of coming up with new ways to engage her students.

> With the student that I'm working with now, I've found that a lot of times she will tell me about an incident, her home life, her school life, and I will kind of file that away in my memory. A day or a week later, I'll read something in the newspaper, or I'll see a comic strip in the newspaper that's related to what she was talking about, and the next time I meet with her, I show her that. We go through the article, and I can explain words she doesn't understand, or we can talk about idioms, or I can have her summarize the article for me, and it helps her work on her English. At the same time, it shows her the connection between what's happening in her personal life and how this can actually take a printed form. I think that it's helped her a lot. (Anna)

Anna is a marvelous example of someone in the second half of life who taps into her intelligence and experience to create a positive learning experience for her students. Not only does she teach vocabulary, grammar and reading comprehension strategies, but she also looks for ways to help her students relate what they are learning in the classroom to their lives outside the classroom. Her patient and kind-hearted demeanor often invite her students to share what is going on in their lives. When this happens, she listens intently to their stories, tries to react without being judgmental and offers words of advice and encouragement. Once the face-to-face classroom time is over, her brain is still at work throughout the week, scanning the world around her for bits of insights that she might bring back to the classroom. By incorporating authentic language materials that are relevant to her students' experiences, she makes the language lesson come alive. Her students benefit from a more meaningful language learning experience, and Anna draws a deep sense of satisfaction from her creative endeavors.

Benefits of Multicultural Experience

What types of social interaction promote creative thinking? Research suggests that social interaction that involves exposure to foreign cultures may enhance creativity (Leung *et al.*, 2008). The experience of living abroad, for instance, encourages relativistic thinking and enables individuals to apply unconventional approaches to solving problems (Maddux & Galinsky, 2009). Multicultural experiences facilitate a different view of the world and challenge long-held assumptions about human behavior and the realities of life. People who open themselves up to different cultures and play down the need for firm answers are better able to engage with the world around them in creative ways than those who do not (Leung & Chiu, 2010). The insights gained from multicultural interactions allow new connections to be made between neurons, extending the scope of people's creative capacity.

Suzanne: From Elderhostel to TESOL

Suzanne exudes energy and vitality. A retired librarian, Suzanne describes herself as currently having two professional occupations – one as an ESL instructor and the other as a part-time archivist. After receiving her master's degree in TESOL in her late sixties, she has been teaching ESL to adults at local community colleges. In addition, Suzanne has been working one day a week managing the archives for a non-profit organization. A mother of three grown-up sons and grandmother of nine grandchildren, she maintains a very active lifestyle. When I asked about her children, she exclaimed, 'My children are, God, they're old!' The eldest of her three sons is 50. As was typical for women in the 1950s, she was married right after college and gave birth to her first child nine months later.

> I worked as a librarian when I graduated from college, but that only lasted 6 months. In those days, you weren't even supposed to work when you showed. When my oldest son was 16, I went back to library school. It was very boring just taking care of children. I was never very good at it. I would much rather be doing something else. I worked half-time at the local library, Mondays and Thursdays from 1 to 9 and then every other Saturday. Then as soon as the children were old enough, I went into academic librarianship. I was at [university a], and then I got divorced. Then I could really move, and I went to [university b] in Indiana, and then to [university c] in New York, and then to [university d]. It was all university. It was all science. (Suzanne)

Suzanne remarried in 1990 and moved to Maryland, but her second husband passed away 10 years later. After retiring from her librarian career in 1998, she tried to keep herself busy by taking music theory courses at a local community college. When I asked what motivated her to study music theory, she said, 'I just love the way music is put together. It's like a puzzle. I really enjoyed that'. She also participated in several Elderhostel programs in hiking, biking, kayaking and skiing. Founded in 1975, Elderhostel, also known as Road Scholar, provides people over the age of 60 with low-cost educational and cultural programs. Participants experience a variety of learning opportunities, from cultural tours to study cruises to outdoor activities. It was while participating in an Elderhostel folk dancing program that Suzanne decided to pursue a degree in teaching ESL.

There was a woman there, and she had on a T-shirt. It was in Czech, and it was about teaching English as a Second Language. I said, 'Oh!', and she said, 'Yes!' She had just graduated, and she was my age. And I said, 'Oh, at your age, you did that?' And she said, 'Oh, it doesn't matter how old you are. You can do that'. And I thought, alright. Even though [TESOL] was something in the back of my mind, this was kind of what put me over the edge to do it. (Suzanne)

Emboldened by seeing someone her age pursuing a post-retirement career in TESOL, Suzanne decided that she could study to become an ESL teacher as well. It took her several years to complete her master's degree in TESOL, but when she finally got her degree, she was able to secure part-time ESL teaching positions in community colleges relatively easily. She has been teaching ESL for about eight hours per week ever since. When I asked her to describe the students she has taught over the years, Suzanne could hardly contain her excitement and talked animatedly about them.

My favorite courses I taught were in [city x]. I love my students in [city x], because it's a really authentic group of people. They've been through the mill. One of my students was an Ethiopian Christian priest, and he had several of his parishioners with him. You'll find in [city x] a lot of these kids who escaped from Africa. They have such stories to tell. They've had such lives, that you can't imagine. And they're just terrific people. One of my students, I remember, was from Mali. It was from him that I learned that that's where most American jazz musicians came from. Their music is very similar to American jazz. All these things you learn from these students! I had one woman student, I just love this, who had started out as a hotel maid, and she got together her money. She was running a cleaning service that she had people working for. It was the American story. It's just so much fun to run into that. You see, that can still happen in the 21st century. People can come with nothing and recreate themselves. (Suzanne)

By characterizing her students as 'a really authentic group of people' with 'such stories to tell', Suzanne explains how her interactions with them have opened her eyes to new realities. She is fascinated by 'all these things you learn from these students' and inspired by stories of those who achieve their goals through hard work. Her encounters with immigrant students, many of whom have maintained a positive outlook on life despite extraordinary hardships and adversity, contribute to her own optimistic view of the world and to her emotional and physical well-being. Overall, teaching ESL has been an excellent post-retirement career choice for Suzanne, who has always sought out intellectually stimulating activities.

Jonathan: Coming into a new place with an alien culture

While multicultural experiences can provide many benefits, they often take us out of our comfort zones. When we are in a foreign country, we may experience culture shock and feel disoriented in the absence of familiar things. The language, food and behavioral norms that we typically take for granted are often lost in a foreign culture, leaving us feeling unsettled and out of place. Consider the cross-cultural experience of Jonathan, a career librarian with a PhD in philosophy, who recently spent one month in Ecuador teaching English to adult Ecuadoran students. The following is an excerpt from a note that Jonathan sent from Ecuador to one of his friends in the United States.

> As soon as you set foot in the new environment, time seems to speed up. What was habitual has to be considered consciously now because any detail might turn out to be different.... Even handling a cup of coffee is challenge because the cup is just slightly different than any cup I've seen in the past three years, plus while thinking of the cup, I'm also trying to figure out what the server just asked me—was it about whether I was taking it out? Did it relate to sugar or stirrers or cup lids? And, how can I get a napkin? Should I tip? All this distracts from basic motor control, so I spill the coffee on myself, or have to shift my carrying case in order to hold the coffee better, and then walk into the door frame. After getting coffee once, I feel strong pressure to do it exactly the same next time since I won't have to do all the first-time-in-my-life thinking that I did last time. (Jonathan)

In this excerpt, Jonathan describes his distorted sense of time and how his brain is constantly put to work by having to think consciously about decisions he would normally breeze through at home. Processing Spanish input is mentally exhausting, as he is not very proficient in the language. Every encounter with a stranger is laborious, as he lacks knowledge of the expected norms of behavior in this society. He feels physically awkward and clumsy, having to perform routine acts consciously rather than habitually. Even something as ordinary as buying a cup of coffee becomes a demanding mental exercise in this new setting. But as he fumbles and makes a mess, his brain creates a new schema to account for the experience, and the next time he faces a similar situation, he would likely adapt his behavior so as not to make the same mistakes. Though difficult and uncomfortable, new learning will have taken place, and neuronal connections that did not exist previously will have been created.

In fact, after two weeks of his stay in Ecuador, Jonathan was able to use his accumulated knowledge to purchase a briefcase on his own, an event he considers as constituting the 'next level of complexity' in this new setting. His note to his friend continues as follows.

For example, I just today found time and figured out an approach to buying a portfolio briefcase. It took an hour of going from one stand to another, haggling, analyzing, and finally purchasing the best one I could find for $54. You can tell me if my head was still buzzing at purchase time, when you see the result. It is all leather, with uncountably many zippers and sections and straps. It is big enough for the computer and all my other stuff without looking outsized. (Jonathan)

As Jonathan's experience attests, being in a foreign environment can be rather unnerving. But it is precisely these new experiences outside one's comfort zone that stimulate the brain to innovate, make adjustments and invent unorthodox solutions to problems. Even in the midst of feeling confused and out of control, Jonathan is able to celebrate small successes like this and gradually build a repertoire of skills to function in this environment. His horizon is broadened to include possibilities he may not have considered before, and his confidence grows as he navigates the subtleties of everyday events in the new setting.

The Dangers of Negative Age Stereotypes

As exciting and invigorating as it may be for older adults to engage in creative thinking and mentally stimulating pursuits, not everyone chooses to participate in these activities. What explains the reluctance of some adults? One contributing factor is that as people age, they become more and more accustomed to the way things are. After decades of doing things more or less the same way, people often find it difficult to break out of their routine in search of unknown adventures. It requires a considerable amount of determination and effort to shake things up, to move to a new environment and to feel uncertain and vulnerable again. Thus, one of the reasons that older people do not seem creative is that they frequently forego opportunities in which their intellectual capabilities could be challenged (Enayati, 2012).

Another, perhaps more important reason is that we live in a youth-oriented society, where being young is celebrated and old age is frowned upon. Age stereotypes, or negative views about older people abound, and we tend to focus more on what is bad about aging than what is good about it. Rather than viewing old age as a time of wisdom, self-realization and satisfaction, we are more inclined to regard it as a time of decline, decrepitude and dependence. Internalized age stereotypes make people think that they are no longer capable of new learning and innovation, and older adults who believe they are 'over the hill' or 'past their prime' are more likely to give up without trying when presented with a new challenge.

In an influential paper, psychologists Claude Steele and Joshua Aronson introduced a concept called 'stereotype threat', which refers to being at risk of confirming a negative stereotype about one's group as self-characteristic

(Steele & Aronson, 1995). In several experiments, Steele and Aronson (1995) showed that African American college students performed more poorly on standardized tests than White students when their race was emphasized. When race was not emphasized, however, African American students performed better and equivalently with White students. Stereotype threat can undermine the academic performance of African Americans who think that their behavior might be viewed through the lens of racial stereotypes and can even lead to significant negative health outcomes among them (Blascovich et al., 2001; Steele, 2010).

There are positive stereotypes at work as well. For example, a common cultural stereotype holds that Asian Americans have superior mathematical skills compared with other ethnic groups. Could this positive stereotype work to their advantage? In an interesting study, psychologist Margaret Shih and her colleagues investigated the math performance of Asian American women (Shih et al., 1999). When it comes to math performance, Asian American women present an interesting test case, because while they are subject to a positive stereotype due to their ethnic status as Asians, they are also susceptible to a negative stereotype about women (i.e. 'Women are not good in math'). The authors found that Asian American women performed better on a math test than a control group when their ethnic identity (i.e. positive stereotype) was activated but performed worse than the control group when their gender identity (i.e. negative stereotype) was activated. If performance on academic tests can be enhanced by activating positive social stereotypes (or harmed by activating negative social stereotypes), then it is no longer a purely cognitive phenomenon. It is as much social as it is psychological.

Likewise, the concept of stereotype threat has strong implications for how people see themselves and develop their potential in the second half of life. Individuals who confirm negative age stereotypes as self-characteristic perform worse than those who hold positive views of aging on an array of cognitive and physical tests (Levy & Leifheit-Limson, 2009). People's perceptions of their own abilities are a powerful predictor of what they can accomplish, and seniors with positive age stereotypes are 44% more likely to fully recover from a bout of disability (Levy et al., 2012) and live a longer life (7.5 years longer on average) than those with negative age stereotypes (Levy et al., 2002). Levy (2009) argues that interventions aimed at changing older people's attitudes toward aging can have significant health implications and demonstrates the potential for such interventions through laboratory experiments that activate positive age stereotypes.

We are often unaware of how age stereotypes shape our perceptions of older people. Like racism and sexism, ageism – negative beliefs about people in a particular age group – frequently operates below the level of consciousness and forms early in life (Levy, 2003). Young people are not directly affected by their own stereotypes about older adults until they become older themselves, and when they do, their views about older people may have a negative effect on them. A recent study found that negative age stereotypes held early in life predict negative health outcomes among older individuals (Levy *et al.*, 2009). In a cohort of 440 participants, aged 18–49, those who held negative age stereotypes earlier in life were significantly more likely to experience a cardiovascular event over the next 38 years than those who did not hold such stereotypes. Furthermore, in a younger subset of 229 individuals, aged 18–39 years, those with more negative age stereotypes at baseline were twice as likely to have a cardiovascular event after age 60 than those with more positive age stereotypes (Levy *et al.*, 2009). Based on these results, the authors conclude that programs aimed at reducing the negative age stereotypes of younger individuals could benefit their cardiovascular health when they become older.

Since the way we think about aging has strong implications for our physical and mental well-being, helping people understand the harmful effects of age stereotypes should be a policy priority in a rapidly aging society. The fact is that everyone is aging, and all of us can think of ways in which to fight negative age stereotypes and reinforce the positive aspects of aging. Just as racism and sexism hurt everyone, ageism harms both younger and older populations, and we need to encourage people to reach their full potential and provide them with opportunities to expand their intellectual and creative capacities. To think of older adults only in terms of decline and disability is to overlook their value as a resource of enormous potential (Cohen, 2000: 21). When we dismiss that potential, we squander a huge portion of our society's assets to our detriment.

Toward a More Positive View of Human Potential in Later Life

I opened this chapter with the research on the remarkable plasticity of the human brain. We saw that the brain keeps growing throughout the lifespan and continually reshapes itself in response to new experiences. The brain is always adding to its base of knowledge and capabilities, even as physical functioning weakens gradually over time. As a result of accumulated experience and learning, the aging brain has distinct advantages over the younger brain in areas such as problem-solving, social relationships and creative thinking. Having access to a wide range of lessons gathered over a longer lifespan, the older brain has the capacity to innovate and create in extraordinary ways if provided with adequate incentive. In addition, older adults have the advantage of being able to regulate their emotions better than younger adults and refrain from impulsive emotional responses. Older adults are also more likely to stay calm in the face of life's challenges and focus on the positive aspects of their lives. As we will see, all of these attributes of older adults are exceedingly valuable assets, especially for a profession that requires as much patience, level-headedness and empathy as teaching.

Strong social networks have a profoundly positive impact on the health of the mind and body in later life. We saw in this chapter that people with high levels of social activity are at lower risk of illness and mortality and are less likely to experience declines in cognitive functioning than those who are socially disengaged. Teaching and learning English are very much a collaborative endeavor between teachers and their students, and both groups have valuable insights to contribute to this social process. Multicultural relationships fostered in the ESL classroom are emotionally enriching, as they bring together the experiences and perspectives of people from different cultural backgrounds and can act as catalysts for the creation of new ideas. In order to be effective, teachers need to be able to meet their students where they are and consider the materials that they are trying to teach from the students' perspectives. This requirement drives teachers to tap into their intellectual potential in ways that broaden their horizons as well as those of their students.

At a stage in life when many people plan to sit back, relax and spend their hard-earned retirement in leisure, the individuals in my study have made the choice to put their minds and energies to work as teachers. In my interviews, one of the most consistent reasons that people gave for teaching ESL was that it is fun and keeps the mind active. While all study participants find the process of preparing and delivering lessons to be quite challenging, they also find the exchange of ideas and conversation in the classroom to be hugely rewarding. By engaging with people from diverse cultural backgrounds and looking for effective ways to reach their students, they not only fulfill their desire to make a positive difference in the lives of others but also satisfy their built-in human drive to innovate, think and create.

4 The Role of Prior Work Experiences in Choosing TESOL

Not many children grow up thinking that they will become an ESL teacher (a teacher, yes; but not an ESL teacher). Instead, many ESL teachers discover the profession by volunteering as literacy tutors in the community, helping neighbors who speak little English or working or traveling abroad. Consequently, TESOL attracts latecomers with experiences in other professions. In this chapter, I explore how prior work experiences in different fields contribute to individuals' decisions to pursue TESOL. I briefly review entry requirements to Master of Arts (MA) TESOL programs and describe the diverse educational backgrounds and job histories of the participants in my study. I show how personal dreams and aspirations are shaped and reshaped by changing life circumstances and how TESOL is incorporated into people's visions of what they want to be and where they want to go in the second half of life.

Requirements for Entering TESOL Programs

As a professional field, TESOL has a relatively low barrier to entry, which appeals to people looking to switch careers. Applicants to TESOL programs do not need to demonstrate that they have had significant previous coursework in English. Unlike some of the other professional graduate studies, which require considerable undergraduate coursework in specific content areas (e.g. science courses for applicants to medical or dental school), TESOL does not require substantial preparation in any particular discipline. MA TESOL programs are open not only to English majors but also to applicants with bachelor's degrees in a variety of other fields. Typically, admission requirements include the following:

- An undergraduate degree in *any major* with a minimum GPA of 3.0.
- A statement of purpose.
- Letters of reference.
- Standardized test scores (e.g. Graduate Record Examination [GRE] in the United States).
- TOEFL for international applicants.

In evaluating applications, reviewers look for strong academic preparation as evidenced in grade point averages and test scores, a genuine desire to help English learners and cross-cultural sensitivity. While teaching experience is not a requirement in most programs, some familiarity with students in various learning situations is considered helpful.

That TESOL is broadly accessible to individuals with a wide range of backgrounds is a special draw for people who wish to work in international settings but lack the specific content expertise desired by host countries (e.g. forestry/natural resources; oceanography; foods, nutrition, dietetics). For instance, one of the participants of this study, Ruth, is pursuing a master's degree in TESOL so that she can join the Peace Corps.

> I've wanted to do Peace Corps from the time I first heard about it when I was in 6th grade. Peace Corps was 2 or 3 years old at the time. It was brand new. It was like a year after Kennedy was shot. My 6th grade teacher had a daughter who was in Ethiopia. And I just thought that that was the neatest thing to do, helping people dig wells for pure water or something. I want to go to a place not very developed. I've always lived in the Eastern U.S., and I want to experience a culture that I wasn't born into. I want to work with a needier segment of the world. (Ruth)

Ruth is enrolled in the Peace Corps Master's International (MI), a program that offers MA TESOL coursework with an extensive internship through the Peace Corps. Students begin their coursework in the United States and design an independent academic project, which they then carry out while they complete their Peace Corps field assignment. When I asked Ruth why she chose to incorporate TESOL into her Peace Corps experience, she said she had originally wanted to do work involving biology and earth science. However, MI programs in those fields required undergraduate coursework in the sciences, which she did not have.

> I had also thought about doing an MI in science. I wished that I had gotten a degree in something like ecology, because I've always been fascinated by bugs and animals and plants. I'm a nature freak. There is an MI program through [university X], but they said you had to have a B.S. But mine was a B.A., not a B.S.[1] (Ruth)

Ruth decided that it was impractical to do another bachelor's degree and felt that an MI in TESOL would satisfy her desire to help people in need in another part of the world and experience a different culture at the same time.

Aside from the fairly general entry requirements, what contributes to the perceived accessibility of TESOL is the belief that English speakers already possess intimate knowledge of the content they wish to teach. Compared to teaching a content area subject like high school mathematics, teaching one's native language to speakers of another language seems like a simpler task to most people. In the current study, all participants, except

Martha, are native speakers of English.[2] When asked why they decided to teach English (as opposed to another subject area), the participants typically responded that since they already spoke English, they felt confident about teaching it. They also pointed out the growing demand for English teachers throughout the United States and around the globe, and how their teaching of English could address that need. Because so many people in the world want to learn English, the participants in the study believed that their knowledge of English was a marketable skill, a valuable 'commodity' in a globalized world (Heller, 2003). Below, Jonathan discusses what it means for him to be a 'native English speaker'.

> [My students in Ecuador] seemed to be quite taken with the idea of having a native English speaker. Even though the Ecuadoran teachers had very good English, they weren't native English speakers. My being a native English speaker seemed to have a lot of cachet, and I was kind of pleased with that. Like for no fault of my own, I seemed to be popular on that score. It's like an unearned privilege somehow. I almost felt guilty about that, you know, why would they give me more respect than other people who had worked really hard to learn good English and teach English? (Jonathan)

Here, Jonathan describes how he felt both pleased with and guilty about the preferential treatment he received in Ecuador over Ecuadoran English teachers who are English learners themselves. The view that native speakers are superior in linguistic competence as compared to non-native speakers and that they are owners of proper, authentic language is very common throughout the world (Doerr, 2009). But as people who have ever tried to teach ESL without formal training quickly discover, native speaker status in no way guarantees one's success as a teacher of English. In fact, many non-native English-speaking teachers of English are credited with a more conscious knowledge of English grammar and with language learning experience that they can share with learners. Thus, they can serve as good models and empathize with the language learners they work with (Braine, 1999). In order to be effective as an ESL teacher, one must acquire pedagogical knowledge, which includes how to present language and cultural material in ways that facilitate student learning; how to help students practice speaking, listening, reading and writing in a second language; and how to assess students' growing linguistic competence. One also needs to develop sufficient understanding of the linguistic and cultural backgrounds of the students to be effective as an ESL teacher.

Educational Backgrounds of the Participants

Table 4.1 summarizes the educational backgrounds and job histories of the study participants. The sample includes substantially more women (24)

Table 4.1 Educational backgrounds and job histories of the study participants

Name*	Age	Sex	Educational background	Previous job(s)/career(s)	Current job(s)
Andrea	57	F	BA in French with a minor in German	Bank employee; underwriter at an insurance company; language teaching methodologist for a federal government agency	Language teaching methodologist for the federal government
Anna	61	F	BA in Spanish; MA in Spanish Linguistics	Foreign language specialist for a federal government agency	Part-time adult ESL instructor
Barbara	57	F	BA in Fine Arts and Education	Graphic artist and sign painter; editor and proofreader; quality control inspector for home builders; substitute Spanish and French teacher; short-order cook; stablewoman; waitress	Graphic artist and sign painter; editor and proofreader; quality control inspector for home builders; part-time adult ESL instructor
Bill	53	M	BS in Political Science; Master of Business Administration	Import/export business; corporate trainer	Full-time elementary school ESL teacher
Bonny	57	F	BA in English	University admissions coordinator	University admissions coordinator; part-time adult ESL instructor
Clara	60	F	BA in French Literature with minor in German Literature; BS in Mechanical Engineering	Filing files in an insurance company; car mechanic; Port Authority employee; engineer	Engineer; volunteer adult ESL teacher
David	63	M	BA in English	Family business buying and selling used steel drums; selling exotic birds; worked in electronics for a telephone company; self-owned business in painting houses; counselor for the mentally retarded; US Navy; tutor; writing advisor	Undergraduate academic coordinator

(continued)

Table 4.1 (*continued*)

Diane	65	F	BA in Humanities; MA in Romance Languages	Court transcriber; translator (Italian, Spanish, French); information specialist; consultant; human resources director; trade association work; copyeditor; yarn shop co-owner	Part-time adult ESL teacher
Elaine	53	F	BA in Art History; Doctor of Chiropractic	EFL teacher in Italy; chiropractor	Chiropractor
Elizabeth	71	F	BA in Music with a minor in English and Foreign Languages; MFA in Music Performance and Costume Design; Juris Doctor	Voice instructor; costume designer; administrative assistant for a non-profit organization; paralegal; attorney; English for specific purposes instructor	English for specific purposes instructor; contract editor; cross-cultural communications workshop facilitator
Ginny	57	F	BA in Psychology; Bachelor of Architecture	Architect; stay-at-home mom	Part-time adult ESL instructor
Helen	54	F	BA in English; MA in Human Resources Development	Environmental activist; fundraiser; recruiter for a newspaper company; organizational development job at a bank; worked in a bakery; substitute teacher	Part-time family literacy instructor
Henry	45	M	BS and MS in Mechanical Engineering	Engineer	Full-time high school ESL teacher
James	60	M	BA in Music with a minor in Spanish	Jazz musician; incense maker	Full-time elementary school ESL teacher; incense maker

(*continued*)

Table 4.1 (continued)

Name	Age	Sex	Education	Previous careers	Current position
Joan	70	F	BA in Political Science	Civil rights activist; community organizer; program administrator; projector director for a HIV/AIDS study	Community organizer
Jonathan	65	M	BA in Humanities; MA in Library Science; PhD in Philosophy	Philosophy instructor; reference librarian	Library director
Joni	47	F	BA in English	Paralegal; stay-at-home mom; receptionist; supermarket cashier; school health room technician	Full-time elementary school ESL teacher
Julia	54	F	BA in Psychology; Master of Social Work	Social worker	Stay-at-home mom; part-time adult ESL teacher
Lesley	56	F	BA in Elementary Education and Human Development; BS in Information Systems/Computer Science; MA in Instructional Systems Design	Travel agent; software engineer/corporate trainer/project manager at a telephone company; customer service agent for an airline company	Starting a long-term fifth-grade substitute teaching position at a public school
Lynn	49	F	BA in International Relations with a Latin American concentration; Juris Doctor	Attorney	Part-time adult ESL instructor
Margie	52	F	BA in German; MA in International Business	Au pair; paralegal; credit analyst for a bank; contracts administrator; stay-at-home mom	Stay-at-home mom; part-time adult ESL instructor
Marianne	67	F	BA in Interior Design; BS in Child Psychology; Master of Social Work	Social activist; neighborhood renovator; day-care center director; administrator at a law firm; social worker	Social work consultant; part-time adult ESL instructor

(continued)

Table 4.1 (*continued*)

Martha	45	F	BS in Elementary Education	Stay-at-home mom; substitute teacher	Stay-at-home mom; substitute teacher
Patricia	54	F	BA in English	Sales/merchandising for a cosmetics company; volunteer work while raising three children	Full-time middle school ESL teacher
Paula	54	F	BS in Biology; PhD in Biology	Tenure-track assistant professor in Neurobiology	Part-time adult ESL instructor
Ruth	57	F	BA in Human Development and Family Studies	Model builder/industrial designer; stay-at-home mom; community organizer; ESL tutor	Part-time adult ESL tutor
Sonia	45	F	BA in German	Social group work; housing coordinator; English as a foreign language (EFL) teacher in Austria; program director for a non-profit organization; administrative assistant	Administrative assistant
Suzanne	73	F	BA in History; MA in Library Science	Academic librarian at various universities	Part-time adult ESL instructor; part-time archivist
Theresa	58	F	BA in History; MA in Journalism	Secretarial jobs; newspaper reporter; freelance writer; editor; high school teacher	Graduate assistant; part-time adult ESL teacher
Tom	64	M	BA in English	Manager for international operations for a federal government agency	Retired and living in Florida

*All participants were given pseudonyms.

than men (6), which is typical of teacher education programs in the United States. The participants range between 45 and 73 years of age and are well educated. Because an undergraduate degree is a minimum requirement for the MA TESOL program, all 30 participants have at least a bachelor's degree from a four-year institution. In addition, 4 participants have two bachelor's degrees each, and 12 have a master's degree. There are also two participants with a PhD, two with a law degree and one with a doctor of chiropractic degree. Although all 30 participants have a bachelor's degree, not everyone entered college immediately after graduating from high school. In addition, some entered college, dropped out and then returned to school many years later to finish their degrees.

In terms of undergraduate education, almost everyone majored in the arts, humanities and social sciences; only three participants have science or engineering degrees. Six majored in English, while five majored in a foreign language (e.g. German, French or Spanish). This translates to about a third of the participants having majored in a language-related discipline, whether it was English or another language. TESOL tends to attract people with a certain level of comfort with language and social interaction, and this participant pool reflects that. For example, James, who majored in music as an undergraduate student, states, 'I just like languages. I'm a humanist'. Barbara, who was a fine arts major in college, asserts, 'I feel very comfortable with language. I enjoyed teaching Spanish and French when I was subbing. It was fun. So I thought, well, I know English. I could teach that'. Aside from languages, the participants had majored in a wide variety of disciplines in the humanities and social sciences including history, psychology, international relations and political science. Almost everyone was a non-education major; only three participants majored in education as undergraduate students.

Job Histories of the Participants

As can be seen in Table 4.1, the participants in my study have worked in a variety of jobs in a wide range of fields, from corporate to non-profit sectors, from salaried positions to self-owned businesses, from blue-collar to white-collar jobs, from part-time to full-time work. While few of them have held one job for 20, 30 or 40 years, almost everyone has moved in and out of multiple jobs and careers, often in unrelated fields. Some of the women stopped working full-time when they had children, and two of the men had their education and employment interrupted by military service. A closer look at the job histories of the participants reveals that, by and large, teaching is not a totally novel enterprise. What is noteworthy about the participant pool is that more than a third have had some form of direct teaching experience prior to coming to TESOL, as part of their jobs in one form or another (e.g. corporate trainer, counselor, program director). In addition, most of the participants have taught ESL as volunteer teachers or tutors in local communities at some point in their lives. Thus, it was evident that, in choosing TESOL, the participants did not make their decisions blindly, but made deliberate considerations based on firsthand experience with English learners.

For most of the participants in the study, the process of deciding on the kind of work they wanted to do did not happen neatly in college. Neither did their job histories have clear, well-defined trajectories. Decisions to pursue certain lines of work over others were often complex. They were pushed and pulled by personal interests and changing life circumstances as well as the need to make a living. Finding fulfilling and suitable work often took time and required individuals to experiment with different jobs. Discovering one's passions and gifts was a dynamic process, as individuals continually developed in adulthood and personal interests evolved over time. Chance encounters and unexpected opportunities occasionally opened doors previously unknown, and what seemed like a terrible misfortune at first sometimes turned out to be a blessing in disguise. The first-person accounts of the study participants offer a glimpse into their dreams, hopes and fears, and how they have coped with life's challenges. The following excerpts capture some of the ways in which they characterized their careers.

> I would lump my career into three major areas. I did import/export in medical supplies for 3, 4 years. Then I got a job in international training, conducting trainings at conferences. I have been teaching ESL at [an elementary school] for 5 years. (Bill)

> I worked in New York as a costumer in the 70s. Then I worked 10 years as a paralegal, 20 years as a lawyer. I'm currently teaching ESL in two programs. (Elizabeth)

> My whole purpose in life has been to avoid working 9 to 5. And so, I pretty much have. TESOL is the very first thing I've done that had any economic, practical, immediate application. (Diane)

> I'm a sign painter and graphic artist. I do editing and proofreading. I also do quality control inspections for a home builder. I have many jobs, none of them full-time. I substitute taught and painted signs. I was a short-order cook. I worked in a stable. I've been a waitress. I've had jobs but I've never had a career. (Barbara)

The different job histories of Bill, Elizabeth, Diane and Barbara reflect the broad range of life experiences of the study participants. Below, I provide a closer look at the career paths of these four individuals and how they have arrived at TESOL.

Bill: A corporate trainer turned ESL teacher

In college, Bill was a political science major who was aspiring to become an attorney. A brief stint at a law firm, however, showed him that much of the work that lawyers did behind the scenes (when they were not in the courtroom) was unexciting and rather tedious. Having had an interest in international affairs, he then thought about becoming a foreign service officer. But after some research into foreign service careers, he decided that it would be more practical to pursue his international interests in the corporate sector. He applied and was accepted into business school and completed his MBA degree with a concentration in international business. Upon graduation, Bill worked for a few years importing and exporting medical supplies using connections he had in Venezuela. The business contacts he developed in that job subsequently led him to a corporate training position organizing international conferences and conducting training seminars. Bill really enjoyed this work and was planning to make a career of it, but his hopes were dashed when his firm downsized, and he was let go. The field of international training was undergoing a major transformation at that time, from a model based on in-person training to one incorporating greater amounts of distance learning. Preferring personal interactions over online communications, Bill found himself at a crossroads. Should he continue his work in training by adapting to distance learning or switch to a different career?

While he looked for another training job, Bill tried substitute teaching in elementary and middle schools for a year. When asked what drew him to public schools, he said it was relatively easy for him to find substitute teaching positions with his educational and work credentials. He also desperately needed to earn some money right away to support his wife and three children. Though his initial venture into public schools was motivated more by financial need than a true passion for working with children, it was while substitute teaching that he discovered TESOL. He observed some ESL teachers in the schools and became very interested in teaching students of immigrant families, who he thought seemed 'so hungry to learn' and 'so appreciative' of their teachers. He subsequently sought the advice of several ESL teachers at different schools in the district, all of whom suggested that he get a master's degree in TESOL.

Upon his acceptance into our MA TESOL program, Bill took courses in the evenings while substitute teaching. One year into the program, he was able to secure a full-time training job in instructional design and did that work while he finished his TESOL coursework. Then, shortly before completing his MA, he was offered a full-time ESL position at a public elementary school, where he has been teaching for five years. When asked how he felt about transitioning from the corporate world to public school education, Bill commented:

I'm mostly happy that I took that path. As a training consultant, I was making more than twice the money I was making when I first started teaching ESL. But even with the pay cut, my wife was glad I went into TESOL, because I was having a hard time finding a training job. Since I didn't have a regular full-time job for a while, she knew if I went into education, even if it doesn't pay as much, that it would be stable. That's what she liked. (Bill)

Having a family to support (with children aged 15, 11 and 8), Bill needed a job with benefits and a stable income, albeit a considerably smaller one than what he used to make during his corporate days. Job security in public education was a big draw for Bill and his family, and it was also what some of my other participants found attractive about teaching ESL in K-12 schools. Aside from Bill, four other participants were teaching ESL full-time in public schools at the time of the interview.

Elizabeth: 'The world is my stage'

Elizabeth, aged 71, finds herself in a different life stage than Bill. She does not have a family to support; her adult daughter and two stepchildren are grown up and independent. Elizabeth currently spends about a third of the year in foreign countries teaching English to scientists and engineers from around the world. Before coming to TESOL, she had done some very different kinds of work, including designing costumes for Off-Broadway theatre productions and working as a poverty lawyer. A voice major in college, Elizabeth had trained to become an opera singer. Many people who heard her intensely rich and colorful voice vowed that she would become the next Renata Tebaldi, one of the most beloved opera singers of all time. But a routine medical visit led to the doctors' discovery of nodes on her vocal cords, which, even if treated, would prevent her from performing as a singer. Her voice was never as strong as it used to be, and she was forced to switch to a different kind of repertoire at first and eventually give up singing altogether. Having dreamed of becoming a professional singer for as long as she could remember, Elizabeth was utterly devastated.

But her love of the opera could not be extinguished so quickly, and Elizabeth looked for ways in which she could work in concert halls and theatres. After some research, she decided that she would enjoy making the costumes that singers wore on stage and enrolled in a Master of Fine Arts (MFA) program in costume design. When asked what it was like to transition from music performance to costume design, she said it was 'extremely frustrating and satisfying': frustrating because she had to completely retool her skill set, but satisfying because once she started building costumes, her intimate knowledge of opera singing helped her design costumes that not only looked good on stage but also allowed singers to use their bodies in ways that produced full, rich sounds. She explained:

> When people are singing on stage, it's different than when they're acting on stage. They have to use their body differently, because they're producing that kind of sound. So you can't build period costumes that actually cinch people up. With the way they made costumes, women couldn't make a peep. So you have to make it look right, but you have to give them the room to breathe. You have to be able to do that kind of designing for people who have to use their bodies in that way. (Elizabeth)

Upon completion of her MFA, Elizabeth moved to New York City to work for an Off-Broadway theatre as a costumer. She thoroughly enjoyed her work as a costumer. While she could no longer sing, she felt she was nonetheless playing an important role in creating art. The many hours she spent each day designing and making costumes allowed her to imagine donning the outfits and enthralling the audience with her performance. But life changed once again when her daughter was born. Elizabeth was now responsible for the safety and welfare of another human being, and Manhattan seemed less and less like a suitable place to raise a young child, especially for low- to moderate-income families like hers.

After much soul-searching, she moved to Maryland with her family and started working as an administrative assistant in a non-profit organization that advocated for individuals with disabilities. The connections she developed there subsequently led her to a paralegal position at a law firm, which provided free legal services to low-income people. While Elizabeth believed that her work at the law firm was rewarding, she became increasingly frustrated that she could not represent her clients beyond the administrative hearing level as a paralegal. This motivated her to get a law degree. She was in her late forties when she became a licensed attorney, and she worked for another 20 years in poverty law until her retirement in 2008.

When I asked Elizabeth how she felt about changing careers again (this time, from theatre to law), she had a more tempered response. Unlike her previous switch from music performance to costume design, which she felt was drastic and painful, she saw a great deal of similarity between her work in theatre and the courtroom.

> You know, law is theatre. Because when you go into a courtroom, you're telling somebody's story. And you are there to convince the judge or the jury. You are, in a way, on stage, because it is your job to get the facts out there and get them out there in a way that convinces people. And for that, I think you have to have a little bit of theatre in you. It's a performance, and you're giving somebody else a voice. (Elizabeth)

Although a much different kind of performance than opera, Elizabeth clearly saw representing clients in a courtroom as a performance. Having long lost her ability to sing opera, Elizabeth had found another stage, on which she could 'give somebody else a voice'.

As gratifying as her work in costume design and poverty law has been, however, Elizabeth still relives her early dream of becoming an opera singer.

> I guess I'm a pretty happy person, but even today when I listen to opera, and I hear people singing something I used to be able to sing, it still brings me to tears. I can feel it, but I can't do it. I don't think that's ever going to go away. But it's okay, because I can appreciate what other people are doing. When I hear [the singers], I know what it takes to produce that sound. Even to this day, there's something about it that is just overwhelming. But it passes, you know, and the music is still beautiful. (Elizabeth)

When she retired from her legal work, Elizabeth had a new work chapter waiting for her in the world of TESOL. Actually, teaching English had overlapped with her work as an attorney for several years. In 1999, she was able to spend six weeks helping non-native English-speaking scientists and engineers with their English in an international program where her husband was on the faculty. She realized that she did not have the necessary skills to help them effectively, and after talking with a friend who was a schoolteacher in Maryland, she decided to obtain formal training in how to teach ESL. Elizabeth currently teaches ESL and facilitates cross-cultural communications workshops held in different countries each year. At 71, she wishes that she could do this work for another 20 years but admits that that is probably not realistic. She compromised by saying, 'I'll settle for five to eight'.

Diane: 'TESOL draws together all the strands of everything I've learned'

Diane, aged 65, could often be seen knitting during my classes in the TESOL program. A co-owner and manager of a yarn shop in Maryland, Diane explains, 'I come from a family where nobody sits still. You do not just sit in my family. You always have something in your hands, you're always doing something'. During the interview, Diane used a knitting analogy to justify her decision to become an ESL teacher: 'It brings all the threads together from things that I'd done before. I mean, a little linguistics, a little language, grammar from an entirely different point of view'. Diane describes herself as a 'heavily humanities person' who takes profound interest in 'what people view as useless knowledge'. Upon her graduation from college, Diane had enrolled in a PhD program in Romance philology at a university in Pennsylvania. She met her husband there, got married and relocated to Washington, DC with him. By then, she had completed all the requirements for her degree except her dissertation.

> We moved to Washington, and I was supposed to write the introduction to my dissertation, in which I was to say why *The Anglo-Norman Verse Prophecies of Merlin in Two Redactions* was important. There was Watergate, the oil crisis, and the Saturday Night Massacre, and I couldn't think of a simple reason. So I just stopped. (Diane)

Diane never finished her PhD. The early 1970s were a turbulent time in the United States, and she simply could not see how her dissertation could be useful in a society that was undergoing so much political and economic turmoil. While she had always been interested in the study of languages, she could not justify spending hours on end each day writing about a topic that seemed so far removed from the immediate realities of the world she lived in. But eager to put her language expertise to practical use, Diane found a job at a court reporting firm.

> I worked as a transcriber, which was fascinating, because they did the Watergate hearings, and I got to type up all the testimony for that. Then I worked for [an organization] translating environment-related newspaper articles from Italian and Spanish and French. I became a consultant for a small consulting firm downtown. I got tired of that and went back to the court reporting firm, where I was personnel and human resources director. Then I worked for a big trade association for 5 years and earned, honest to goodness, money for the first time in my life and had a big office. A friend and co-worker started an editing business, and I did book design and copyediting and developmental editing. (Diane)

As someone whose 'whole purpose in life' has been to 'avoid working 9 to 5', Diane often took jobs that allowed her to have a flexible schedule and use her talents in languages (e.g. transcribing, translating and editing). These jobs were attractive, because 'You work when you work, and you don't when you don't'. She also liked the fact that she could spend time with her two children when they were young. With her children both grown up and out of the house, Diane now spends most of her time managing her yarn shop and teaches ESL to adults at a local literacy council and in university intensive English programs. When asked how she would rate TESOL in relation to other jobs she has had in her life, Diane was quick to place it at the top.

To the extent I've had jobs, I think [TESOL] is probably the best one other than the really early days of editing. I don't mind the pay. You don't go into it for the money, but it really is very satisfying. The job I hated most was the job that paid the most. You couldn't give me enough money to make me go back to work for the trade association. (Diane)

Barbara: A graphic artist who 'retired' out of college

Barbara, aged 57, describes herself as having had many jobs but none of them on a full-time basis. Coming from a family of intellectuals with highly accomplished older sisters, Barbara said she 'grudgingly did the college thing'. She graduated in 1974, with a bachelor's degree in fine arts and education. Hoping to get a job as an art teacher, she applied to different school districts but received no offers; it was at the height of an economic recession. So, for two years, she sang and played guitar and mandolin in a five-member bluegrass band and gave concerts all over the United States. When her tour ended, she searched for a job where she could apply her art training and came across commercial sign painting. While painting signs was not what she had originally set out to do, she was quickly drawn to the intensely physical nature of the job. In fact, she liked it so much that she has been painting signs for more than 20 years and even runs a sign painting business from her house.

Barbara thinks that in her heart she is a 'blue-collar worker' and a 'craftsman' who is good at working with her hands. She admitted, 'I like getting dirty.... I'm not very graceful, but I like that whole body kinesthetic thing. I like being active and moving'. When asked how her art training in college helped her in sign painting, she explained that sign painting was actually very different from what she had learned as an art student in college.

Mine was all fine art, as opposed to commercial art, which were very separate entities back then. So I can sketch and draw, I know about color and design and layout, but everything you do in sign painting is as an apprentice. You get a job and work for somebody and learn. You do everything from digging holes to climbing ladders and painting letters on the sides of buildings while cars whiz by the ladder. (Barbara)

As much as she enjoyed sign painting, however, it was still a part-time position, and she needed to supplement her income in other ways. Over the years, Barbara has worked in a variety of positions as a short-order cook, a waitress, a stablewoman, an editor, a proofreader, a quality control inspector for a home builder, a fundraiser and a substitute Spanish teacher.

But none of these jobs were full-time, regular positions with benefits, which led her to conclude, 'I'm never going to be able to retire, because I've never had a job that gives me a retirement'. She griped that one of her older sisters even teases her by saying, 'You retired right out of college, and now you have to get a job and go to work'. When asked what her dream job would be, Barbara replied that, more than anything else, she would like to paint and create art. But she was quick to point out that doing art the way she envisions it is not financially viable.

> In my heart of hearts, what I would really like to do is just sit in my house and paint and do art. But it's just not practical. And I love working with horses, but it's just not practical. You have to do something that's practical. But of all the things that I've done, I don't like sitting in an office and working at a computer all day. It's just not something I could do. I don't think I could be a public servant, you know, sitting behind a desk. It's just not my thing, pushing papers. And I don't want to be a physical laborer anymore, I've outgrown that. So, I like the challenge of teaching. (Barbara)

Finding enjoyable work that pays a decent wage has been a perennial struggle for Barbara. Now, as she looks into the future and plans for a time when she would no longer be able to dig holes and climb ladders, TESOL serves as both a potentially rewarding line of work and a source of income.

What do People Want from Their Work?

In his book, *Working*, Studs Terkel (1974: xiii) asserts that work is a search for 'daily meaning as well as daily bread, for recognition as well as cash, for astonishment rather than torpor; in short, for a sort of life rather than a Monday through Friday sort of dying'. He adds that people desire to find meaning in their work and have an impact in the world. His collection of first-person narratives provides an intimate look at what ordinary people do every day in their work and how they feel about what they do. In the following, I explore how the participants in my study feel about the jobs they have had. I discuss some of the factors that contributed to their like or dislike of various jobs and how TESOL combines many of the desirable attributes of the work they have done.

Jobs that people disliked

On the whole, the jobs that the participants in my study disliked had the following characteristics: uninteresting work, work that is repetitive and monotonous, excessively long hours, stressful work, gender discrimination and being unrecognized or devalued by coworkers and supervisors. When the participants changed jobs, these were among the top reasons. But moving to a different job did not always solve the problems. Sometimes, people would leave a set of problems in one job, only to encounter a different set of difficulties in another.

> I would rate ESL 8 or 8.5. I would rate my other jobs 0. They were just money-making, treading-water kinds of jobs that I had until I figured out what I really wanted to do. (Joni)

> The first job I had was with a small architectural firm. The work was a little bit boring. The partners do the major things, and then you're like putting the details on where the toilet is. Then I got a job at a firm which had 65 people. It was so cut-throat and extremely competitive. And I can tell you that a lot of places did not want a woman to be their face. We were expected to put in overtime, 60 hours. (Ginny)

> The company got through divestiture, and we had turnover in management. I had done a presentation for some high-level muckety-mucks, and I was packing up my gear to leave and they sort of forgot I was there, and they started talking about the next reduction in force. And they were talking about hundreds of people like they're pawns, like they're worthless. There was absolutely no consideration of the fact that these were people whose lives were going to be turned upside down. I hated it. It was horrible. (Lesley)

> Then I was an administrator at [university x]. It wasn't working for me. I was like pushing papers around. (Joan)

> Office work, and government paperwork, and just the admissions office work is not very fulfilling. It's very frustrating to be working in the office all day. (Bonny)

None of the participants liked work that led only to a paycheck – 'just money-making, treading water kinds of jobs', as Joni put it. Before coming to TESOL, Joni had worked as a paralegal, and when she had her children, some part-time work as a supermarket cashier, a receptionist and a school health room technician. When I asked her to rate these jobs on a scale from 1 to 10 (with 1 being the worst and 10 being the best), she rated all of them 0. While she certainly appreciated the extra income she was able to bring home, she was doing these jobs just to survive. She never really looked forward to going to work; she went simply because she had to make money.

Like Joni, others yearned for something more than a paycheck. They wanted to experience purpose, fulfillment and variety, but there were obstacles to achieving these goals. For Ginny, it was sexism. When she graduated with a bachelor's degree in architecture in 1975, it was a time when there were very few women architects. In her graduating class of 90 students, only 3 were women. Ginny was strongly discouraged from going into architecture by her parents and relatives, who could not see a woman working as an architect. But Ginny was determined to study architecture and pursued it anyway. Upon graduation, she worked for about nine months in an unpaid position in which she helped to redesign a small section of a hospital. Then, she followed her husband to his new job in Arizona, where she was able to secure a paying job in a small architectural firm. Much to her dismay, however, she was given only minor roles in the company and was never included in the bigger decision-making. When she later moved to a larger architectural firm, it was the same story. In a highly competitive and male-dominated environment, women were given very few opportunities to advance but were still expected to put in 60-hour weeks.

Being devalued by coworkers and supervisors was a major source of grievance among the participants. Lesley talked about how demoralizing it was to be caught up in corporate mergers and acquisitions. When she started working as a software engineer for one of the major telecommunications companies in 1983, she considered herself very lucky. These were companies that people wanted to work for when they graduated from school, and that their children went to work for when they reached the right age. 'You wanted to work for the company for your whole life, and the company in return treated you well and offered you an employment package that made you feel like you were valued', she maintained. But as her company went through divestiture, and with the arrival of new management, everything changed. Lesley once heard a manager tell employees at a meeting that if they were working for the same company for more than five years, they were not worth anything. Gone were the days of lifetime employment and company loyalty. Relentless focus on the bottom line and cost-cutting were the new order of the day. All employees, no matter how skilled and valuable, were considered dispensable and were expected to figure out how to move on when their services were no longer deemed necessary.

Organizational bureaucracy and the seemingly endless paperwork associated with administrative jobs also turned many people off. Joan and Bonny complained of 'pushing papers around' in the office. Indeed, lack of variety was a major complaint among office administrators. As Theresa put it, 'doing the exact same thing every day of the year' does not appeal to many people. She said that when she first became a newspaper reporter, she could not wait to get to work. She thought it was the best thing that had ever happened. But after several years, she 'outgrew' newspaper reporting and did not want to do it anymore. So she worked as an editor for some time. When she got tired of that, too, she knew it was time to change to something completely different. Suzanne, who has had an illustrious career as an academic librarian, agrees, 'Everybody's sick of what they're doing by the time they're 60. I mean, you just get tired of it. And you need to have someplace else you can go'.

Jobs that people liked

The jobs that the participants in my study enjoyed had the following characteristics: interesting work, autonomy, meeting new people, addressing issues that one cares about, problem-solving and helping other people. Although the participants did not want to be stressed because of their jobs, they did not necessarily look for easy work. In fact, people enjoyed being challenged with difficult tasks as long as they could see that their work was meaningful and contributed to a worthy goal.

> I ran my own corporate travel office in a technology firm. I worked for a travel company, but the office was mine. It was a one-person thing. My job was to make their business travel reservations, the flight, the hotel. And it was just fun. I had a whole lot of autonomy, and I got to meet a lot of people. (Lesley)

> It's peaceful, making incense with all the nice fragrances, the fruits, the musks, and the flowers. I use an old chicken house that was on my parents' farm. When I go out there and start to mix the fragrances, it's very peaceful and relaxing. (James)

> A woman approached me one day and said, I need a project director for an HIV AIDS study at [name of university]. It had to do with IV drug users, women with HIV. That put me in connection with the issues that I had been concerned about. So the HIV AIDS work was bringing me back in touch with that. (Joan)

> What was good about fixing cars? Oh, unlike French or German, there was one right answer. The machine dictated reality, and it was your job to find out what reality the machine was in. It was very outside oneself. That was so appealing. It was also intuitive. You would get to the point where you would just be able to feel what was going on with the machine. (Clara)

> Maybe it's just where I come from, my culture, where we like to help. You know, Minnesota Nice is a real thing. I don't know if it's on our driver licenses yet, but it really is. Last time I heard, over 60% of people in Minnesota volunteer. They do something. Maybe it's my background, the way I was brought up. I enjoy helping people. I like talking to them. (Marianne)

In defining meaningful work, Adina Schwartz (1982: 635) refers to the notion of 'autonomy', which involves 'planning effectively to achieve one's aims instead of simply reacting to the circumstances'. According to Schwartz, autonomous people take responsibility for the decisions that they make and revise their goals and methods by observing the consequences of their choices. Having autonomy and exercising control over one's own goals, schedule and tasks was an important element of satisfying work for the study participants. Lesley shared that her most favorite job of all time was her travel agent job. For two years, she ran a one-person operation in a technology firm, where she was in charge of making travel arrangements for the whole company, 'from the president all the way down'. She had a great deal of autonomy and earned the gratitude of many employees, who liked her service so much that some even asked her to make their personal travel arrangements. By sending people where they needed to go, Lesley felt that she played an important role in helping them get things done. Her research into different cities and countries was fun and informative, introducing her to places she would otherwise not have known. Years later, when she worked for an airline company and could fly anywhere in the world for free, she actually visited many of these places herself.

Similarly, James, aged 60, described the joys of being one's own boss. A professionally trained jazz musician, James had dropped out of college to play in a band for 10 years. He wrote music, played the saxophone, made studio recordings and gave concerts all over the world. During that time, he met some Muslims in Philadelphia who sold him incense wholesale, which he took on the road and sold to other bands and people he met. When his tour ended and he was resettled in Maryland, James decided to learn how to make incense. At first, he bought his incense sticks locally, for which he paid a high price, but when he started importing container loads of sticks directly from Hong Kong, he was much more competitive. James's incense business has done very well for the last 37 years, and for a while, he even had two full-time helpers working for him. When one of his aunts passed away in 2003 and left him $46,000, James decided to use the money to return to school and finish his degree. He now has both a bachelor's degree and an MA in TESOL and is teaching ESL at a public K-8 school. Although he can only make incense on a part-time basis, it is still a great source of peace and satisfaction for him.

Another element of satisfying work for the participants in the study was having the opportunity to address issues that they cared about. When Joan started college in 1956, there was a growing political awareness on university campuses about civil rights issues. Having grown up in the suburbs in relative comfort, Joan had had no idea that these issues existed. But on campus, she met 'students who were aware of the world, who knew what was happening in South Africa, in Algeria, and the Civil Rights activities happening in the South'. She subsequently became very active in political youth organizations, raised money for students in the South and organized civil rights events and conferences. For the next several decades, she worked as an activist and a community organizer, 'inspired by the courage, dedication, and ideas that people were putting forward'. Always 'pulled by the inner city and social justice issues', Joan did a lot of work involving families, schools and communities in urban neighborhoods. Though it was quite challenging at times, she always found her community organizing work fulfilling, because it directly addressed social issues that she cared deeply about.

Aside from working on issues that one considers important, the study participants enjoyed the mental stimulation of problem-solving. Clara, aged 60, is an engineer with two bachelor's degrees, one in French and German literature and the other in mechanical engineering. When she graduated with her first bachelor's degree in French and German literature, she got a job filing for 40 hours a week in an insurance company in San Francisco. One day, as she was walking down the street, she saw a mechanic who was fixing cars and trucks in a garage in his house. Strangely attracted to the idea of working with automobiles, Clara became his apprentice and started working in the garage two days a week and filing three days a week. Soon, she was working full-time at the garage and earning a subsistence fixing cars. When asked what she liked about fixing cars, she replied that it was like solving a puzzle. She relished the challenge of identifying what was wrong with the car and correcting it. The objectivity that came with working with machines – finding that 'one right answer' – was supremely appealing, leading her to eventually pursue her second bachelor's degree in mechanical engineering. She was 38 when she finished that degree and has been working as an engineer ever since.

Finally, helping other people was a significant source of satisfaction among the study participants. Marianne, aged 67, who currently works 20 hours a week as a social work consultant for disaster relief workers, described her upbringing as a Minnesota Lutheran and spoke of helping people as an important goal in life. As a social worker with many years of experience in child protection services, she has seen 'the real down and dirty of the world'. Her work would often drain her emotionally and sometimes make her sick. When I asked her why she is still doing social work at age 67, she replied that, even with all the challenges, she enjoys being helpful to people. While she cannot solve all the problems, she likes the fact that she can provide relief to those who need it. Likewise, her part-time ESL teaching is motivated by her desire to be helpful to another vulnerable population – adult immigrants.

Why teaching English is attractive

The reason that the participants in this study have decided to pursue TESOL is that it combines many of the desirable attributes of the jobs they have had (or wish they had). These include meeting new people, being intellectually stimulated, having autonomy, gaining a broader perspective about the world, seeing the fruit of one's labor and being appreciated.

The best thing about teaching ESL is meeting interesting people and broadening my horizons. The other thing that's very good about it is that there's a lot of independence. The classroom is my kingdom in a way. (Ginny)

The great thing about teaching ESL is that you constantly get new people and new topics. (Theresa)

The actual time spent with students is by far the most rewarding. When you see something that happens that you caused to happen, it's just very exciting. (Joni)

I love seeing the light bulb go off and seeing the 'Aha' moments and the progress students make. (Henry)

You asked how I dealt with the stress of being a social worker. Nature is very grounding for me. Driving on the ground is also grounding. Seeing that there are different kinds of people in this country or in the world is also grounding. Some people have worse lives than you, and some people have better lives. My mom had this saying, 'If you've got a roof over your head and enough to eat, it's a really good day'. And I think you have to see other people to get that perspective. (Marianne)

One of the things that I've been able to see is how offhandedly and badly immigrants are treated by their American employers. One of my middle-aged women students works as a housekeeper for a family in McLean. They call her Virginia. But her name is Maribel. The students come to the Literacy Council, and everybody treats them with respect. That makes a big difference. (Diane)

As can be seen in these excerpts, the individuals in this study felt empowered by what they could accomplish in the classroom. Ginny aptly described her classroom as her 'kingdom', and the participants enjoyed the sense of autonomy and freedom that came with their jobs as teachers. They were thrilled when they saw visible improvements in their students' spoken and written English and felt gratified that their efforts as teachers played a definitive role in that progress. With every new class came a new group of students with different backgrounds and a diverse set of needs, which required the teachers to tailor their instruction. That different students brought different meanings and interpretations to existing lessons was eye-opening to the teachers and broadened their horizons. In short, no one found teaching to be dull. Teaching was always dynamic.

The individuals in this study also felt that they were making a positive difference in the lives of their students, which made their work meaningful. Immigrants, often a vulnerable population with few economic resources, are sometimes poorly treated and taken advantage of by majority populations. Given this reality, social advocacy on behalf of immigrants was thought to be as important as teaching them English. The study participants felt that their work as ESL teachers was not confined to the classroom, but also extended to the communities. Driven by civic-minded purpose, they eagerly deployed their education and skills to bring about positive change in the ways that immigrants are viewed and integrated into American society. Their advocacy was gratefully acknowledged by their students. Some of the participants talked about their students bringing them 'gifts from the heart', such as handmade crafts and homemade foods.

Conclusion

In this chapter, I explored how prior work experiences contribute to individuals' decisions to pursue TESOL. I described the diverse educational backgrounds and job histories of the study participants and how TESOL became incorporated into their visions of what they want to do in their lives. The 30 participants have had a wide range of occupations in different sectors of the economy, spanning professional to blue-collar work, corporate to non-profit jobs and full-time to part-time work. Many had switched careers at least once before they came to TESOL. As individuals with the benefit of hindsight, the study participants made sense of the significance of the work they have done and imagined the kind of work they wished to do in the future. Each person had a unique story to tell and savored recounting their varied pasts. But as diverse as the individual narratives were, what held all of them together was an underlying search for meaning and enjoyment in work. Regardless of the kind of work people did, they wanted their labor to lead to something more than a paycheck. They yearned for their efforts to be connected to a greater purpose and impact in the world.

For all of the participants, pursuing TESOL was the outcome of a deliberate and careful consideration, an endeavor to which they were now prepared to commit their time and energies. Prior experience in a variety of jobs has given them a better understanding about themselves: the kinds of jobs they fancy or turn away from, their work habits and the ways in which they relate to people of different backgrounds. Their stories sometimes reveal regrets over roads not taken and lessons learned from mistakes, but they also bring to light a clearer sense of self developed over time.

The question now arises, 'If the individuals in this study had been introduced to teaching ESL when they were younger, would they have gone into it'? The answer is, 'Perhaps'. Some people could have chosen teaching as young adults and made a long career of it. However, what makes these individuals different from younger teachers and potentially very effective is that they have a surer sense of who they are, they know that their time on earth is limited and they are anxious to make their work count toward something meaningful. They are driven by a sense of purpose and are motivated to make a positive and lasting difference in the lives of their students. They are a group with enormous potential to bring about positive social change. Building on the wisdom accrued from a lifetime of experience in other fields, these individuals are ready to transform the ways that language is taught and learned. In the next chapter, we will see how they react to the ESL concepts and materials taught in the teacher training program. We will see how their creative thinking and prior experience contribute to advancing the field of English language teaching.

Notes

(1)   The bachelor of science degree is typically abbreviated as BS in the United States and BSc in Britain and Australia.
(2)   Martha was born in South Korea and started learning English at the age of eight when she immigrated to the United States.

5 Constructing a New Professional Identity

Research shows that the prior experiences of career changers have considerable influence on their developing sense of self as teachers (Freeman & Johnson, 1998). Professional and personal identities held earlier in life are often reflected in the ways in which teachers plan and carry out instruction and interact with students and colleagues (Goodson, 1992; Goodson & Walker, 1991; Williams, 2010; Zeichner & Gore, 1990). In this chapter, I describe the study participants' reactions to concepts covered in the teacher training program and how their prior knowledge and experiences help them make sense of this new information. I examine how they see themselves as teachers of English learners and reconcile the various professional identities they have constructed in other careers. We will glimpse the inner conflicts they experience as they cross seemingly irreconcilable disciplinary boundaries and transition from being experts in their previous careers to being novices in TESOL. Based on these discussions, I will make a case for recognizing the wealth and diversity of career-change teachers' experiences and show how doing so contributes to both individual professional development and advancement of the TESOL field as a whole.

Communities of Practice

How do people become teachers? What kind of learning is necessary to become an effective teacher? Educational theorists, Jean Lave and Etienne Wenger, coined the term 'situated learning' to show that learning is a social process that is embedded within activity, context and culture (Lave, 1996; Lave & Wenger, 1991; Wenger, 1998). Like other sociocultural theorists (e.g. Vygotsky, 1978), Lave and Wenger conceptualize learning as a fundamentally social phenomenon, which occurs in interaction between people rather than simply in the minds of individuals. They view learning as a process of increasing participation in different 'communities of practice', that is, groups of people with a common interest in particular areas or domains. Lave and Wenger (1991) maintain that newcomers to a community of practice are 'legitimate peripheral participants' who construct an identity within the community by being immersed in its practices. They argue that learning is a process of identity formation. By engaging in the social practices of the community, participants learn not only the technical skills, but also the implicit knowledge that is required for identifying as members of that community.

According to Norton (1997: 410), identity refers to the ways in which 'people understand their relationship to the world, how that relationship is constructed across time and space, and how people understand their possibilities for the future'. Current understanding of identity revolves around three central ideas (Varghese et al., 2005). First, identity is not a fixed, stable, unitary and internally coherent phenomenon but is multiple, shifting and in conflict (Leung et al., 1997; Rajadurai, 2010). Second, identity is not context-free but is embedded in the social, cultural and political context. People do not establish identities by themselves but construct them through social interaction with others (Duff & Uchida, 1997; Nieto & Bode, 2011; Pavlenko & Blackledge, 2004). Third, identity is maintained and negotiated through language and discourse (Gee, 1996; Schecter & Bayley, 1997).

Wenger (1998) shows that people belong to many communities of practice, some as full members and others in more peripheral ways. For some, participation may be central to their identities; for others, it may be more incidental. These various forms of participation contribute to the production of identities. Wenger argues that, in order to effectively construct an identity of belonging in a community of practice, new members must broker across the boundaries of other communities of practice to which they previously belonged and negotiate the various identities they constructed within each community. He explains that the job of brokering across the boundaries of different communities of practice is one of the most difficult tasks that individuals face. This is because it involves translation and alignment between perspectives, and it requires reconciling different identities that people construct within the various communities of practice so they can coexist in relative harmony.

For people who are entering TESOL from other careers, this is a new community of practice to which they attempt to gain membership as newcomers. Learning to become an ESL teacher requires not only being immersed in the day-to-day practices of this professional community (i.e. learning how to teach English to speakers of other languages), but also identifying with the standards, beliefs and values of its existing members. This sometimes poses a challenge for people who come from other communities of practice with ideas and attitudes that are vastly different from those of TESOL. For example, for some career-change teachers, the emphasis that TESOL places on cooperation and collaboration comes as a culture shock. I often hear from my career-change teachers how 'everybody's so helpful in TESOL' and how 'teachers are so willing to share their knowledge and resources with one another'. While cooperation is a value that many members of the TESOL community may take for granted, it may feel like a foreign concept to people who have built their careers in more competitive fields.

Another challenge facing career-change teachers is negotiating the tensions inherent in being an expert in their previous careers and a novice in TESOL. In her study of career-change teachers, Williams (2010) used the term 'expert novice' to describe the conflict between career changers' identities as old-timers in other communities of practice and as newcomers in the field of teaching. Williams showed the ways in which one career-change teacher drew on a range of experiences gained from her previous careers to contribute to her learning as a student teacher, and how the teacher training program challenged many of her existing beliefs and enabled her to negotiate new meanings about learning and teaching. Experiences in teacher education both enhanced and frustrated the career-change teacher's learning and the construction of her identity as a new teacher. Williams showed that two crucial elements were necessary for her learning: social and academic support and recognition by others that she brought to teaching valuable and relevant skills from her previous career.

In what follows, I examine the tensions inherent in being an expert novice in TESOL and how my study participants perceived the processes of brokering across the boundaries of different communities of practice. Many of Lave and Wenger's key ideas are applicable to the experiences of the study participants and provide a useful analytical lens through which to examine the connection between learning and identity as they relate to career-change ESL teachers. I will show how different identities are reflected in the ways the participants respond to TESOL materials and how they construct and negotiate new identities as they become legitimate participants in the TESOL community.

Entering a New Community of Practice

Going back to school as an older adult is an adventure for many people, often accompanied by feelings of excitement and exhilaration. Education later in life can jump-start a new career or take an existing career in a personally more meaningful direction. Since older adults tend to be more focused on their purpose for learning, they are more motivated to work hard and not be embarrassed by their own ambitions. In the interviews, the study participants spoke of the pleasure of learning new things and expanding the mind, and the sense of freedom that comes from not having to obsess over grades as they might have done in their youth. They talked at length about how enjoyable it was to interact with younger classmates and to be challenged and stimulated by different perspectives. Tom, Margie and Elaine used the word 'fun' to describe their experiences of being in school again and said that what they were learning was meaningful and contributed toward a purposeful goal.

My experience of going back to school, obviously, was different because I was older. You're in a little different situation, you have a more accurate perspective of what's going on, and so it makes you a better student than when you were younger. You can actually enjoy yourself more. It becomes less about the grade and more about the learning. So that frees you up and makes it a lot more fun. (Tom)

I love mingling with younger people. I'm always at the library before your class, and Agnes and Maung come in. It's just a fun dynamic. They bring a different perspective and something new. It's what I've always liked about being in school. You're learning, you're interacting, and you're growing. (Margie)

Being in the TESOL program has been a lot of fun. I'm by nature very intellectual. I always liked school and loved going to classes. I like taking notes and reading things. If I could just take classes and not worry about degrees, I would just be a perpetual student. (Elaine)

While the participants in the study were generally thrilled with the idea of being a student again, some worried that they might not remember how to write papers and take exams or how to act in class with students who are much younger. Lynn, who practiced law for 20 years as a licensed attorney before coming to TESOL, confessed that it was difficult for her to go back to school in her late forties. Even though she was always thoroughly prepared for class and was one of the top performers in the TESOL program, she confessed that she felt intimidated by her classmates who came with more teaching experience.

Going back to school was not easy. It was hard being in classes with people in their 20s. It was very difficult for me. My memory doesn't retain things like it used to, and homework was difficult. It was difficult for me, because most of the people had teaching backgrounds. I felt that the TESOL program catered to those with teaching experience, and I definitely felt at a loss. I felt inferior, because I didn't have a teaching background. I was intimidated, because teaching takes a different set of skills. It's a very specific set of skills. (Lynn)

The recognition that teaching requires a different set of skills than those that she had developed in her previous career placed Lynn in the position of a novice, which contributed to her anxiety. Despite the fact that she was an established expert in the legal world, Lynn felt that the professional competencies she possessed as a lawyer were not readily transferrable to the field of teaching. In her view, she was a beginner placed at a distinct disadvantage when compared to people who came to TESOL with more classroom experience.

TESOL teacher training programs typically draw participants from a wide range of teaching backgrounds. Some people, like Lynn, enter these programs with little or no previous teaching experience, while others come with many years of experience in formal classroom settings. Since experienced teachers tend to be older, career changers who are entering the field of teaching for the first time are sometimes mistakenly perceived by their peers as having many years of teaching experience. They are also seen by their students (i.e. English learners) as having significant classroom experience because of their older age. Correcting these misperceptions often involves explaining what one used to do before coming to TESOL and acknowledging that one is new to teaching, which places the career changer in a vulnerable position. As a few of the participants put it, it makes one 'feel like a baby again', lacking a sense of control and authority as a teacher. Lynn explains:

> I tell my ESL students that I used to be an attorney, and they are just floored by it. They have such a high regard for attorneys that they think there's something wrong with me that I would give up a legal career to be a teacher. I keep it as a social lesson, that I went back to school in my 40s and learned a new career. They're floored that I don't have years and years of experience teaching, and they're floored that I was an attorney for 20 years. (Lynn)

Julia, whose career in social work spans several decades, recounted her feelings of insecurity and nervousness as a new social worker, and how it took many years for her to become a full-fledged, skilled professional. Although her self-confidence grew and her identity as a social worker became more firmly established with increasing years of experience in the field, as she embarked on a new career in TESOL, her earlier feelings of being a novice surfaced all over again.

> I remember when I was new in social work, I wanted to be very experienced. I would look at the people who are very experienced and just envy them because I wanted to be there, you know. And I feel that about myself now as an ESL teacher. (Julia)

Julia's comments revealed that she was aware of her different identities. She was an older student, an experienced professional and a beginning teacher. The perceptions of other people played an important role in her developing sense of herself as an ESL teacher. She did not construct a new professional identity by herself but did so through social interaction with others (Nieto & Bode, 2011; Pavlenko & Blackledge, 2004). She speculated that other people would expect her to be good at teaching because she was older and more experienced, an assumption that added to her anxiety.

The Value of Previously Developed Skills in Teaching ESL

Part of the difficulty that older adults face in entering a new community of practice is that previously developed competencies and skills are not readily recognized by existing members of the new community (Crow *et al.*, 1990). Career changers themselves may not realize that the skills they have developed in their previous careers can be valuable in their new job. However, some of the participants in this study acknowledged that working in a previous career influenced the kind of teacher they wanted to be. This was evident in the way they approached their students, the lessons they developed and the methods they used in teaching. For example, Lesley explained how her experience in airport customer service has prepared her to work with students of diverse backgrounds.

> I've interacted with a lot of different people from a lot of different cultures. I can look at things from someone else's perspective. That's how I approach pretty much everything. If you can understand where the other person is coming from, then you can calm them at the airport, or offer them alternatives that will help them. You can say things that can diffuse a tense situation. I think that's what makes me a good teacher. [My customer service work] has really helped me to develop that part of myself, because if you are working with a small group or one-on-one with a student, you can notice what things are important and meaningful to your student and you can frame the instruction that way. That's kind of what I do with customers. You get a sense of why they're angry, what's important to them, and who they are. Even in a short conversation, that's very possible. (Lesley)

It is apparent from this excerpt that one of Lesley's strengths is her ability to relate to people from different backgrounds. By looking at things from other people's perspectives, she is able to understand what is important to them and present the situation in ways that could help them. Research suggests that career changers develop a range of interpersonal skills and insights into human nature that can be beneficial in their teaching (Mayotte, 2003). From their prior life and work experiences, career changers often bring a deeper understanding of human behavior to teaching and tend to build strong relationships with students and colleagues (Williams, 2010). Lesley seems to be one such individual, who is able to see the relevance of the people skills developed in her previous career. She is able to make the connection between her experiences and her new role as an ESL teacher.

Joan is another teacher who sees the relevance of her previous work to her new job as a teacher. She believes that her experience as a civil rights activist and a community organizer has shaped the ways in which she interacts with immigrant students.

> I think my experience working in low income communities puts me in a place where I can help students understand issues around social inequality. My civil rights work has helped me sort out issues with racism in this country, with stereotyping, and with the relationships between whites and blacks or between black Americans and black Caribbeans. When Latinos or Asians experience some kind of discriminatory remarks, I think I am able to put that in a framework and not write it off. So that's what excites me about teaching and having a group of students. (Joan)

Joan believes that it is important for teachers to explicitly address the issues surrounding poverty and racial discrimination that many immigrant students face. Although racism and discrimination are difficult topics that often make people uncomfortable, Joan thinks that it is important for teachers to help students learn about them and make sense of what they are experiencing in the wider community. By building her lessons in class around issues that are socially relevant to students, Joan is able to make their learning more meaningful. Both her choice of reading materials and the manner in which she facilitates discussions in class reflect her conviction. Joan explains:

> I'm reading this book, *Putting the 'Movement' Back into Civil Rights Teaching*. It's a compilation of very inspiring essays written by teachers and by people who were involved in the Civil Rights Movement. One of the things it shows is how people find their voice within certain subjects. There are a couple of articles about teaching young kids about violence or slavery and how some people want to put that behind them and don't want kids to learn it. But kids of every age are interested in knowing about that tension, the struggles, and the challenges, and that turns them on to learning rather than having just vanilla stuff fed to them. (Joan)

Similarly, Paula spoke about how her training as a researcher has helped her in her teaching of academic writing to ESL students. A published author of many peer-reviewed journal articles in neuroscience, Paula has a great deal of experience writing collaboratively with other scientists. All of the articles she has published have undergone multiple iterations of drafting, revising and editing based on the feedback of collaborators as well as peer reviewers and editors. She has honed her skills as a writer over many years and is very used to process-based writing, a hallmark of present-day writing instruction.

I can think logically and critically, and it's helped my writing immensely. I can write very well, and it's helped my critiquing of writing. It has that crossover into writing instruction. (Paula)

Teaching writing to second language learners of English is a daunting task for many teachers. Although many pre-service ESL teachers have some form of teaching experience, relatively few have specifically taught ESL writing. Traditionally, the majority of ESL teacher education programs have placed more emphasis on developing students' oral and reading skills than on their writing skills. Writing has often been the last skill to be taught in ESL classes after listening, speaking and reading (Shin, 2006).

While writing instruction is a weakness and a source of anxiety for many ESL teachers, Paula feels that it is one of her biggest strengths as a teacher. Her confidence in her ability to write and help students improve their writing comes largely from her prior training as an academic writer. Even though TESOL and neuroscience may seem worlds apart to most people, Paula is able to make the connection between her previous experiences and her new role as an ESL teacher. The challenge for teacher education programs is to help individuals who are not able to make such connections to do so. That career changers bring valuable skills from their previous careers to the job of teaching ESL students should be explicitly acknowledged and celebrated in teacher education programs. I return to this point later in this chapter.

The Value of Immigrant Experiences in Teaching ESL

Aside from the knowledge and skills gained in previous careers, some participants believe that their life experiences as either immigrants or children of immigrants shape their view of the kind of teachers they want to be. For example, Martha, who came to the United States at the age of eight from South Korea, believes that her experience as a former ESL student is helpful in her work as an ESL teacher. In the interview, she recalled the difficulties she experienced upon her arrival in the United States in overcoming culture shock and learning a new language. She spoke of her feelings of isolation and loneliness as a newcomer student and the mental exhaustion that came from having to process second language input all day. She talked about how hard her parents worked to provide for the family and how they were always tired. With little knowledge of English and American culture, they often did not know how to make sense of the notes that Martha brought home from school or appreciate how much English she was able to learn. Martha believes that all of these experiences make her particularly well-suited to work with English learners and their families.

I think I relate better to ESL students, because I was once an ESL student. Some people have to imagine how they feel, but I don't have to imagine. I know. For example, some teachers want immigrant parents to be involved in a certain way in school, but I know they are probably just like mine, busy trying to survive and learn the new culture. I know I'm not going to get that much parent involvement from them, not because they don't care, but because of where they are in life. Things like that just make sense, and there's a comfort level there. (Martha)

In the same way, Ginny recounted her experience of growing up in a multilingual household with family members constantly switching between different languages. Her Armenian parents spoke English with an accent, which she was encouraged to correct, and the family always had a Spanish-speaking maid in the house. From an early age, she was exposed to multiple languages and ways of communicating, so she felt comfortable around language learners. Explaining grammar points and correcting mispronunciations came naturally to her, and she felt good about helping people learn English. Later, when she got married, she and her husband adopted two children from Chile and formed a multicultural family of their own.

My father spoke French, Turkish, Armenian, and English. My mom had grown up in Cuba and spoke Turkish, English, Spanish, and Armenian. They switched all the time between English, Turkish, and Armenian. I grew up with parents who had accents and not very good English. My father said, 'If you hear me make a mistake, please correct me'. So I grew up correcting people's English. (Ginny)

For some participants, experiences living overseas influenced the way they viewed and interacted with immigrants in the United States. A child of a foreign service officer, Helen was born in Reykjavik, Iceland, and grew up in a number of different countries in Europe and Africa. To follow her father's work, her family had to move every two years. 'When I was growing up, America was not my home', she stated. 'To this day, it doesn't feel like my home'. When I asked her where her home was, she replied:

Well, I don't really have a home. That's a very sad story, and I could cry right now (laughter). Since 11th and 12th grade, I've lived in the United States, but I still don't feel like I'm an American unless I go overseas.... I'm not unhappy being an American, but I realized recently that I really feel most comfortable with expats, because that's what I am. Even in my own country I'm an expat. And so I am not a typical American. (Helen)

Helen's assertion that she is 'not a typical American' and an expat in her own country is an identity statement that resonates with displaced and transnational populations. Like Helen, many immigrants feel that they belong neither in their home country nor in the new society. Living in the intersection of two cultures, they are pushed and pulled by various forces of assimilation, traditional values and family pressures, which often leave them confused and lost. Helen feels that her experience as an American expat living overseas gives her a unique lens through which to view the lives of immigrants in the United States.

When I lived in Africa, I experienced a small trauma related to black/white prejudice. I know how prejudice can creep up on you without you even realizing it. Because I've experienced that, hopefully I can be more sensitive translating that into compassion for people who feel very threatened by the idea of us becoming a multicultural country. (Helen)

It seems that, to Helen, being an ESL teacher is more than just about teaching language. It is also about being a cultural ambassador, promoting tolerance and mutual understanding among different groups of people. The cultural knowledge that Helen has gathered over the years thus serves as a valuable resource in her work as an ESL teacher.

Brokering Between Different Communities of Practice

While the skills and competencies developed in previous careers and life experiences are seen by some participants as being valuable to TESOL, not all prior experiences are integrated so seamlessly into the field of teaching. Several of the participants find brokering across different communities of practice to be very difficult. For example, Clara described the process of transitioning from engineering to TESOL as 'a real culture shock' and 'an emotional challenge'. Her difficulty involved, at one level, suddenly having to interact mostly with women in the teacher training program, which she was not accustomed to as an engineer. In the male-dominated field of engineering, Clara had developed a set of strategies for talking and behaving around male coworkers that would not put her at a disadvantage.

In her book, *Talking from 9 to 5: Women and Men at Work*, Deborah Tannen (1994) describes the different ways in which men and women communicate in the workplace and how differences in conversational styles influence people's perceptions of others' skills and abilities. For example, women tend to be more indirect in their speech, which makes them look as if they are less confident and competent than men. Women also tend to end their statements on a high note, as if they are asking a question. This makes them sound tentative and unsure. However, when they learn to speak like men to compensate for these female tendencies, they are sometimes accused of being aggressive, bossy or even unfeminine. Thus, women face a dilemma in the workplace: How should they talk so as not to appear incompetent, or too masculine? Striking a balance between male and female tendencies in speech requires constant monitoring and adjustment of one's own speech, which can be stressful. In Clara's case, having trained herself to do this for many years, she now finds herself at a loss as to how to act in a professional setting with mostly women. Women who have always worked in female-dominated fields such as teaching may not be as sensitive to the difficulties faced by women working in male-dominated fields.

On another level, Clara's difficulty involved meeting a different set of expectations for relating to classmates in the TESOL program. Engineering programs typically focus on individual mastery of content through lectures and problem-solving. Discussions and collaborative learning activities, characteristic of teacher education courses, are not a major emphasis in engineering classes. Furthermore, engineering classes are typically graded on a curve, and classmates are often seen as competitors rather than as collaborators. Coming from such background, Clara described how difficult it was for her 'not to be threatened' by her classmates in the TESOL program.

> Your class on teaching reading and writing was an emotional challenge, because I'm used to going to classes and being somewhat competitive in learning content and mastering material. Your class involved a lot of personal interaction, and it was a real challenge for me not to be threatened. After a while, I sort of realized that it wasn't such a bad challenge. You know, I can deal with this. The program was a real shock after engineering school. I mean a pleasant shock for the most part, but a real culture shock. For the longest time, I haven't been in a group of women. In my field it's mostly men, there's a certain setup, and you act a certain way. (Clara)

While she was eventually able to let her guard down and interact more freely with her classmates in the TESOL program, Clara admitted that it took her some time to see her classmates as collaborators. Her experience shows that crossing disciplinary borders requires not only learning new content but also acquiring new manners of communicating, behaving and interacting with other members of the professional community. In order to effectively construct an identity of belonging in a community of practice, new members must negotiate the various identities they have constructed within each community of practice (Wenger, 1998). When the perspectives vary widely, as was Clara's experience, reconciling those identities can be a major challenge.

Similarly, Ginny spoke of the spirit of cooperation that permeates the world of TESOL as nearly inconceivable in the field of architecture. 'Unbelievable' and 'in shock' were the words she used to characterize her experience of crossing the boundary into TESOL. As a woman in another historically male-dominated field, Ginny had had to fight sexism and constantly prove her worth as a professional. In an industry where many people guard their knowledge and resources fiercely, Ginny had been accustomed to figuring things out on her own and not expecting to receive help, even when she desperately needed it. But teaching ESL has opened her eyes to previously unknown possibilities for interacting with colleagues that are far more affirming and helpful than any she had previously experienced.

> When I started teaching ESL at [community college X], [my program director] showed up in the classroom on the first day, and he was unbelievably helpful. He said if I had questions about the next class I could call him. And he'd answer right away. It was such a contrast from architecture. I was almost in shock about how helpful people were. I mean everyone is so cooperative. Can I watch your class to get ideas? Sure! Can you show me your syllabus? Of course! What book do you use? Come in and look. I mean, people are willing to give you their time and advice. It's just unbelievable. It's a very different work environment. (Ginny)

Ginny's assertion that TESOL is 'such a contrast from architecture' and 'a very different work environment' shows that she is actively comparing the two fields. By highlighting what is good about TESOL, she seems to be aligning herself with TESOL and constructing a new identity of belonging in that community. Becoming a TESOL professional involves identifying with the values that are considered important by existing members of the TESOL community, such as cooperation and helpfulness. As Ginny increases her participation and becomes a core member of that community, it is likely that she will in turn transmit these values by making her knowledge and resources available to other teachers.

Wenger (1998) explains that brokering across different communities of practice often involves introducing elements of one practice into another. But as he points out, elements of one repertoire may be quite inappropriate, incomprehensible or even offensive in another community. When Lynn started taking courses in the TESOL program, she found that some of the concepts she was introduced to were critically at odds with what she knew from her former practice as an attorney.

> One time I got into a very heated argument with one of my favorite professors in the TESOL program about what a lie is and isn't. She was coming from a cultural perspective that in certain cultures people say

things knowing it's not necessarily true because they don't want to hurt someone's feelings or they want to save face. Therefore, not only is it okay to not tell the truth, it's expected that people not tell the truth. I was coming from a prosecutorial background, where my job was to catch inconsistencies, however small, because if they're telling one lie, they're probably telling other lies. She ended up being one of my very favorite professors, but we had some very difficult confrontations in that class. (Lynn)

This excerpt illustrates the emotional struggle that Lynn went through to reconcile conflicting views about what constitutes a lie. In her work as a prosecutor, Lynn had been trained to take evidence provided by a witness at face value. If the witness was later found to have made a false statement under oath, that person could be charged with perjury. Telling a lie, however small, was a grave matter, the consequences of which could be dire. A lie was a lie, no matter how well-intentioned it might have been. Thus, the idea that certain cultures are more accepting toward lies clashed powerfully with Lynn's existing beliefs, leading to some heated arguments with her professor. While Lynn acknowledged that this professor later became one of her favorite instructors in the program, it is clear that her principles as an attorney were seriously challenged from this experience.

In reconciling her former identity as a lawyer and her new identity as a teacher, Lynn was conflicted about the need to be open-minded about what members of the TESOL field consider important and the need to stay true to the identity she had constructed as an attorney. While she wanted very much to develop a sense of belonging in TESOL, she did not want to do it at the cost of undermining her other identity. This inner conflict was an ongoing struggle for Lynn throughout the teacher education program. She shared that, on one occasion, another instructor in the program had made highly critical statements about federal immigration policies. As someone who had made a career working for the federal government, Lynn became quite upset. She explains:

I have a unique perspective. I know that I'm not as liberal as most of the people in this field. I'm not saying that I don't believe in those things. I do. I just have a different perspective about it. I've seen too much. (Lynn)

By asserting that she has a 'unique perspective' and is 'not as liberal as most of the people in this field', Lynn places some distance between herself and her colleagues in TESOL. At the same time, she is careful to align herself to her TESOL colleagues by pointing out that she does believe in the things that they believe in (e.g. advocating for immigrants). These seemingly contradictory statements suggest that reconciling identities can be a complicated process (Norton, 1997). Lynn herself seems to realize the apparent contradiction in her statements and justifies her views by pointing out that 'I've seen too much', referring to some of the more serious criminal cases she handled as a prosecutor, which contributed to her perspective.

Likewise, Paula, a trained biologist, believes that her views are often in conflict with those of her TESOL colleagues. Specifically, she finds that scientific theories are misunderstood and misrepresented by non-scientists.

> I get irritated sometimes when I feel like people aren't being logical. I have to squelch myself on occasion when I'm at a professional conference and somebody says something that's just totally off the wall scientifically, and I say to myself, 'Now's not the time to make a point'. Some well-educated young women were debating about if they taught some students something for several generations, students four or five generations later would learn it easier. And I was like, 'This is Lamarck! This is Lamarck! This is crazy!' But I said to myself, 'This is not the time to teach them biology'. (Paula)

Named after the French biologist, Jean-Baptiste Lamarck, Lamarckism is the idea that an organism can pass on characteristics that it acquired during its lifetime to its offspring. In modern evolutionary biology, Lamarck's theory about the heritability of acquired characteristics is all but rejected. Here, Paula is exasperated by the fact that what she considers to be non-science is treated as being scientific by some people in the TESOL community. Rather than correct these misperceptions, she mostly keeps her thoughts to herself so as not to appear condescending and antagonize potential colleagues. While refraining from making scientific comments could be Paula's way of gaining acceptance into the TESOL community, it is not without an emotional cost, since it entails silencing an integral part of her identity as a scientist.

However, when she is given a safe opportunity to display her knowledge without fear of being rejected, Paula offers a bit of constructive criticism for how experimental research could be improved in TESOL. She explains how some of the TESOL research she has come across has a seriously flawed design.

> The other place where my science background comes out and I think this is good, is that I'm extremely critical of experimental design. I read some of the published studies in TESOL, and half the time I shake my head. This is not the way to do it. There's this problem, and there's this problem. Some of it has to do with doing research in the humanities, where you can't control every variable. I understand that. But some of it is just inexcusable. The proper controls are not there, there are inferences drawn that aren't merited, and so on. (Paula)

Paula's criticism of poorly designed experimental research involving language teaching and learning can be pretty difficult for long-time TESOL professionals to stomach. It could be especially discouraging to established professionals who have relied on published research to inform their work for many years. Nonetheless, it is precisely this type of critical lens that is necessary in order for the field to advance its knowledge and ensure quality in its scholarship. Since TESOL research is used to make important pedagogical and policy decisions that potentially affect millions of language learners worldwide, it is all the more crucial that high standards be applied to designing the studies.

A profound conceptual change involves introducing perspectives from one community of practice into another, what Wenger (1998) calls 'boundary encounters'. Such encounters can transform the way each community defines its own identity and practice. Vital to the success of the boundary encounter is the role of highly skilled brokers like Paula, who straddle different communities of practice and facilitate the exchange process. Thus, the increasing presence of career changers in TESOL is a positive development for the profession, one that should be welcomed and embraced by existing members of the TESOL community.

Affirming Identities Through Collaborative Learning

How can career changers' knowledge and skills be recognized and validated in TESOL? How can their sense of belonging in the new community be nurtured? One way this may be accomplished is through collaborative learning activities in teacher education programs. Unlike individual learning, collaborative learning helps students to capitalize on one another's knowledge and skills (Dillenbourg, 1999). Collaborative learning takes place when groups of students work together to search for understanding, meaning or solutions or to create a product of their learning (Smith & McGregor, 1992). It may include collaborative writing, peer feedback, group projects, reciprocal teaching, debates and guided discussions among other activities (Barkley et al., 2005). What is particularly positive about collaborative learning is that it engages students of all backgrounds, providing individuals with opportunities to share their unique knowledge and perspectives acquired in their previous careers and lived experiences for one another's benefit (Barkley et al., 2005).

Research shows that group projects and peer feedback, two popular collaborative learning techniques used in teacher education programs, offer many advantages. Group projects can help students pool knowledge and skills to tackle complex tasks together and establish a shared identity with other group members (Caruso & Woolley, 2008). They can also help students receive social support to take risks and look for novel approaches to solving problems (Mannix & Neale, 2005). Furthermore, students gain a strong sense of audience and experience a wide range of ideas and perspectives when they receive peer feedback (Peterson, 2008). Peer feedback can generate supportive dialogue among students and produce multiple insights that go beyond the information given by the instructor (Nicol, 2010). In the following, Elizabeth describes how she benefited from giving and receiving peer feedback on weekly writing assignments in a reading and writing methods course I taught online one semester.

> Tony is brilliant. I read everything he wrote—he, and Charlie, and Marianne. Every time I read their stuff, I learned so much. Of course, I learned from you, because it's your course. But I totally believe in that kind of connecting with other people in the class. It's got to be with other people who are thinking about this stuff, who are doing this stuff, because you're never going to know it all. These guys, they don't know how much they have helped me. (Elizabeth)

In this excerpt, Elizabeth highlights the importance of learning from peers and 'connecting with other people in the class'. Conversations that lead to a shared repertoire and the negotiation of shared meanings are essential for the formation of professional identity (Wenger, 1998). Here, Elizabeth's comment about connecting with 'other people who are thinking about this stuff, who are doing this stuff' makes it clear that peer feedback facilitates the kind of conversation that leads to a shared repertoire.

Because of the substantial number of career-change teachers in our TESOL program, peer-to-peer learning frequently takes place among individuals from different age groups and employment backgrounds, adding to the richness of insights. Tony, one of Elizabeth's classmates named in the above excerpt, is 41 years old and is contemplating a change from his full-time job in a student accounts office in a university to a career in TESOL. Marianne, aged 67, has a social work background, and Charlie, who is in his early thirties, has been teaching English as a foreign language (TEFL) in South Korea for 11 years. Elizabeth and Tony discovered their common interest in science by working on a group lesson plan together.

> When you put me and Tony together in the lesson plan group, I said, 'Oh, thank you, God'. He and I both like to read a lot. He asked me, 'What are you reading now?' And I said, 'Well, I've been reading this thing called "Packing for Mars"'. I found out that when he was younger, he had been in a junior astronauts club. He thought the article was pretty interesting, so I said, 'Why don't you go online and read a couple more chapters and see what you think? This has a little science, you know, maybe you'd find it interesting'. And he really liked it. I was so glad that he was willing to do the lesson on micro gravity. (Elizabeth)

As a result of her interaction with Tony and Marianne in the course, Elizabeth subsequently invited both of them to work with her in a summer ESL program where she has been teaching for more than 10 years. This case illustrates how learning to become a teacher is about making connections and that one of the most important jobs of the teacher educator is to facilitate the formation of such connections.

Conclusion

I began this chapter with the argument that learning to become a teacher is fundamentally a social process that involves constructing a new professional identity within the teaching community. Based on Lave and Wenger's (1991) framework of 'communities of practice', I suggested that constructing an identity of belonging in TESOL entails gaining not only the technical skills of TESOL, but also the implicit knowledge that is required for identifying as a member of that community. I described how the participants in this study broker across the boundaries of the different communities of practice to which they belong and negotiate the various identities they construct within each community (Wenger, 1998). We saw that while some participants could readily see the value of their previously developed competencies and experiences in their new careers as teachers of English learners, not everyone was able to do so. For some people, reconciling the divergent perspectives of different communities of practice was a significant challenge, often involving a considerable emotional cost. Sometimes, the practices of different communities were so dramatically opposed to each other that reconciliation was nearly impossible.

I showed how the participants took different approaches to resolving conflicts in identities. Lynn openly debated matters that conflicted with her existing beliefs and challenged the practices of those who had been working in the field for many years. She was not afraid to question accepted practice in TESOL and refused to have the views of others imposed on her. In contrast, Paula chose not to draw attention to her own views. Her strategy involved concealing her former identity so as not to alienate potential colleagues. In all of the cases, the participants found negotiating the tensions between their various professional identities to be a rather demanding task. There was a general feeling, particularly among those who were established experts in other communities of practice, that the needs of career changers were not being met adequately in the teacher training program. Their frustration stemmed largely from having their previous skills and experiences unrecognized, misrepresented or misunderstood by members of the TESOL community.

Perhaps the most important conclusion to be drawn from this discussion is the need to explicitly recognize the previously developed knowledge and skills of career-change teachers (Williams, 2010). Lynn's comment that the TESOL program catered more to those with a teaching experience is an important issue that needs to be addressed. Lynn was aware that although she was highly accomplished as an attorney, she was still a novice in TESOL and needed help and reassurance to develop a sense of herself as a competent teacher of English learners. Career-change teachers do not necessarily receive the support they need, because they are often viewed as experienced in teaching due to their age and prior experience (Mayotte, 2003). It was apparent from Lynn's description of her experiences that the faculty in the TESOL program may have assumed that she was able to manage the requirements of being an ESL teacher on her own due to her age, when in fact she needed constant encouragement and support.

What kinds of help could benefit career-change teachers? A large part of the support needs to center around providing them with the time and space to articulate the relevance of their previously developed competencies to their new work (Mayotte, 2003). Because career and life experiences have considerable influence on how individuals develop as teachers (Zeichner & Gore, 1990), an exploration of the connections between previous experience and TESOL is crucial to the construction of a new professional identity (Williams, 2010). It is imperative that teacher educators create an atmosphere in which career changers feel comfortable about sharing their knowledge and skills. This can be partly accomplished through collaborative learning activities in teacher education courses, such as group projects and peer feedback that can help establish a shared identity among individuals of different backgrounds. These enable all participants, both career changers and non-career changers, to recognize the diversity and richness of experience that each person brings to the TESOL community and help them build on these experiences.

Another strategy might be to incorporate autobiographies in teacher education courses. Several researchers have highlighted the significance of autobiographies in the construction of teacher identities (Antonek et al., 1997; Goodson & Walker, 1991). Goodson (1992: 116), for example, maintains that teachers' lives cannot be separated from their identities as teachers, and therefore from their practice as teachers: 'Life experiences and background are obviously key ingredients of the people that we are, of our sense of self. To the degree that we invest our "self" in our teaching, experience and background therefore shape our practice'.

As a teacher educator, I would not have known the career backgrounds and life experiences of the 30 participants had it not been for this study. While conducting a full study like this one is not always feasible or even necessary, teacher educators can design assignments or provide forums in which students can describe their work experiences and think of ways in which their knowledge and skills developed in previous jobs might be incorporated into their teaching. Mayotte (2003: 692) refers to such practices as 'stepping stones to success' or 'footholds [that] include opportunities to relate their current experiences to past ones and [to] build upon them'. Including such activities in teacher education courses would not only promote the identity development of career-change teachers but also contribute to the learning of non-career-change teachers and teacher educators. More broadly, doing so has the potential to shape the ways in which the field of TESOL defines its own identity and practice.

6   Learning to Teach

In this chapter, I explore the study participants' classroom experiences, the instructional decisions they make and the reasons behind their decisions. Delivering a well-planned and engaging lesson to a diverse group of students can be a daunting task for anyone who is new to teaching. Research shows that learning to teach is a complex, long-term process that requires careful training and reflective practice (Johnson & Golombek, 2002; Richards, 2008). It is a socially negotiated process, constructed through experiences with students, families and administrators as well as other members of the teaching profession (Johnson, 1999). We know that one's success as a teacher depends on a wide range of factors, such as the knowledge, beliefs and experiences that teachers and students bring to the classroom; teachers' approaches to designing lessons and conducting the sequence and flow of classroom activities; and contextual variables such as class size and composition, physical setting, school leadership and parent involvement (Freeman & Richards, 1996; Johnson, 2000; Liew, 2013).

The job of the teacher is complicated by the fact that teachers play multiple roles in schools: as instructors, curriculum writers, administrators, classroom managers, counselors, researchers and social workers. In fact, teaching consists of 'not one but several other professions, combining the skills of business management, human relations, and theater arts' (Danielson, 1996: 2). Given the complexities of the profession, how do the participants in this study develop as teachers? How do they react to the demands of the job? What choices do they make and why? This chapter describes the participants' experiences as classroom teachers and the lessons they learned from working with students and colleagues. It describes their strategies for coping with stage fright, tackling classroom management issues, and planning and delivering lessons. It addresses questions such as: What do the study participants know about teaching and learning, and what do they learn as they gain classroom experience? How do they articulate their developing knowledge? What motivates them to teach the way they do? What challenges do they face, and what support do they need in order to overcome them?

Changing Views about Teacher Learning

Traditionally, teacher education has been based on the idea that knowledge about teaching and learning can be transmitted to teachers by others (Freeman & Johnson, 1998; Johnson & Golombek, 2002). In the knowledge transmission model, teachers were viewed as empty containers waiting to be filled with pieces of theoretical and pedagogical knowledge dispensed by 'experts' – teacher educators and educational researchers – who define what good teaching is and show teachers what they should do. Teachers were then expected to apply this abstract, decontextualized body of knowledge to any teaching situation they found themselves in. It was assumed that the more research-driven knowledge was provided to teachers, the more their teaching performance would improve (Holmes Group, 1986). Teachers played little role in the creation of knowledge about teaching and learning. Their individual perspectives and understandings of what makes good teaching were largely ignored.

However, research in recent decades has shown that the way in which teachers actually use their knowledge in classrooms is highly personal and interpretive (Golombek, 1998; Johnson & Golombek, 2002). Ethnographic investigations of teachers working in classes have revealed that teachers do not simply implement pedagogical techniques they learn in teacher education programs, they also generate knowledge and construct their own explanations of what works and doesn't work in their own classrooms (Freeman & Johnson, 1998; Tsang, 2004). How teachers use their knowledge in their teaching depends on contextual factors. For example, new teachers quickly find out that a pedagogical method that may be effective in one setting with one group of students may not be effective in a different setting with a different group of students. No matter how engaging and successful a given lesson may be, it has to be adapted to the diverse needs of learners in order to be effective.

Consistent with sociocultural theories that emphasize the fundamentally social nature of cognition and learning, knowledge about teaching has been shown to be socially constructed in individual experiences and contexts (Lave, 1996; Lave & Wenger, 1991; Wenger, 1998; see also Chapter 5). By participating in the social practices and contexts of schools, teachers construct their own understandings about the learning process and the complexities of human interaction (Kanno & Stuart, 2011; Richards, 2008). Teachers' prior knowledge and beliefs about teaching are a powerful factor in how they interpret what goes on in their classrooms (Freeman & Johnson, 1998). Consequently, more and more teacher educators see their job as 'reshaping teachers' existing knowledge, beliefs, and practices rather than simply imposing new theories, methods, or materials on teachers' (Johnson & Golombek, 2002: 2). Teacher educators are increasingly focusing on the internal thought processes of teachers, and why they do what they do, rather than simply looking for outward signs of the application of theories and techniques taught in teacher education programs. More and more teacher educators see teachers as 'producers of legitimate knowledge', capable of infusing 'outsider' knowledge of teacher education generated by researchers with 'insider' knowledge about what works in real classrooms (Johnson & Golombek, 2002: 3).

Following this framework, I provide below a descriptive account of how the participants in this study have come to learn what they know, and how they use that knowledge in a variety of educational settings. We will see how they view themselves as teachers, and how their beliefs, dispositions and knowledge are reflected in the ways they design and deliver lessons and interact with students. Specifically, I consider how they articulate the following four perspectives:

- Teaching is hard work.
- Teaching is performance.
- Teaching requires the ability to manage classrooms.
- Good teaching empowers students.

I first begin with the participants' views of teaching as a labor-intensive process.

Teaching is Hard Work

Many of the participants felt that teaching was one of the most challenging jobs they have had. While they generally found working with ESL students to be a hugely meaningful endeavor, they were often overwhelmed by the many demands of the job, especially during the initial stages of teaching. They discussed how time-consuming it was to prepare lessons and grade student papers, and how stressful it was to be always 'on top of everything'.

Being an ESL teacher is a lot harder than being a librarian. What makes teaching hard is knowing what your students are thinking and always being on top of everything. Some things the students know more about than I do. I mean, why do I prepare so much for this course? I've already taught it twice, but I just feel like I have to be on top of everything. And it's hard. (Suzanne)

Teaching is a ton of work. I bring home stuff all the time. I plan very slowly. I think I've gotten better at grading the writing. But I take forever. It's also the lesson planning that takes forever. (Ginny)

To do it right, you really need to put in a lot of prep time. And you need to be able to juggle your schedule so that you have the time to do a good job of it, prepare thoroughly enough that when you're up there in front of the class, you really give them something worthwhile. (Anna)

Teaching is exhausting for me, just exhausting. You know, by 3:00 in the afternoon, it's migraine time! When we teach, we teach from 8:00 to 3:00, six contact hours with the same group every day, and you're the only teacher. It is exhausting. (Andrea)

Part of the participants' difficulty with teaching may have to do with their lack of specific experience with planning lessons and managing classrooms. Research shows that as teachers learn to teach, they move through certain developmental stages (Grossman, 1992). During the initial teaching experience, teachers may focus solely on what they need to do to cover the lesson plan and maintain classroom control. As they gain more experience and procedural knowledge about how to manage classrooms, they gradually focus more on *what* they are teaching and *how* to present the material. They also begin to adapt instructional activities to meet the needs of individual students. Thus, the focus shifts from just covering the material to looking for ways to promote student learning.

Having taught several adult ESL classes at various community colleges, Suzanne now recognizes the critical role that students play in the teaching and learning process. She knows that students are not blank slates waiting to be filled with knowledge imparted by teachers. They are unique individuals with prior knowledge and experiences, which influence the way they react to the content being taught. She knows that it is not enough for her to simply tell students what they need to know. She also needs to communicate the relevance of the content in ways that make sense to them. Because she believes that the success of her lessons depends on how the content is internalized by the students, 'knowing what your students are thinking' is also very important. For this reason, Suzanne observes her students for any signs of difficulty and makes constant adjustments to the lesson as it unfolds. Her mind does not rest during class, as she tries to move seamlessly from one activity to the next, maintaining the rhythm and intensity of student engagement and preempting problems before they occur. Even though she has taught the course twice before, she still prepares extensively for the class, because she knows that different groups of students are likely to react differently to the same material. All of these factors contribute to Suzanne's view that being a teacher is 'a lot harder than being a librarian'.

Ginny also found teaching to be 'a ton of work', on which she spent a great deal of time outside of class. Although grading students' writing has become somewhat easier over the years as she learned what to look for, lesson planning still 'takes forever' and is exceedingly laborious. Similarly, Anna puts in 'a lot of prep time' in order to give her students 'something worthwhile'. Because she believes that good teaching involves helping students acquire knowledge that could benefit them, she tries to make the most of her class time by preparing her lessons thoroughly in advance. Similar to Suzanne, Anna's attention is focused on what students actually take away from her lessons rather than simply following the curriculum. During the many years that she was a student, she no doubt sat through some classes that seemed like a waste of her time. As she embarks on her own teaching career, Anna seems determined to make sure that she gives her students a positive learning experience worth their time.

Finally, several of the participants commented on how exhausting it is to teach all day. Andrea stated that classroom instruction requires huge amounts of mental energy. Similar to what Suzanne articulated about 'being on top of everything', Andrea feels that her mind is constantly activated while she is teaching. After a whole day of intense concentration in the classroom, she would often go home with a migraine. For this reason, she prefers working one-on-one with students to whole-group instruction.

Teaching is Performance

In addition to their view that teaching is labor-intensive, some of the participants saw classroom instruction as a performance. They likened teachers to actors and the classroom to a stage, with students participating as the audience. They felt that it was their job as teachers to act and be entertaining in order to engage students in the learning process. The claim that teaching is performance is by no means new. Analogies between teaching and performance are often made by educators who recognize that effective teaching relies on the theatrical techniques of scripting, rehearsal, improvisation, timing, stage presence and critical reviews (Pineau, 1994). Some claim that the best teachers are those who behave in a manner similar to actors by internalizing the roles they wish to play and dramatically portraying the importance of the content to students (Barney & Pilmer, 2012). As no action on stage is carried out without a purpose, good teachers are seen as those who can breathe life into even the most mundane classroom activity, such as taking attendance or returning homework. For these reasons, some teachers take acting lessons in order to improve their teaching (Gregory, 2006).

In examining the notion of teaching as a performance, some researchers have turned to the insights provided by speech act theory. Speech act theory is based on the idea that people use words not only to present information but also to carry out actions. J.L. Austin (1962), a British philosopher of language, argued that speakers use language to *assert* things as well as to *do* things (thus the title of his book, *How To Do Things With Words*). According to Austin, any utterance can be identified as either a *constative* or a *performative*. Constatives include all descriptive utterances, statements of fact and definitions that intend to report, inform and state (Searle, 1969). They are statements that, by referring to objects, facts, events or states, may be judged to be true or false. For example, the statement 'The forest was on fire' would be true if in fact the forest was on fire. If the forest was not on fire, this sentence would be false.

In contrast, *performatives* cannot be evaluated for their truth value. Performative utterances such as naming, betrothing, sentencing and confessing perform an action (Austin, 1962). For example, the declaration 'I now pronounce you man and wife', uttered by a minister at a wedding, effectively establishes a marriage. Likewise, answering 'Yes' to the question,

'Do you promise to clean your room?' confirms a commitment to clean the room. The effects of such *performatives* depend on the presence of what Austin (1962) calls 'felicity conditions':

(1) *Convention*: The speaker must be authorized by law or social convention to enact the authority invested in his words.
(2) *Intention*: The speaker must sincerely intend to carry out what his words say.
(3) *Interpretation*: The addressee must understand and acknowledge what the speaker intends. (Austin, 1962: 18)

Therefore, if a marriage declaration was uttered by someone without proper authority to enact such a ceremony, it would not be felicitous. In the same way, it would be infelicitous to break a promise. Social conventions require that people keep the promises they make.

Austin drew a further distinction between *illocutionary* and *perlocutionary performatives*. Unlike illocutionary performatives (like the betrothing and promising examples discussed above), perlocutionary performatives (such as amusing, inspiring, scaring, convincing and persuading one's audience) cannot be enforced by social conventions and may produce consequences that are different from the speaker's intentions. For example, the act of amusing people does not guarantee that they will be amused, however amusing one's words may be. Likewise, one's effort to persuade someone to do something may not always produce the desired outcome, no matter how persuasive the speaker may be. Put in another way, the effect of perlocutionary acts is external to the speaker's performance and is based on the feelings, thoughts and actions of the listener. This is where the 'art' of teaching might come in.

Drawing from speech act theory, Liew (2013) argues that the performative nature of teaching lies crucially in teachers' use of *perlocutionary acts* to inspire and motivate students. He contends that teachers are committed to 'doing things with words' and do not merely utter constatives; that is, they do not simply present information. Rather, teaching consists of speech acts that seek to produce certain effects on the feelings and actions of the students. Thus, it is not enough that students merely understand the teacher's speech. What the teacher says should also bring about certain cognitive, affective or behavioral changes in the students. Liew (2013) argues that the job of the teacher is to facilitate student learning through well-positioned perlocutionary acts, which he calls *pedagogical perlocutions*. The following excerpt from my interview with Martha illustrates pedagogical perlocutions.

Public speaking is something that really excites me. At various times I've been asked to speak to the women at our church. I'm a mentor mom for MOPS (Mothers of Preschoolers). It's a support group for young mothers who just got married and are having children. I speak about things like relating to their husbands and their children. When I stand up and give my presentation, I feel really good about it. It brings out the teacher in me, because I'll bring my props and try to present in a way that engages them personally and helps them remember. (Martha)

Martha begins by stating how much she enjoys public speaking and giving presentations. She particularly relishes having opportunities to address recently married women at her church as a mentor mom. Giving presentations to the young mothers 'brings out the teacher' in her, because it gives her a chance to incorporate a variety of pedagogical techniques (e.g. the use of teaching aids such as pictures, videos and objects) in her sessions. She also tries to 'present in a way that engages' the audience by providing concrete, practical examples of relating to one's husband and children and by creating an atmosphere in which the participants feel comfortable about sharing their own experiences. Rather than talking *at* the participants and telling them what they need to do, she tries to talk *with* them and listen to what they have to say. Learning is highly personal in this type of situation and has the potential to produce genuine affective and behavioral changes. In fact, after her presentations, Martha follows up with the young mothers, whose changed outlook and actions give her a sense of satisfaction.

While some participants like Martha were highly adept at engaging their audience, others felt unsure about their ability to 'do things with words'. Below, Suzanne and Patricia describe their struggle with the performance aspect of teaching.

I think the best teachers are real performers like Philip. And I'm not a performer. I don't really enjoy that part of it so much. I find it stressful. I feel as though I need to be better at it than I am. The teachers that students really like are the ones that keep them amused. I think I'm not as good at that as I'd like to be. (Suzanne)

I hesitate to say this, but the biggest reason I never wanted to teach is that I have stage fright. I just did not want to be on stage all the time, which is exactly what you are when you teach. You're acting. You're on stage. No doubt about it. It's not that I can't be entertaining. It's just that having all that undivided attention is hard. I never liked being the center of attention. I don't like it when people are looking at me. I always made it a point to not look too nice when I went places, because I didn't want people going, 'Ooh, look at her. She looks great'. I don't want to look that good. (Patricia)

Suzanne asserts that 'the best teachers are real performers like Philip'. Philip is a popular instructor in our TESOL program, sought after by students for his sense of humor and down-to-earth manner. Students find him very approachable and often come to him for professional and personal advice outside of class. Here, we see that Suzanne's view of good teaching is based on her knowledge about Philip, whom she judges to be highly skilled at keeping students entertained. Because she believes that she is 'not as good at that as I'd like to be', she finds this aspect of teaching to be stressful.

The ability to entertain students is something that Patricia also considered important. She believes that as a teacher, she is 'on stage all the time' and at 'the center of attention', which makes her uncomfortable. She believes that her students look to her to be entertained, and that it is her responsibility to make this happen by 'acting' and being 'entertaining'. As the sole teacher in the classroom with many eyes fixed on her, she feels the pressure to give the students a good show. Since she does not like people looking at her intensely, this has been an area of difficulty for her. When I asked her how well the TESOL program has prepared her for teaching ESL in middle schools, she replied:

> I think I was very well prepared. The only part I was not well prepared for is the teaching aspect. People assume, because I'm older, I know how to teach. But I had never taught before. I'd taught one on one a lot, but I'd never taught in a classroom setting. I didn't feel like I got a lot of background in that. I mean it's the sort of thing you pick up on the job anyway, and you come up with your own systems. But it took me five years. I actually feel like I know what I'm doing now. (Patricia)

Part of the reason that Patricia did not feel prepared to teach may have been due to the fact that she did not do a teaching internship, as students typically do in teacher education programs. Because she was hired as a full-time ESL teacher before she finished the program, she did not have the benefit of transitioning gradually into classroom teaching. Although all new teachers have to learn some things on the job, a formal student-teaching experience could have eased her transition to full-time classroom teaching. Nonetheless, Patricia's comment that it took her five years to 'feel like I know what I'm doing' suggests that the ability to entertain and motivate students is something that can be cultivated through practice even by those who have stage fright. It also shows that learning to teach is a long-term developmental process, built through experience in actual classrooms (Johnson & Golombek, 2002).

In addition to experience, however, overcoming one's fear of being in the spotlight requires courage and resolve. Several years ago, Clara saw an ad in a newspaper calling for volunteers to teach English to adults at a local community center. Because she had wanted to get involved in her community for some time ('because if you just live in your apartment and go to work, you don't really see what's happening around you'), this seemed like a perfect opportunity. Clara was also confident that she could manage teaching a class one night a week without disrupting her full-time work as an engineer. So she signed up as a volunteer teacher in an introductory ESL class, and for three years, has been teaching English to recently arrived immigrants who speak little or no English. Clara describes what it's like to teach this class.

> The first day of class you go in the room, and all the students are just petrified. And then by the end of the class, they can all say, 'Good evening. How are you?' And they're so enthusiastic! Teaching was really an avenue for me to just be funny or to make jokes, to act out, and to act. It's very emotional. I mean, in order to make the class fun, you really have to be sensitive to where people are coming from. You have to draw people out. The main thing is you have to just stand up and make a fool of yourself and hope that the students will follow. (Clara)

Clara describes her students as being 'just petrified' on the first day of class. They may be worried about making a living in a new country and paralyzed by so many uncertainties about their future. They may feel overwhelmed by having to learn a whole new language as adults while also juggling work and family responsibilities. Fear and anxiety are palpable in this beginning ESL class, as students do not know where to begin or what to expect, and some are afraid of making mistakes in English and looking stupid. Into this tense setting enters Clara, who immediately puts the students at ease. With her exaggerated facial expressions and gesticulations that border on being comical, she introduces herself to the students and communicates her desire to get to know them. She models conversational expressions that she would like her students to learn that night and encourages them to repeat after her while providing plenty of positive feedback and reassurance along the way. At first, there are some hesitations and false starts, but before long, the students realize that they are speaking English and communicating with their teacher and with one another. This is a huge victory and affirmation for people who started the evening speaking no English at all.

For Clara, teaching is 'very emotional', because one has to 'be sensitive to where people are coming from' and be able to 'draw people out'. Because she knows that her students are frightened, she infuses humor and non-verbal communication (e.g. looking foolish, acting) into her lessons to lower students' anxiety. To connect personally with her students and to let them know that it is okay to make mistakes when learning a new language, she makes a fool of herself. This, incidentally, is no small feat for a woman engineer who, for many years, has trained herself to suppress her emotional tendencies in order to compete in a professional world dominated by men. It is a daring move for someone who has disciplined herself to be cautious and guarded in her interactions with people.

As Clara gathers her courage to act and to entertain, however, she realizes that she has little control over how her actions will actually be interpreted by her students. After everything she has done to amuse and motivate them, she can never guarantee that they will be amused and motivated. All she can do is 'hope that the students will follow'. This statement shows her understanding that the effect of her perlocutionary acts is outside of her performance and ultimately depends on the feelings and thoughts of her students. Because she can never know for sure how they will judge her attempts to be funny, teaching is an emotional gamble, which results in her feeling exposed and vulnerable. It is very much a performance that requires practice, faith and constant reflection.

Teaching Requires the Ability to Manage Classrooms

Another way in which the study participants viewed teaching had to do with managing student behavior in the classroom. Effective classroom management is widely viewed as one of the most important jobs of teachers, because it contributes significantly to student learning (Reupert & Woodcock, 2010; Stoughton, 2007). In fact, research shows that teachers' actions in the classroom have twice the impact on student achievement as do school policies regarding curriculum, assessment, staff collegiality and community involvement (Marzano & Marzano, 2003). At the same time, classroom management is the most significant area of concern for pre-service teachers, particularly during the internship (Bromfield, 2006) and is a deterrent to joining the profession (Priyadharshini & Robinson-Pant, 2003). Difficulty with classroom management is also one of the most common reasons given by teachers for leaving the profession (Fisher, 2012).

While classroom management can be defined in a number of different ways, it typically involves actions that the teacher takes to 'establish order, engage students, or elicit their cooperation' (Emmer & Stough, 2001: 103). Other definitions include promoting 'positive social interaction, active engagement in learning, and self-motivation' (Burden, 2003: 3), and 'actions taken to create a learning environment conducive to successful instruction' such as 'arranging the physical environment, establishing rules and procedures, [and] maintaining students' attention to lessons and engagement in activities' (Brophy, 2006: 17). According to Evertson and Weinstein (2006: 4), classroom management has two distinct purposes: 'It not only seeks to establish and sustain an orderly environment so students can engage in meaningful academic learning, it also aims to enhance student social and moral growth'.

Marzano and Marzano (2003) argue that the quality of teacher–student relationships is critical in classroom management. They point out that the most effective relationships are characterized by specific teacher behaviors: exhibiting appropriate levels of dominance and cooperation and being aware of high-needs students. Teachers can show appropriate dominance by establishing clear behavior expectations and using an appropriate tone of voice. Teachers can foster cooperation by providing flexible learning goals, taking a personal interest in students, making eye contact and encouraging all students to participate in class discussions. In addition, Marzano and Marzano (2003) point out that because 12%–22% of all students suffer from mental, emotional and behavioral disorders, teachers should have a repertoire of specific strategies for meeting some of their needs, including creating behavior contracts and providing immediate rewards and consequences for aggressive students; dividing tasks into manageable parts for students with attention deficit; and counseling socially inept students about acceptable social behaviors.

In the current study, classroom management was found to be a significant source of anxiety for some of the participants. During her first week of classes in the TESOL program, Lynn received a phone call from a local public school system asking whether she would be interested in a job as a teacher's assistant in a high school ESL class. Since she was thinking about volunteering in the schools anyway, she was pleased at the possibility of actually being paid for her work. When she arrived at the school, however, she was told that she would get a class of her own instead of assisting a teacher. When she informed the school that she was in her first week of the teacher training program and did not have teaching experience, the school assured her that she would be fine, since she has a law degree and had worked as an attorney for a long time. They told her that given her extensive work experience, she would have no problem handling the students. Lynn took the position despite her reservations, believing that she could learn on the job. But she quickly realized that taking this job was not a good idea.

I remember my first week. I had to run out of the classroom in tears. I was in the bathroom crying, thinking I used to prosecute criminals, and these 16-year-old punks are making me cry? What the hell did I get myself into? I always thought teaching high school would be incredible. So this was perfect for me. But I had to create a midterm, all the assignments. I was clueless. And then there was one student who had been suspended no fewer than 12 times. The Russian students would get into fights with this student. And then there was a woman who was rushed to the hospital. It had something to do with witchcraft. I wasn't teaching. I was doing daycare for special-needs students. If I were in my 20s, teaching high school would be it. But I don't want to do this in my 50s. So I dropped the K–12 certification. (Lynn)

As someone newly entering a teacher education program, Lynn was clearly not prepared to assume responsibility for teaching this class. It would have been challenging to teach a class like this even as a student teacher with full support from a mentor teacher and a university supervisor. But being thrown into a classroom with many high-needs students with no one to turn to for help, she was completely overwhelmed. The school probably should not have given Lynn her own classroom, because she was just beginning to be trained as a teacher. The school's decision reflects the common assumption that older adults with successful previous careers will transition into teaching with ease (Mayotte, 2003). People also generally assume more from older teachers than from younger teachers and think that they will have better control of students by virtue of their age and experience (Williams, 2010). But this assumption can have costly consequences. In Lynn's case, she found her experience at the high school so traumatizing that she decided to abandon K-12 certification altogether and teach only adult ESL.

Was Lynn's decision to give up teaching high school premature? Could she have made a different choice if she had more teaching experience going into the job? Although it is difficult to know for certain, there is some indication that a gradual induction into teaching with a higher degree of mentoring and support could have helped her to stay in the job (Allen, 2005). In his book, *Outliers: The Story of Success*, Malcolm Gladwell (2008) examined the lives of exceptionally successful people to find out how they achieved their prominence. He found that rather than natural talent or IQ, it was the amount of time that people spent practicing a chosen profession that accounted for their excellence. Specifically, he found that it took about 10,000 hours for individuals to achieve mastery and become experts in their field. For new teachers, 10,000 hours translate to about five years in the classroom, and those first five years are often the most challenging (Fisher, 2012). This is also when many newly licensed teachers decide to quit teaching; about half leave the profession in the first five years (National Education Association, n.d.). Since the likelihood of teachers leaving the profession declines significantly after that time (Allen, 2005), providing teachers with the necessary support in their first few years is crucial.

My interviews with the study participants confirmed that four to five years is about the amount of time required for them to get their teaching stabilized, with classroom management commonly identified as an area of major difficulty during that time.

I'm not good at classroom management. I spoke to [instructor X] and five other people last December about how I had horrible classroom management. I told them that my students were wild, they didn't listen, and they spoke up. I was just really bad at it. I think I'm finally getting it, but I've been teaching for 4 or 5 years. And it's just been a challenge all the time. (Ginny)

To this day, teaching scares me. I still go into classrooms and think, how did I do it? It's just so intimidating to me to walk into a classroom full of kids. I think it's just the number of kids and the possibility that they could really take over the class if they wanted to. I just relate much better one on one or in a small group. (Joni)

Ginny's remarks reveal that managing student behavior has been a continuous struggle for her for the last four to five years she has taught ESL. She characterizes her classroom management skills as 'horrible' and 'really bad', with students not listening to her and speaking up without being called on. Although she believes that she is now 'finally getting it', she recognizes that this is an issue that will require a long-term, developmental approach. Similarly, Joni believes that she has some way to go in improving her classroom management skills. Although she has been teaching for four years and is now a tenured teacher in her school district, she confessed that she is still afraid of walking into 'a classroom full of kids'.

How can new teachers be supported to develop in the area of classroom management? The problem for many teacher educators in teaching classroom management is that pre-service teachers often prefer to receive recipe-like directions for addressing behavioral issues rather than learn about the central principles that guide human behavior (Reupert & Woodcock, 2010). Bromfield (2006: 189) cites a training survey which found that pre-service teachers requested 'step-by-step strategies to deal with bad behavior and a discussion of options for different situations'. The trouble with mechanistic approaches to classroom management, however, is the tendency to oversimplify the nature of students' behavioral difficulties and disregard important contextual factors (Reupert & Woodcock, 2010). In order to prevent classroom management problems, one needs to appreciate the contexts and beliefs that drive both students' and teachers' behaviors (Charles & Senter, 2008). By understanding what motivates students to conduct themselves the way they do, teachers can not only correct misbehavior but also prevent behavior problems from occurring in the first place. Indeed, effective teachers deliberately plan to create a positive classroom environment (Beaman & Wheldall, 2000). Their energies are focused on producing lessons that engage students and keep them actively involved in the learning process.

In the interviews, Lesley shared her philosophy of handling disciplinary issues in her classes. She believes that good classroom management is not about establishing and enforcing rules but rather about helping students make the right choices.

> I'm not a good disciplinarian. All they have to do is look sad, and my plan goes out the window. I'm perfectly fine with providing direction, but I don't like to tell people what to do. I always like to give people a choice. Even if they're not really getting a choice, I like to present it as a choice. I mean, honestly, you always have a choice. [I say to airline passengers who are angry about their canceled flights,] 'You can either not go, or you can do this'. They're not good choices, but it's always a choice. So when I'm dealing with my students, I like to have them feel like they're making a choice. I think I can be pretty persuasive, but I still like them to feel like *they* have decided to do it. (Lesley)

Here, we can see her prior experience as an airline customer service agent shaping her classroom management style. By presenting classroom cooperation as a choice, Lesley steers her students toward a desired outcome without appearing authoritarian. This seemingly gentler approach is based on her knowledge of herself and how she responds empathetically to students who appear to be having trouble. 'All they have to do is look sad', and she doesn't follow through with her plans to discipline them. Since students who figure this out can potentially use this knowledge to avoid being disciplined, Lesley has adopted a strategy that shifts her students' focus from just complying with her demands to making good personal choices. Lesley believes that, when presented with a choice (even if it is a pseudo-choice), students feel that they are in charge of the situation and are more likely to take responsibility for their own actions. She believes that it is not just *what* she tells her students, but *how* she presents the information that can make a difference in their behavior.

Lesley's strategy of providing students with a choice can be characterized as a preventative classroom management strategy. Unlike corrective strategies (e.g. giving students a time-out, issuing threats or warnings or referring students to the principal) that react to misbehavior after it has happened, preventative strategies (e.g. establishing a regular routine, teaching appropriate behavior as part of the lesson) create a positive classroom environment by promoting good behavior. While preventative strategies have been shown to be effective in managing classrooms, research shows that pre-service teachers do not employ preventative strategies as frequently as they do corrective strategies (Reupert & Woodcock, 2010). Furthermore, many schools and teachers tend to be control oriented and use more corrective than preventative measures in managing student behavior (Furlong *et al.*, 2000). Given the preponderance of corrective strategies in schools, Lesley's preventative approach is all the more noteworthy and underscores the role of prior work and life experience on career changers' development as teachers. In this case, Lesley's knowledge of human behavior from years of working in customer service was clearly evident in the way she related to her students.

Good Teaching Empowers Students

In addition to their view that classrooms should be managed effectively for learning to occur, some of the study participants believe that teaching should be about empowering students. They discussed the importance of helping students become competent and confident users of English and equipping them with the necessary tools to be able to achieve their personal goals. This sentiment was particularly strong among those who work with adult students. They believe that adult learners bring a wealth of life experiences and ways of knowing and have a keen desire to learn and succeed. Because most adult learners are deeply committed to their educational pursuits and are motivated to learn, the study participants believe that it is important to invite adult learners to participate in making decisions about what they will learn and how they will develop personally and professionally (Bland, 2003).

Research shows that adult language learning is most effective when it occurs within the context of a community (Larotta, 2009; Wrigley et al., 2009). When adult learners feel that they belong in the ESL program, they are more likely to invest in their learning and take ownership of the curriculum. Larotta (2009) stresses that learning a language is not just an exercise in mastering isolated skills such as speaking, listening, reading and writing, but rather a process through which learners develop new identities and a new understanding of the world that incorporates the language. Human relationships are crucial in promoting successful adult learning, and a partnership between the teacher and the student is especially important (Bland, 2003). Below, David explains how he promotes a sense of community in his classes and builds partnerships with his students.

> I've always had good teacher ratings at the end of the semester. My students have always given me good evaluations, even in my first semester, because I always take the approach that I'm a human being teaching other human beings. I tell my students, 'I'm sharing what I know with you. Let me know how I can help you and be of service to you'. I set up that atmosphere. (David)

Rather than simply telling his students what they need to do to be successful, David tries to involve them in the learning process by asking them how he can help them achieve their personal goals. In doing so, he assumes the position of a helper and a facilitator rather than an instructor. I had the opportunity to observe an advanced speaking and listening class that he taught at a local community college and see his philosophy at work. The session I observed was one of the last classes of the semester, in which his students conducted a debate on immigration reform in the United States. His five adult students were from different countries in Asia: Korea, Nepal, China, Myanmar and the Philippines. Everyone had come to class directly after work; two students were in their work uniforms from Panda Express and Dunkin Donuts. Despite the fact that this was an evening class and people seemed tired, there was a spirit of camaraderie among the students, as they chatted and laughed with one another.

David explained to me that because all five of his students aspire to get college or professional degrees, learning academic English is very important to them. However, they lack confidence in speaking English, and they feel discouraged when Americans do not understand their speech and they have to repeat the same utterance over and over again. Thus, throughout the semester, in addition to teaching English pronunciation and intonation, David taught his students specific techniques that they can use if they are not understood the first time, such as slowing down and enunciating words, using synonyms for words that they have particular difficulty in pronouncing and rephrasing sentences. As David reviewed the rules of the debate, he reminded the students that he is not only interested in what they argue but also how they make their case. He stressed the importance of projecting one's voice, maintaining an upright posture and using appropriate gestures to support the points they are trying to make. He encouraged them to listen carefully to the arguments made by the opposite group, take good notes and decide how to refute the other side's views.

The two groups took turns presenting their arguments and counterarguments. The students had done research on the topic and prepared PowerPoint slides complete with charts, photos and graphics. Although they had some difficulty with grammar and pronunciation, they were clearly able to articulate key aspects of this complex topic in English. For example, the Nepali student asserted, 'Amnesty is FORgiveness for illegal imbrigants. In our view, it's not good for legal imbrigants. Many people want to come to the United States legally'. The Filipino student argued against him by saying, 'Illegal immigrants are humans. Therefore, we need to treat them HUmanely'. While David made on-the-spot corrections of some of the students' language errors, he was careful to comment on the substance of their arguments and praise them for their efforts. For example, he commended the Burmese student, 'I'm so pleased that your pronunciation has improved a lot. I remember you used to always say "DEveloped". Now you say it correctly'. The student was visibly pleased to receive this compliment and thanked David multiple times.

At the end of the class, the Korean student produced a small jar of kimchee wrapped carefully in four layers of plastic bags. When the other students asked her what was inside, she opened the bags, one after the other, and explained, 'This is for David. I made it this morning. It's fresh. Winter kimchee is the best. Summer kimchee not so good. You can put kimchee in pancakes, in soups. Mmm.... It's so good'. The Chinese student told me after class that even though she used to be scared to talk in English before taking this class, she was not afraid anymore. The strategies she learned in this class have been very helpful and have given her a lot of confidence in making herself understood by English speakers. Overall, David's humanistic approach to teaching seemed to resonate deeply with his students, who appreciated their teacher for what he has been for them – a trusted advisor, coach and partner in their education.

Empowering adult immigrants to have control of their lives and achieve their aspirations is what motivates Marianne to teach adult ESL. She believes that lack of English skills puts adult immigrants at a distinct disadvantage and prevents them from reaching their full potential. In particular, she lamented the presence of a severe language gap between parents and children of immigrant households and described how its effects were felt during the housing market crash of recent years.

> What really pushed me into teaching ESL was the housing crash, when the bubble burst. In our law firm, we had a homeowners association. We were in foreclosing and had so many immigrants who had been taken advantage of by mortgage companies. They bought way more house than they could afford, didn't speak English, didn't know how to read the contracts, and didn't know how to work with money. Since they didn't speak English and their children did, the kids translated. So the children were learning that they were losing their homes before their parents did. I pitched a fit over that one with my firm, and they finally hired someone who spoke Spanish, but can you imagine the damage? It was just breaking everybody's heart, and I was practically doing therapy in the lunchroom with the paralegals. It was overwhelming for everyone. I just hated that anybody would be taken advantage of in that way. I mean, they've come here for jobs and to give their kids a better education. I absolutely hate the concept of a lost generation. Why does the first generation have to sacrifice everything? It's not necessary. It's just a language issue. (Marianne)

As can be seen in this excerpt, parents' lack of English skills can be a source of stress for the entire family. It is not uncommon for school-aged children to be asked to serve as interpreters in potentially sensitive situations (e.g. parent–teacher conferences, at the doctor's office) when there is no one else who speaks both the native language and English. While parents may be embarrassed that they have to rely on their children for things that adults should normally be able to do, children may also be frustrated that their parents are dependent on them for even the simplest tasks (Shin, 2005). For parents, their lack of English skills sets in motion a vicious cycle. It forces them to take two or three low-paying jobs, which in turn leave them little time and energy to attend English language classes. Since they cannot spend adequate time studying the language, their English never improves. Although parents want to be able to understand what their children are learning in school and help them with homework, lack of time and knowledge of English gets in the way of their full participation in their children's education. Parents often feel powerless, even as they work their bodies to the limit hoping to secure a good future for themselves and their children.

To Marianne, teaching should be about providing students with the necessary tools to be effective in their roles as parents, workers and citizens. Her experience working at the law firm with immigrants who were losing their homes has taught her that the tools that her clients needed most were English literacy and numeracy skills. These are well-reflected in her adult basic English classes, as she explains:

> You should see how hard I teach money in my classes. Half of my students don't know there are five nickels in a quarter or two nickels in a dime. They don't understand the currency. More than I expected, they are late getting into banks. A lot of them run on cash. They just hand somebody a large bill and take whatever change that comes back to them. So in my class, I've got all these pictures of currency, and we spend time buying and selling, writing checks, and balancing checkbooks. I do maybe more financial literacy than other teachers because of that. It's just amazing to me how many people have been here for ten years and don't know the currency, because no one's ever taught them. (Marianne)

Marianne teaches perhaps 'more financial literacy than other teachers', because she has witnessed firsthand how devastating it can be for immigrants and their families to not have this knowledge. Her classes help adult students learn not only how to speak, read and write English but also how to take charge of their finances, which can be hugely empowering.

As a former military spouse and later a divorced single mother with two daughters, Marianne has had her own struggles in life. Nonetheless, she learned a new career as a social worker later in life, and for more than 20 years, has helped countless individuals overcome challenges of their own. The help that she provides her clients (and now her students) is practical and constructive, and she relates to them with respect and compassion. Her students obviously appreciate what she does, as they often give her hugs and present her with gifts and food they have made. To them, Marianne seems to be more than just a language teacher. She is also a loyal ally and a trusted counselor.

Conclusion

In this chapter, I explored the study participants' experiences as classroom teachers, the instructional decisions they make and the factors that drive them to make those decisions. I discussed how they have come to learn what they know about teaching and learning, and how they use their knowledge in a variety of educational settings. By and large, they find teaching to be a highly complex process that requires thorough planning and impeccable execution. As career changers, many of them view teaching as one of the most intense, emotional and difficult jobs they have had. They mention how laborious and time-consuming it is to prepare lessons and grade student papers and how mentally exhausting it is to have to be 'on top of everything' all the time. They believe that what makes teaching especially demanding is that it depends on a practically limitless number of personal and contextual variables, which interact in myriad ways to influence how students learn (Liew, 2013).

The way in which the participants use their knowledge in teaching and interpret what goes on in their classes is highly personal (Golombek, 1998; Johnson & Golombek, 2002). Coming from a variety of backgrounds and life experiences, each of the 30 participants experienced teaching in different ways. While public speaking excites some of them, others are terrified of standing in front of a class full of students. Some associate teaching with a theatrical performance and feel insecure about their ability to 'act', to motivate, amuse and inspire their students. They believe that good teaching requires more than reading from a well-written curriculum script: *How* one presents the material can sometimes make all the difference in the world. In many of the interviews, the focus was very much on student engagement and what teachers can do to facilitate learning. Teaching and learning are thought to be a multidimensional enterprise and much more than a one-way transfer of information from teachers to students. Because the participants feel that real learning is likely to occur when students care about the subject, they seek to deploy speech acts that would engage not only the students' minds but also their hearts (Austin, 1962; Liew, 2013).

While teaching is thought to be a challenging undertaking, the men and women in this study ultimately believe that it is a satisfying and worthwhile effort, deserving of their time, creativity and energy. Driven by a sense of purpose, they mobilize the knowledge and resources they have at their disposal to prepare lessons that would give their students 'something worthwhile'. They put fearful newcomer ESL students at ease by infusing humor into their interactions, and strive to create a classroom environment in which all students feel welcome and valued. Their knowledge of human behavior acquired from years of working in various people-intensive fields is evident in the ways in which some of them relate to their students, particularly as they address issues around classroom management and work to build a strong classroom community.

The study participants' teaching is in no way perfect. It is, in fact, continuously developing. Perhaps what sets these teachers apart from other, younger teachers is that they have a more practical view of the purposes for learning and a keener sense of their own strengths and weaknesses as teachers. These teachers, by virtue of their age and life experiences, are perhaps better attuned to the reality that teaching cannot be reduced to a predictable scientific schema of causality and conventionality (Liew, 2013). They strongly believe in the importance of nurturing human relationships and building personal connections – elements that are not easily quantified yet are critical for student success. It is perhaps this aspect of their work that has the potential to make the most difference in students' lives.

7 Launching a Career in TESOL

In this chapter, I describe the post-program activities of the participants in the study. Upon completion of their teacher training programs, how do people launch their teaching careers? What does the job market look like for career changers with TESOL training? What opportunities become available as one acquires new pedagogical skills and credentials? I first describe the state of the ESL job market and the occupational outlook for ESL educators in the United States. I then discuss how the men and women in this study are faring as teachers in various educational settings including K-12 schools, community colleges, literacy organizations and community-based English language programs. I examine the degree of job satisfaction in each setting and consider some of the major difficulties that the participants experience related to instruction, complying with educational laws and policies and developing professionally. In addition, I explore the circumstances of those who are biding their time and currently not teaching for a variety of personal, familial and financial reasons. I describe what these individuals are doing to keep connected to TESOL and continue to grow as professionals. I first describe the ESL job market.

State of the ESL Job Market

As indicated in Chapter 1, English learners are the fastest-growing segment of the American school-aged population. Figure 7.1 shows that while total pre-K-12 enrollment has generally stagnated, growing only about 7% from 1998 through 2009, the enrollment of English learners has increased by 51% over the same period. The English learner population is expected to continue on the path of dynamic growth over the coming decade. It is projected that by 2020, there will be 17.9 million school-aged children of immigrants (ages 5–17) in the United States (Fry, 2008).

School districts across the United States are experiencing considerable difficulty filling their ESL teaching vacancies (US Department of Education, 2014). An analysis of nationwide teacher staffing indicates that 36 states and the District of Columbia have had shortages of ESL or bilingual teachers since 2000, with some states reporting chronic difficulties in finding necessary numbers of ESL instructors for eight or more years (Terrazas & Fix, 2009). While states and districts have explored a variety of strategies to meet their teacher staffing needs (e.g. providing incentives for professionals in other fields to enter teaching, helping

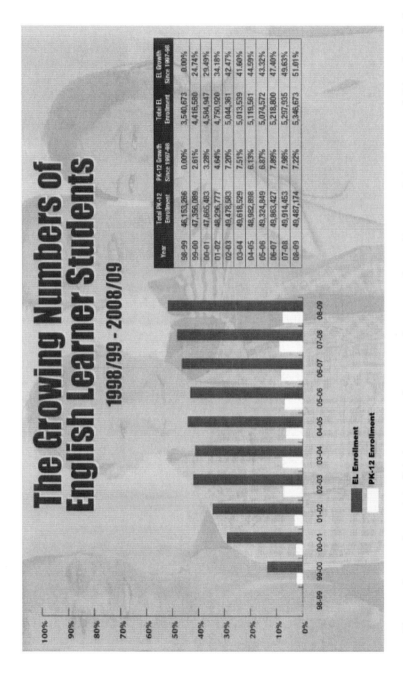

Figure 7.1 The growing numbers of English learner students 1998/1999–2008/2009 (Source: US Department of Education, National Clearinghouse for English Language Acquisition and Language Instruction Educational Programs [NCELA], 2011)

teachers from other countries who are living in the United States to obtain the appropriate credentials and recruiting foreign teachers through the US government's temporary worker program or teacher exchange programs), these strategies often do not address immediate needs because of the lengthy investments typically necessary for teacher education and licensing (Terrazas & Fix, 2009).

The fact that ESL teacher shortages are an enduring challenge facing schools and school districts should appeal to people who are considering entering the field. Over the coming decade, the overall job outlook for ESL teachers is quite strong. Although opportunities will vary by region and the level of funding for educational staffing in different locales, job prospects for ESL teachers are likely to remain robust given the rapid enrollment growth of English learners. In addition, schools are facing the largest teacher retirement in history – about half of American teachers are expected to retire over the coming decade (National Commission on Teaching and America's Future, 2011). While employment of elementary school teachers is projected to grow by 12% from 2012 to 2022, teachers with certifications to teach in critical teacher shortage areas, such as ESL and special education, are expected to have better job opportunities (Bureau of Labor Statistics, 2015a). During the same period, employment of secondary school teachers is projected to grow more slowly (6%), but again, middle and high school teachers with certifications to teach critical teacher shortage areas such math, science, ESL and special education are expected to have better job prospects than those certified in other content areas (Bureau of Labor Statistics, 2015b).

The job outlook for adult ESL teachers is equally strong. A Migration Policy Institute report on adult language instruction in the United States estimates that 5.8 million legal permanent residents are in need of English language instruction to pass the naturalization exam and be able to participate in civic life (McHugh et al., 2007). In addition, 6.4 million undocumented immigrants are in need of English language instruction to acquire work permits and obtain legal permanent resident status; and 2.4 million youths aged 17–24 require English instruction in order to begin post-secondary education without remediation (McHugh et al., 2007).

Much of this need is currently not being met. Only 921,548 adults were enrolled in federally funded, state-administered ESL programs in 2009/2010 (US Department of Education, Office of Vocational and Adult Education, 2011). In addition to federally funded programs, English instruction is offered by a variety of community-based programs, private language schools and academic institutions (Center for Applied Linguistics, 2010). Even with these programs, however, the demand for affordable, high-quality English classes far outstrips supply. Across the country, there is an urgent need to build capacity for ESL, adult basic education (ABE) and workforce preparation classes to help immigrant adults improve their English and achieve their personal and occupational goals (Schaetzel *et al.*, 2007). As staffing these classes with qualified teachers becomes crucial in many places, the demand for adult ESL teachers is likely to increase. In fact, employment of adult literacy and high school equivalency diploma teachers is projected to grow by 9% from 2012 to 2022 (Bureau of Labor Statistics, 2015c).

Job Search Experiences of the Participants

The strength of the ESL job market is reflected in the job hunting experiences of the participants in the current study, as nearly everyone was able to secure a teaching position when they wanted. Out of the 30 participants in the study, 5 were working as full-time ESL teachers in K-12 public schools at the time of the interview, with 3 more on track to teach K-12 ESL in the near future (the 5 K-12 ESL teachers were actually hired before they were finished with the TESOL program as part of a statewide effort to alleviate a critical shortage of ESL teachers in public school systems in Maryland). Seventeen were teaching adult ESL on a part-time basis in community colleges, literacy organizations or community-based English language programs. The remaining five participants were not teaching at the time of the interview for a variety of personal reasons but expressed a desire to teach adult ESL sometime in the future.

In assessing their work as teachers, the study participants stated that teaching ESL was one of the most satisfying jobs they have had. A few described it as *the* best job of their careers. All of the participants, even those who were not teaching at the time of the interview, were glad that they received TESOL training and thought it was a good investment of their time, money and energies. They believed that the TESOL program has generally prepared them well to work with English learners and equipped them with the tools necessary to be effective in the classroom. For instance, Patricia had the following to say about her TESOL training and her middle school ESL position: 'This job really requires my education. I feel like I'm using everything I've learned in the TESOL program'. When asked what the best part of teaching ESL was, the participants consistently named the following: (1) having the opportunity to interact with the students and make a lasting difference in their lives; (2) being appreciated by students; and (3) having flexible hours (in the case of adult ESL).

Despite these positive assessments, however, significant concerns were raised by the K-12 ESL teachers in the study regarding their relationships with general education teachers and administrators in public schools and meeting federal and state educational standards, particularly as they related to preparing students for high-stakes standardized testing. Those working in adult ESL settings were dismayed by a lack of structure, curriculum and materials in many ABE programs and lamented the relatively low funding priority given to adult education by local, state and federal governments.

While the ability to work part-time was thought by some to be an attractive feature of teaching adults, others who wished to make a full-time career out of teaching adults were disappointed by a severe lack of full-time positions in adult ESL. In what follows, I discuss each of these challenges and the ways in which the participants have dealt with the realities of their day-to-day work as educators.

One Profession, Multiple Paths

My interviews with the study participants revealed that the pathways to launching their careers in TESOL were varied and not always straightforward. The choices people made and the timing associated with their decisions were influenced by a host of factors including financial constraints, family responsibilities and life circumstances. For instance, one of the main reasons for some people's selection of K-12 ESL over adult ESL was the ready availability of full-time positions with benefits in public schools. The individuals who chose the K-12 option did not necessarily want to teach only children; all of them could see themselves working with adults as well. But the need to have a stable income with benefits was a primary driving force behind their decision to pursue the K-12 route. As James put it,

> Teaching elementary school was not at the forefront of my mind. Actually, teaching adults was. But the way my life had been, I was not financially prepared for old age. I plan to teach 5 years in [name of public school system] because, after 5 years, I can keep certain things for the rest of my life, like health insurance and a small retirement. Then I might go teach overseas. (James)

Compared to public schools, full-time benefited positions are much rarer in the world of adult ESL. Most adult ESL teachers get paid by the hour or by a set amount for each course they teach, and they may or may not be compensated for the time they spend outside of the classroom preparing lessons and grading student assignments. Since it is difficult to make a living by teaching adult ESL as a part-time instructor, most people hold other jobs to supplement their income. In the current study, 10 out of the 17 adult ESL instructors had jobs that were unrelated to TESOL. For example, Bonny works as a full-time university admissions coordinator and teaches one adult class in an intensive English program. She explained her situation as follows:

> Right now I need the day job at the university. I'm finding that most of the teaching jobs that are coming out in adult ESL are for part-time work without benefits. And I have to have the benefits. So, I'm just

going to keep teaching one class at the [intensive English program]. Office work is not very fulfilling, and sometimes it's frustrating. I would rather work with students…. If I could work with students full-time and get the benefits, that would be great. But then, I don't know if I have the stamina. I see some of the younger teachers, and they're so energetic. (Bonny)

When I asked Bonny whether she would quit her day job if she could get a full-time teaching position, she initially responded that she would be inclined to do so, and then quickly added that she may not have the energy to teach more classes. This reservation was based on her observation that some of her younger colleagues in the intensive English program seem to be a lot more dynamic than she is. Bonny's concern may have originated from her insecurity as a novice teacher and could very well diminish over time as she gains more classroom experience. But it shows how people's career decisions are often complex and shaped by personal aspirations as well as private fears.

While some people were disappointed by the fact that full-time adult ESL jobs were hard to find, being able to teach part-time was actually what appealed to others. These individuals appreciated that their part-time teaching positions allowed them to develop other skills, spend time with family and friends and still enjoy all the intellectual and social benefits of interacting with students from diverse cultural backgrounds.

I'm paid $26.00 an hour with my master's degree. That's not a lot, but fortunately, I'm not trying to earn my living teaching ESL. I don't have kids to put through college, they're off the family payroll, and the mortgage is paid for, so it's a good time to do this. I don't mind the pay. You don't go into it for the money, but it really is very satisfying. (Diane)

I'm not really doing this because I need the money. I'm doing it because I really like it. Of all the jobs I've had, teaching ESL is the best thing I've done. I love it, because it sort of marries all of my passions, my interest in languages, and my interest in helping people and being exposed to people of diverse backgrounds, which I've always loved. (Margie)

What I like about teaching adult ESL is I don't have to do it full-time. I can do it just a little bit… I wouldn't like to be teaching children. (Suzanne)

Diane, Margie and Suzanne found themselves in a much different financial situation than did James and Bonny. Both Diane and Suzanne have a retirement income that allows them to pursue their varied interests. In addition to teaching ESL, Diane owns and operates a yarn shop, and

Suzanne works as a part-time archivist one day a week. Margie is a stay-at-home mom and a long-time participant in two different conversation groups in German and Spanish. These women were teaching ESL primarily for personal enjoyment and gratification; they weren't doing it because they needed the money.

However, people who wanted to draw a full-time salary from teaching adults and did not have alternative sources of income struggled to make ends meet with a string of part-time positions. David was one such individual. He explains:

> After I graduated from the TESOL program, I worked in several community colleges. I worked in [community college x]. Then I worked in [community college y] for a long while. And I did a lot of private tutoring, especially when the economy went sour and there were fewer and fewer courses available, and fewer and fewer people coming in. You know how it is. You sign up to teach a course, and you're at the mercy of registration. If you don't get enough people registering, then you're out of work. (David)

Here, David explains how working in community colleges as an adjunct instructor has always been a tenuous enterprise. He often did not know whether the courses he was signed up to teach would actually be offered; sometimes, his courses would be canceled just days before the start of the semester due to low enrollment. Community college enrollment took a particularly hard hit during the Great Recession (2007–2009), when fewer people signed up to take courses than before. When this happened, David did a great deal of private tutoring, but this was not a reliable source of income either, as students would sometimes cancel sessions at the last minute. Then, after many months of 'a constant hustle looking for work', he was offered a contract position as an English teacher for a defense company. For six months, David had been able to settle into a nice rhythm of teaching one group of students in one place every day of the week. Although being in the classroom eight hours a day was rather intense and exhausting, his corporate job paid well and came with health benefits, which he desperately needed.

> They were teaching Algerian soldiers some kind of communication systems. There must have been about 50 of them taking a six-month intensive English language course. There were about half dozen or so teachers, and it paid very well. But the Italians outbid [the defense company], and the Algerians started getting their training some place in Italy. And so that was the end of that. At that point, I was really having trouble finding work to pay my bills. And personally, I didn't want to teach in public schools. Someone asked me if I would be interested in

tutoring Korean kids in [name of town]. And so I developed a reputation among the Korean community, and I was making a good living tutoring these children. But I was working my tail off, driving all over the place and working Saturdays and evenings. It was a great experience but I was working myself ragged and I kept looking for a full-time position. I was still working at [community college y] but I was teaching only a couple of courses because they really didn't have that much. So I was just wearing myself out. (David)

David's break finally came when he was offered a full-time job as a coordinator of a student learning support center at a university, a position he has held to this day.

As a coordinator, I manage and direct people, keep records, and make sure everything is going well. But I miss teaching ESL and having that relationship with the students. I mean, I deal with people, but not on that level. When you're teaching a class, each student means something. And you can recognize the development in each student as they're coming along and you try to help them meet their challenges. I miss that interaction. (David)

As a coordinator at the student learning support center, David spends most of his time doing administrative work and teaches just one course a semester on academic and life skills for undergraduate students who are about to be suspended for failing too many classes. Although the job pays fairly well and provides benefits, he misses interacting with ESL students. To maintain his connection to students, David teaches one course at the community college as an adjunct instructor. Although he now has a bit more financial security, he sympathizes with those who are trying to earn a living from part-time teaching.

I know everybody who's doing what I was doing is struggling like crazy. For me, if I didn't teach adult ESL, it was a matter of either going overseas to teach English or going into public schools. And my health is so bad I couldn't go overseas. I have very serious health problems. And I didn't want to teach in public schools. So at one point I was thinking about just giving it all up and finding a 9 to 5 job that I could live off of. Even if it wasn't teaching, if it wasn't ESL, I would do that. Then this opportunity came along, and I was able to make money and teach adults. But that doesn't happen to everybody. (David)

In the following section, I look more closely at the experiences of the K-12 ESL teachers in the study.

Job Satisfaction in K-12 ESL

The participants in the study who worked in K-12 schools were generally satisfied with their jobs. When asked what they liked about teaching K-12 ESL, they stated that they particularly enjoyed connecting with English learners and having an impact on their academic success. They articulated how rewarding it was to spend time getting to know the children and helping them succeed in school. Above all, they loved being needed and appreciated by their students and were thrilled when they saw visible progress in students' language skills.

> The best thing about teaching ESL is the kids. They're so interesting, and they have a lot to say and a lot to offer. I love to hear stories of what goes on in their lives. I love that I can help them tell their stories. (Joni)

> I love working with newcomers, the ones who have just arrived. They're my favorites, because they need you so much. They're hungry to learn, because they know it's kind of sink or swim and you're the one that's going to help them swim. They're motivated and appreciative, and it's so easy to see them progress over the year. Some of them are just amazing. (Bill)

Bill's preference for working with newcomer students comes from his observation that they are 'motivated', 'appreciative' and 'hungry to learn' – characteristics that any teacher would be pleased to see in students. He portrays ESL teachers as lifesavers, offering critical help to students who are in desperate need of assistance. The fact that newcomer students frequently show great improvement over the course of the year, going from knowing no English at all to being able to produce reasonably well-constructed English in just a year's time, also makes working with newcomers gratifying.

However, when asked what he does not like about being an ESL teacher, Bill shared his frustration that some of the other teachers in his school do not seem to think that he is a legitimate teacher.

> The worst part of teaching ESL is probably the fact that other teachers don't understand your role and the point of ESL. Some of them think you're a glorified assistant. It's a tie between that and students who don't care about learning. (Bill)

Most classroom teachers in the United States have not received specific training in addressing the needs of English learners and have a rather vague knowledge of what ESL teachers do (Valdés, 2001). These teachers tend to identify primarily with the content areas in which they are certified and do not necessarily view themselves as teachers of language learners.

In addition, some of them seem to think that any academic problems that English learners may be having are for ESL teachers to fix.

In many elementary schools, ESL teachers are brought into regular classrooms to work with individual or small groups of English learners while whole-class instruction takes place. In this 'push-in' model (where the ESL teacher 'pushes in' to a class taught by a general education teacher), the classroom teacher may view the ESL teacher as a teacher's aide working on special language issues, when in fact the purpose of this instructional arrangement is for the general education and ESL teachers to plan together to present language and content in a way that's accessible to all students, including the increasing numbers of students who are not yet proficient in grade-level English. In theory, both the content area teacher and the ESL teacher are responsible for teaching everyone in the class, and students are supposed to benefit from having not one, but two teachers with complementary expertise in different areas. But in practice, ESL teachers are more often viewed as supplemental to the main instructional activity and relegated to a lower status.

Because of the power disparity between general education and ESL teachers frequently seen in push-in programs, some ESL teachers prefer a 'pull-out' model, where English learners are 'pulled out' of their regular classrooms for about 30–45 minutes a day and given specialized language instruction in a separate classroom. While a pull-out class enables ESL teachers to focus on the specific language issues of English learners, one obvious drawback of this model is that students have to miss classroom instruction while they are in ESL, and few teachers give students the opportunity to make up missed classroom work. In recent years, schools across the United States have generally moved away from the pull-out model because of increased school accountability for student performance on statewide assessments (Zehr, 2008). Although little research exists on the relative merits of push-in and pull-out programs, many school administrators have embraced the push-in model based on the belief that keeping English learners in regular classrooms will help them learn the content better and improve their performance on standardized tests.

Regardless of what instructional model is used, the fact is that *all* teachers, not just ESL teachers, are responsible for promoting the academic success of English learners. This is all the more true in an increasing number of American schools, where English learners constitute the majority of the student population. Content area teachers who have English learners in their classrooms are *de facto* ESL teachers, because they need to teach the grade-level English that students need to know in order to access the content (Ariza, 2006). However, the K-12 ESL teachers in this study believed that content area teachers do not always empathize with English learners' difficulty in learning academic content through another language and have little understanding of how students' cultural backgrounds influence the way they behave in school.

Patricia expressed her discontent with her non-ESL colleagues, 'What I resent is the fact that regular teachers should be sensitive to ESL students in their classrooms, and they are not'. For instance, American teachers may view a student who does not look them in the eye as rude. Yet, if the student is from any number of cultures where staring people in the eye is considered disrespectful or even confrontational, looking away while talking to the teacher would actually be the polite thing to do. Examples like this go to show how a better understanding of cross-cultural communication on the part of teachers can help prevent unnecessary misunderstandings in the classroom.

Another area of difficulty for the K-12 teachers in the study involved preparing students for statewide standardized testing. With the passage of the No Child Left Behind Act (NCLB) in 2001, high-stakes testing has come to exert increasing pressure on American public school education. NCLB required the creation of standards in each state for what a student should know in reading and math in Grades 3–8. In addition, states were required to set academic achievement benchmarks for Adequate Yearly Progress (AYP) so that by 2014, all students would be reading and doing mathematics at grade level. AYP is defined as the amount of yearly improvement each school and district is expected to make in order to enable low-achieving students to meet the high performance levels expected of all children. With AYP in place, student achievement was measured according to tests designed to match the standards and given to every child every year. In addition, schools with English learners had to administer a standardized test of their English proficiency each year. The results of the English proficiency test were a part of the state's accountability system, as were reading and math test scores. All of these tests were high-stakes, because schools that failed to make the grade faced some serious consequences, including state takeover and restructuring.[1]

NCLB introduced sweeping changes in school accountability by requiring schools to report the scores of different subgroups of students separately. This disaggregation of test scores was meant to ensure that the traditionally underperforming students – low-income students, students of color, students with disabilities and English learners – are no longer hidden in school aggregates. While NCLB's aim to improve the educational achievement of students who had been poorly served by schools was widely praised by the law's proponents and critics alike, its implementation has forced a narrow focus on the subjects that are tested (Council for Basic Education, 2004; Dee & Jacob, 2010). School curriculum and instruction have been increasingly driven by materials that are covered by the tests, while non-tested subjects such as social studies, foreign languages and music have been neglected (National Association of State Boards of Education, 2003). The law has also produced other unintended negative consequences, including the inappropriate assessment of English learners and students with special needs and strong incentives to exclude low-scoring students from schools so as to meet test score targets (Darling-Hammond, 2007).

Prior to the passage of NCLB, states and school districts had more flexibility in determining when to include English learners in statewide testing, and newly arrived students who spoke little or no English were exempt. However, under NCLB, English learners are required to take the state content achievement tests in reading and math regardless of how little English they may know and are expected to meet the same yearly progress targets in reading and math as native English-speaking students. Schools across the United States have reported low scores for English language learners on such tests and have been under enormous pressure to make AYP in English learners' attainment of English proficiency and academic content knowledge (Meier & Wood, 2004).

A number of studies have reported that NCLB's test-based accountability policy has caused educators to move instructional time toward tested subjects, to reallocate time within tested subjects toward the specific content and skills covered on the exam and to increase the time devoted to narrow test preparation activities (Hannaway & Hamilton, 2008). The experiences of the K-12 teachers in this study confirm these findings.

> [The state testing] is terrible. It's horrible. I mean, it takes up a huge portion of what I do. Not just thinking about it and preparing for it, but it affects how I teach and the constraints on what we're able to do. I've heard the principal say with his own mouth, 'If it's not toward the test, if you can't justify it for the test, don't teach it. You don't have time'. I'm glad I chose ESL but, boy, do I wish we didn't have the testing pressure. (Joni)

> Another down side of teaching ESL is you spend the last quarter from about mid-March on testing. And sometimes it drives me crazy. Am I a teacher or a tester? (Bill)

> I hate the testing. It's really stressful. I hate the fact that if my school doesn't make AYP, it is my fault and mine only. Before the ESL kids started getting bussed in, the school always made AYP. We get a lot of pressure from the principal to raise test scores. But I'm always going to be right on the border regardless of who I have, because I've got some kids that are just way ahead in math but are struggling with reading because English is not their native language. And I have some kids who have such interrupted education that they come to middle school with a kindergarten education. So I'm never going to make AYP. (Patricia)

As can be seen in these excerpts, the K-12 ESL teachers in the study experienced significant stress from standardized testing, which affected their classroom practice. They were pressured by their principals to raise student test scores and spend large amounts of time on test preparation, especially during the last quarter of the school year, when statewide assessments take place. The pressures of testing have hurt morale among teachers and have left them feeling disempowered (Meier & Wood, 2004). Because entire schools could be deemed as failing if the English learner subgroup did not make AYP, the teachers felt compelled to increase the time devoted to reviewing test-taking strategies that had little broader educational value (Hannaway & Hamilton, 2008). Despite these efforts, however, some students simply could not meet the target scores, because they either had not been in the United States long enough to catch up to their grade-level peers in English proficiency or they had severely interrupted education in their home countries.

Another negative consequence of NCLB was that students who needed ESL services were being mainstreamed too quickly.

> This year that just ended, I had 20 students. But this coming year, I'm going to have much fewer because of this new state law, where we have to release students when they get to level 5. So they're all released from ESL.... But the ones that we release are not ready to be mainstreamed.... It's just that it's coming from the state, and they're telling us that we have to do it. We used to have a little bit of wiggle room, but not anymore. (Patricia)

Here, Patricia shares how she felt conflicted about releasing students who are not yet fully proficient in English from the ESL program. Because schools with English learners must set increasing yearly targets for the percentage of English learners becoming proficient in English, this creates strong incentives for schools to reclassify students as fully English proficient even when they are not quite ready for academic work without ESL support. Premature mainstreaming of English learners can have long-term negative consequences, as the language demands of school subjects become greater as children progress through the grades (Saunders & Goldenberg, 2010). Henry, a high school ESL teacher, is frustrated to see students with potential not succeed due to lack of appropriate support.

> My students are well motivated, but they don't have the know-how of how to learn at a high level. They have to learn how to keep their papers organized, where to find the resources, how to get to the library..... I don't spend a lot of teaching time on that, because our curriculums tend to be fairly packed. So it's a challenge.... The worst part of teaching high school ESL is the frustration of knowing that the students have all this potential, but they're not going to succeed because of lack of support. (Henry)

One of the biggest challenges facing ESL teachers in K-12 schools is helping students to go beyond intermediate levels of English to achieve the high levels of English literacy required to meet grade-level standards in content areas (Shin, 2013). While many students make fairly rapid progress from beginning to intermediate levels of proficiency in English, few progress beyond the intermediate level to achieve advanced English skills (August & Shanahan, 2006). By rewarding the rapid mainstreaming of ESL students, NCLB has contributed to preventing English learners from receiving the help they need to attain advanced English. For teachers who have the best interests of English learners at heart and are trained to help them, NCLB's emphasis on test-based accountability and rapid sink-or-swim English immersion has been a source of frustration.

There is a widespread view among parents, educators and policymakers that NCLB has not made much of a difference in improving the quality of education in American schools. According to a 2012 Gallup poll, roughly 3 in 10 Americans think that the law has actually worsened the quality of education (Saad, 2012). Many of the current proposals to rewrite the federal education law include similar testing requirements, and it is not clear how they would address the issues facing the nation's schools (Wong, 2015).

Job Satisfaction in Adult ESL

Turning now to the degree of job satisfaction in adult ESL, it was clear that the participants found working with immigrant adults fulfilling and enjoyable. When asked what they liked about teaching English to adults, the participants shared reasons that are similar to those listed by the K-12 ESL teachers in the study: the sense of fulfillment in helping people in need, being appreciated by students and watching students' language skills improve. Along the lines of what Bill articulated about working with newcomer elementary school students, Ginny particularly enjoyed teaching beginners, because she was able to witness substantial progress in their language skills over a short period of time.

> Working at [name of community-based ESL program] was very rewarding. The people were extremely appreciative. I felt, especially with the very beginners, that no matter what I did, I was helping them. (Ginny)

Other adult ESL teachers in the study were drawn to teaching adults who were not literate in their native languages. Below, Diane talks about how much she enjoyed helping some of these students 'break the code'.

> At the [name of literacy council], I don't know if I've changed lives, but I've certainly given people a little handle on things that they were

struggling with. Last summer I taught a low-beginning class with 22 people. At least half of them were not literate in their first languages.... I had a young Ghanaian woman who graduated from an English-medium high school in Ghana. But she could not read, not a letter. And I had never worked with non-literate students. So it was a great adventure, but a couple of them broke the code while I was helping them. And I felt so good about that. (Diane)

Adults who arrive in the United States without literacy in their native language face a more difficult task learning to read and write in English than those who have first language literacy. In order to read, one needs to understand that there is a systematic relationship between sounds and the letters that represent those sounds in written language. Learning how to read involves using these relationships to recognize familiar words and to decode unfamiliar ones. However, adults who are not literate in their native language may not understand these concepts and need to learn the functions of print (Peregoy & Boyle, 2005). They also need to acquire vocabulary and develop oral proficiency in English in order to comprehend what they are reading. For Diane, helping non-literate students to read was enormously gratifying, because she could give them 'a little handle on things that they were struggling with'.

One important difference between K-12 and adult ESL teaching is the lack of formal credentialing in adult ESL. Unlike K-12 educators who have to be certified to teach in public schools, many adult educators begin teaching without the necessary training or credentials for teaching adult learners (Schaetzel et al., 2007). Only a small number of states require adult educators to have pre-service training in teaching adults, and other states are just beginning to examine the credentialing of adult educators (Crandall et al., 2008). Most of the adult ESL teachers in this study started as volunteer teachers before they enrolled in the TESOL teacher training program. In a field where credentialing is not a formal requirement, having TESOL training gave the study participants an advantage when they applied for teaching positions. For instance, Ginny remarked that once she had her TESOL degree in hand, she found it easier to get the teaching assignments she wanted at the community college.

The difference after I got my TESOL degree was that I had more choice of when and what to teach. It's not that it made a big difference, but now [name of community college] gives me the same course over and over again, even though they didn't at one time. (Ginny)

The study participants worked in a variety of instructional contexts with content focuses in different areas including workplace ESL, ABE, English for academic purposes and family literacy. There were large differences in the perceived quality of the programs. Marianne, for example, was very happy with her adult ESL program, which was offered through a partnership among the local county government, the public school system and non-profit community-based service providers. The program provides comprehensive educational and social services to at-risk children and their families (e.g. academic tutoring and mentoring, adult education classes and mental health services) and holds classes in local public schools, which are easily accessible to members of the community. Marianne expressed her admiration for the program:

> What I love about [name of program] is, number one, the people there are really knowledgeable about immigrants, and number two, they pay very well. I have a site coordinator who is bilingual in Spanish and English, and she's wonderful. The program has free on-site childcare and the students pay for their books, but the classes are free. It's conveniently located in the schools in the neighborhoods where people live. It services the parents of kids in the schools. (Marianne)

Marianne believes that this program does a better job of addressing adult students' needs than any other program she has been involved with. By offering free English classes and on-site childcare in local public schools, this program tries to meet the needs of low-income adult immigrants. Moreover, having a bilingual site coordinator who is familiar with the cultural backgrounds of the families makes students feel at ease and encourages participation. Marianne believes that the program offers valuable assistance to the whole family by addressing the academic, social and economic issues that children and parents face.

In contrast to Marianne's eager endorsement of her program, Margie was not at all satisfied with the literacy council where she worked as a volunteer teacher. She shared that the program had little structure and curriculum and failed to meet the needs of the students. It used outdated materials and provided few professional development opportunities for volunteer teachers, many of whom had no formal training in teaching English to adults.

> There really was no curriculum at the [name of literacy council]. The people that had taught the class before us had developed what they thought was a great program. Well, they didn't have any money, so they were using a combination of a picture dictionary and a home-school grammar book, which they could make legal copies of and distribute to students. It didn't matter whether the two made any sense. It didn't matter that they were teaching past perfect to people that couldn't even conjugate the verb 'to be' in the present tense. But they were following this program and were convinced that it was the best thing that they

could have done…. The other thing I saw was that some of the teachers who did volunteer work there had this view that since they spoke English, they could teach English. But that's unfortunately not enough. (Margie)

Many of the problems that Margie saw at the literacy council (lack of textbooks and instructional materials, insufficient professional development for teachers) were due to limited funding for the program. Because there was no curriculum, volunteer teachers with little knowledge of adult learning principles and second language acquisition processes pieced together lessons that were often inappropriate for the learners. Furthermore, because people did not have to be certified to teach in these programs, many operated on the assumption that they could teach English simply because they spoke English. For these reasons, Crandall *et al.* (2008) argue that professionalizing the adult ESL teaching force, in particular, preparing and certifying teachers to work with adult learners, should be an important priority.

Waiting for an Opportunity at the Right Time

Finally, the remaining 5 of the 30 participants in the study were not teaching at the time of the interview for a variety of personal reasons. For Elaine, it was mostly financial.

My biggest roadblock to fully changing to ESL right now is that I have two kids in college and a senior in high school. So I can't trade a profession where I actually make some money to a couple of night classes at the community college. I can't replace that income, so it makes it impossible. The other roadblock for me is that, even if I did consider going into the public school system, I would have to sacrifice a year of work to do student teaching. That's also impossible. (Elaine)

Although Elaine would very much like to stop working as a chiropractor and switch to teaching ESL, putting her children through college took precedence over her desire to launch a teaching career. While she considered teaching in community colleges as well as in public schools, neither option seemed viable, as each would require a significant financial sacrifice.

For Anna, taking care of her sick mother who lives in another state consumed a lot of her energy and prevented her from taking on a teaching position. She had also recently gotten married and moved into a new house.

I was so concerned that after I retired, my life would be empty and I wouldn't be able to find anything useful to do. And here I am, I got married 8 months ago, we moved to a new house, and now we're trying to sell the old house. And I'm taking care of my sick mother. It's like, how am I going to find the time to teach? (Anna)

While the men and women in this study endeavored to make the most of their teacher training, teaching was but a piece in a larger picture of their lives. Life with all its complexities continued, and when there were more pressing issues that required people's attention, teaching often took a back seat. Nonetheless, the participants' experience with TESOL seems to have fundamentally altered the way they see the world, including how they view the work they did prior to coming to TESOL. For example, Joan, a retired community organizer, took on a community organizing consulting job in which she was able to integrate insights from her TESOL training.

My transition to actually being in a classroom is kind of on hold, because all of a sudden I've got work. Everybody's really interested in community organizing, and there are all these jobs popping up, and people are calling me: Will I do this training, will I go here, will I help with this? One of the things I'm doing is coaching these teams of people who are given a grant of $4,000 to do a project that they think will change the dynamics in their community. And one of them is in [name of an urban community]. They're working with elementary school kids in reading, because the kids there do not read at grade level. So I've been able to give them some support around reading issues. Another one of my teams is an ESL team at [name of school]. They've organized a group about Latino cultural issues and how they can integrate their kids into the school. (Joan)

In Chapter 6, we saw how previously developed competencies and skills are reflected in the participants' new careers as teachers of English learners. Here, we see ESL training benefiting Joan's former, more main line of work. Thus, learning a new career later in life affects not only what one decides to do from that point forward but also helps one examine previously held beliefs and practices.

An important point about the individuals in this study who have not immediately launched a teaching career is that, as they wait for an opportune time, they are staying connected to the world of TESOL. They are attending professional conferences, staying in touch with faculty and fellow students in the TESOL program through newsletters and email LISTSERVs and keeping abreast of new developments in the field. They also keep their eyes open for new job openings and maintain their professional networks, so that they can seize the opportunity when it presents itself.

Conclusion

In this chapter, I described the post-program activities of the study participants and how they are launching their careers in TESOL. I discussed how they are faring as teachers in various educational settings including K-12 schools, community colleges and literacy organizations, and examined the degree of job satisfaction in each setting. I showed how the individuals in the study took different paths to achieving their professional goals and how the process of starting a new career was often fluid and dynamic. We saw that not everyone made an immediate and complete shift to teaching. Some of this was a function of the part-time nature of teaching adult ESL; people who needed full-time income often kept other jobs while teaching part-time. For others, family responsibilities or unexpected changes in personal circumstances kept them from launching their teaching careers right away.

In making their decisions, the individuals in the study carefully weighed the pluses and minuses of each option and made what they deemed was the best choice given the situation. Often, one type of work overlapped with another type of work, and the TESOL training that they received had a spillover effect on their previous careers, enabling them to see their former jobs in different ways. New insights were infused into the work that people used to do as a result of the training they received in the field of TESOL. Those who did not immediately embark on a teaching career kept their degree as a form of insurance for a time when they could in fact teach, and people generally tried to balance their personal desires with other constraints and responsibilities.

On the job, the study participants experienced varying degrees of difficulty as they related to general education colleagues, tried to comply with educational laws and policies and tried to provide students with meaningful learning opportunities when there was little structure and support. Despite the challenges, however, they considered teaching ESL a worthwhile effort that led to a high degree of personal fulfillment and satisfaction. For most participants in the study, teaching ESL was more than a job; it was a means to make an impact in the world. Even those who continuously struggled to secure full-time teaching positions in adult ESL agreed that selecting TESOL as a profession was one of the best things they have done in their lives. In sum, there was no denying that the sense of personal gratification and enjoyment they drew from their work as teachers was real.

As adults with life experience and accumulated wisdom, the individuals in the study perhaps have a more pragmatic view of what they can reasonably accomplish in their roles as teachers. As they know that no job is perfect, they do not expect teaching to be completely smooth sailing either. They have more realistic expectations of what it can and cannot do for them. Likewise, while they have high hopes and expectations for their students, they know that progress in language learning, as many other things in life, can be painfully slow. Thus, even as they try to continuously improve their teaching and help every student succeed, they are able to maintain a balanced and sensible assessment of what they and their students can reasonably accomplish. They choose their battles without losing sight of the most important reason for their entering the profession in the first place – the students.

The interviews revealed that the negatives in each situation did not nullify the overwhelmingly positive aspects of working with the students. The individuals in the study have the maturity and wisdom to know that things often change over time and that what they find difficult and frustrating now may not always stay that way. As a result, they are more likely to persevere through the challenges, gain valuable experience and skills, and in doing so, fill the critical need for well-qualified ESL teachers in a nation undergoing rapid diversification of its population. After all is said and done, pursuing ESL still comes out on top, as a good choice and a real avenue to making a lasting contribution to the world. As Diane enthused, 'You sort of have the idea that you want to leave the world a little bit better off, at least some little part of it. And TESOL does that. It's fun to think that I actually get a chance to go out and do something that's both entertaining to me and useful to other people'.

Note

(1)   While the K-12 teachers I interviewed for this study worked with all of the challenges of NCLB, teachers now working in schools have the additional challenges of the Common Core State Standards, which are also tied to assessments.

8   A Vision for Lifelong Learning

The pattern that we see today of adults returning to school to be trained for different careers will only intensify in the coming years. People are living longer and staying healthier, and more and more adults – by choice, necessity or some combination of the two – are working well into what used to be known as the retirement years (Freedman, 2007). In this final chapter, I discuss lessons that I learned from working with increasingly age-diverse groups of teacher candidates and what teacher training programs and institutions of higher education can do to better meet their needs. I describe the need for careful mentoring of new teachers and for rethinking teacher staffing models to allow expert and novice teachers across the age spectrum to work in teams. I make a case for creating a shared vision for lifelong learning that encourages individuals to experiment with new ideas and different types of work, regardless of where they are in the life cycle. We will see what our society stands to gain from recognizing the creative potential of older adults and from adopting policies aimed at helping people to prepare for a variety of careers at different points in their lives.

Needed: A Compelling Vision for Later Life

In his book, *Prime Time: How Baby Boomers Will Revolutionize Retirement and Transform America*, Marc Freedman (1999: 231) contends that we lack 'a compelling vision for later life in this country, a vision both that reflects the new hopes and dreams of third agers and that is capable of inspiring this group to assume new roles in society'. Our society celebrates youth and considers growing older a bad thing. Aging is often associated with decline and decrepitude, and we spend a lot of mental and physical energy seeking to look young. Consider the flourishing 'anti-aging' industry, which 'made a disease out of getting old—and made billions' (Weintraub, 2010). Marketers eager to cash in on the insecurities of aging adults sell everything from anti-wrinkle creams, to pills that claim to regrow hair, to hormone replacement therapies. Despite all the hype and promise of the fountain of youth, however, it is not clear how well these products actually work.

Besides the idea that aging is a disease that needs to be cured, another widely accepted and well-marketed concept is that of a leisured retirement. Freedman (1999: 21) points out that a common view about aging promotes the ideal of a second childhood, 'glorifying leisure and offering up the chance for endless play – often at age-segregated playgrounds with names like "Sun City" and "Leisure World"'. For several decades, housing developers and financial services firms have successfully portrayed retirement as a long-anticipated liberation from responsibility and work and a chance for continuous vacation. Retirement has become a prized destination and a centerpiece of the American dream. Everyone runs toward it, and those who get to it earlier are considered more successful. Freedom from work is seen as the ultimate reward for those who endure many years of hard toil.

But as Freedman (2007) argues in his later book, *Encore: Finding Work That Matters in the Second Half of Life*, what a growing number of older Americans want is not freedom *from* work, but rather freedom *to* work. Four out of five baby boomers say that they expect to continue working past the traditional retirement age, and many of them want to engage in meaningful work that gives back to the community (MetLife Foundation/ Civic Ventures, 2005). The fact that more and more adults are interested in work that contributes to the greater good should be a welcome message in a society where 'children are all too often growing up alone, where we don't have nearly enough people to care for the frail elderly, where we face a teacher shortage of nearly 200,000 over the coming decade' (Freedman, 1999: 17). Older Americans are a vastly untapped resource with potential to address some of our society's most pressing needs, many of which are in the highly people-intensive fields of education, social services and health care. These are precisely the areas in which mature adults with their skills, experience and passion for civic engagement excel and are likely to have the greatest impact. Just as it would be injurious to waste our natural resources (i.e. water, oil, minerals), it is a terrible thing to squander our human resources.

Some government and non-profit organizations are catching on to the potential of older adults in making a social impact. For some years, the US Peace Corps has been ramping up efforts to recruit adults aged 50+. Although the average age of a Peace Corps volunteer has remained relatively young (27 years), 7% of the volunteers are over the age of 50 (Peace Corps, 2010). Big Brothers Big Sisters of America, which helps children from low-income families to benefit from one-on-one relationships with volunteer mentors, has been actively recruiting older mentors as well (Freedman, 2011). Similarly, Experience Corps engages older adults as literacy tutors for struggling students in public schools in many cities across the United States, and the EnCorps STEM Teaching Program in California helps skilled engineering and technology workers to teach science and math to children in disadvantaged communities. These are just some of the organizations that produce what is known as the 'experience dividend', the payoff from tapping into the human capital in people in their fifties, sixties, seventies and beyond (Freedman, 2011).

We need to think of ideas, programs and institutions that can improve communities and offer new possibilities for how millions of adults live the second half of their lives. A big part of that thinking should be focused on providing individuals with opportunities for continuous learning. Many older adults are eager to gain new skills and credentials that will help them move into a new chapter of work. We have an obligation to help them. In the following, I discuss some of the major barriers to integrating learning with life and work and ways to reduce those barriers.

Helping People Return to School

Adults who are interested in preparing for a new career are often deterred from pursuing education and training because they lack time. With family and job responsibilities, most adults can go to school only on a part-time basis, typically during evenings or weekends. Yet, most colleges and universities focus more on educating full-time 18- to 22-year-old students and schedule few classes in the evenings (Eisenberg, 2015). *The College of 2020: Students,* a report from Chronicle Research Services, predicts that given the rapidly aging population, adult education will be the fastest-growing market in higher education for the foreseeable future (Van Der Werf & Sabatier, 2009). Yet, higher education institutions have been remarkably slow in embracing this demographic shift (Vacarr, 2014). Although the number of affluent, white, high school students has been falling steadily, many four-year private colleges, whose tuition revenue depends on these students, have concentrated mainly on educating this shrinking population. Unless they can shift their focus to meet the needs of the changing demographic, many of these institutions are in danger of closing in the coming decades (McDonald, 2014).

Even community colleges, whose main clientele is part-time, non-traditional students, have been slow in meeting the needs of 50 plus learners. Community colleges have traditionally emphasized enrichment courses over workforce training, and schools tend not to tailor their courses for the plus 50 group (American Association of Community Colleges, 2015). Most colleges simply market existing courses to plus 50 students rather than designing new courses or redesigning them with the interests of older students in mind. However, the Plus 50 Initiative, organized by the American Association of Community Colleges, helps community colleges to deliver programs that engage the plus 50 student population with a focus on workforce training. The participating colleges in the Plus 50 Encore Completion Program offer courses that prepare older adults for careers in high-demand fields, such as early childhood education, nursing, counseling, adult basic education and human resources. More programs like this are clearly needed to serve the growing population of adults interested in pursuing public service work.

Adults at various stages of life face different challenges to completing degree and certificate programs. Increasing program completion rates among non-traditional students will require changes in the structure and delivery of higher education (American Association of Community Colleges, 2015). Flexible scheduling is very important to this group of learners, and colleges should look for ways to offer classes in the evenings or at weekends to accommodate students with various work and family obligations. In addition, schools may consider offering online and hybrid courses and extend the business hours of certain administrative offices. Student support services need to be tailored to the unique needs of older adults, and faculty and staff should be provided with professional development on how to create a learning environment that working students feel drawn to. Because human relationships are key to experiencing a great college education, schools should encourage a partnership between the advisor and student that goes beyond basic course scheduling to a plan that fosters personal growth and development (Bland, 2003).

Help provided to older adults returning to school should include financial assistance. What made it possible for some of the participants in the current study to pursue their TESOL training was having access to a sudden influx of cash through a severance package or inheritance money. Clara was able to use her workers' compensation to return to school and get her bachelor's degree in engineering at age 38.

> When I hurt my back, I couldn't do the job and ended up getting fired from [name of employer]. I got two years of workers' compensation and went to [name of a city college] for a year. Then I applied to [name of a private 4-year university] as a transfer student. Workers' comp doesn't count as income, so my scholarship covered 100% of the tuition. (Clara)

For people without such funds or savings, it is usually more difficult to go back to school. A major deterrent to pursuing K-12 public school teaching certification for several of the study participants was foregoing income during their student teaching internship. Sonia financed most of her study through income from her full-time administrative assistant job but had to stop working during the final semester when she did her internship.

> I've been doing administrative assistant work, which has not been my favorite. But it has paid the mortgage and given me benefits. I'll be leaving that job at the end of December to start my full-time student teaching internship in the spring. I won't have income then, so I'm going to have to take out loans. (Sonia)

Some of the participants in this study took advantage of the Golden ID Program, which allows Maryland residents aged 60 and over to take undergraduate and graduate courses at little cost. While Golden ID students pay some fees, tuition is waived at state institutions of higher education.

Nationally, about 60% of accredited degree-granting educational institutions offer tuition waivers for older adults (Brandon, 2009). States that offer tuition waivers for at least some of their public colleges include Alaska, Arkansas, Connecticut, Florida, Georgia, Illinois, Kentucky, Maine, Maryland, Massachusetts, Michigan, Minnesota, New Hampshire, New Jersey, North Carolina, Ohio, Rhode Island, South Dakota, Texas, Vermont, and Virginia, as well as Washington, DC (FinAid.org, 2015). While tuition waivers for the over-sixty population are a welcome assistance to individuals in that age category, they are not offered to working adults in their forties and fifties, who are in the throes of raising children and paying the mortgage. Some of these people may require assistance as well.

Freedman (2011) makes a case for a 'gap year for grown-ups' for midlife and post-midlife adults. He states that the gap year has become an important rite of passage for youth on their journey to adulthood and an opportunity to gain the new perspective necessary for making the most of the next stage in life. A gap year is a time for renewal, an opportunity for young people to stop to rest and think before starting college or entering the workforce. He argues that a gap year for grown-ups would offer the chance for reflection, renewal and redirection. It would provide an opportunity for mature adults to be exposed to new experiences and test potential future roles.

We need to rethink the financial mechanisms that help individuals to prepare for a new career. Federal and state governments can provide leadership in this area by reassessing the structure of financial aid programs, which currently favor full-time degree students (Selim, 2014). Federal Pell Grants, which provide need-based grants to low-income students, are typically awarded to undergraduate students and cover only a small portion of the total cost of tuition at most schools. Undergraduates from the lowest-income families tend to receive most of their financial assistance directly from universities, but the aid is typically available to full-time students only. The working adult learner attending a degree or certificate program part-time is not eligible. While financial aid should continue to serve needy students, a new grant program for middle-income working students could ease the burden of debt for many non-traditional students who are debating whether to enroll and complete their degree (Advisory Committee on Student Financial Assistance, 2012). States could also supplement Pell Grants to help low-income students with tuition costs and provide needs-based financial aid to part-time working students.

Aside from federal and state financial aid programs, individuals should be encouraged to put aside money to fund their education in later life. Freedman (2011) recommends helping people to set up special savings accounts to manage their post-midlife career transitions. Specifically, he proposes creating an Individual Purpose Account (IPA), similar to an Individual Retirement Account (IRA), aimed at facilitating career transitions in one's fifties and sixties. With tax credits and other incentives, Congress could support IPAs as distinct packages designed to make switching to different careers easier, just as IRAs make saving for retirement easier.

Another idea, the Lifelong Learning Accounts Act, would help individuals to save for future education that would facilitate career transitions in later life (Council for Adult & Experiential Learning, 2011). Lifelong Learning Accounts (LiLAs) provide a way for employers and employees to co-finance education and training. Under this program, participating employers match employee contributions into a LiLA, up to US$2500 per year, and third parties such as governments or foundations are encouraged to match contributions. LiLA funds can be used to cover educational expenses including tuition, fees, books and other supplies, and employees and employers that participate in LiLAs will be eligible for a tax credit for a portion of their contributions.

Finally, there are proposals to allow individuals to use Social Security as seed capital to invest in the next stage of their lives. For example, Freedman (2011) suggests enabling individuals to stop and start their Social Security payments, as circumstances change. Individuals could begin taking social security at age 62 or older, use it to subsidize a career transition and then stop taking payments as they return to the workforce. These individuals' later payments would be adjusted actuarially to be revenue neutral so that they are not penalized for returning to work. A more radical approach, Freedman suggests, would enable individuals to take a year or two of Social Security before age 62, say in their fifties, to underwrite a transition year and begin getting full benefits years later in an actuarially adjusted way.

Given the politically charged debate over Social Security reform, proposals like this are not likely to promptly gain broad support. However, the fact remains that many mid-career adults require financial assistance to reach their full potential. We need to continue to think creatively about how to help these individuals.

Supporting New Teachers through Professional Learning Communities

So far, we have considered some of the strategies for making it easier for people to return to school to prepare for a new career. In this section, I examine what can be done to assist those who have finished their degrees and certificates. Specifically, I discuss supporting new teachers through professional mentoring. As career-change teachers begin working in schools, they need as much help as any new teacher. The fact that they are older and have more experience does not mean that they know how to teach. Successfully completing teacher training programs does not make these individuals finished products. Educational researchers and practitioners alike agree that teaching is complex work that cannot be mastered in the short period of pre-service teacher education (Grossman & Davis, 2012). What teachers need is continuous support to grow on the job.

It is widely agreed that a teacher's first year is often the most demanding. While a learning curve is expected in any new field, individuals entering the teaching profession for the first time face a unique set of challenges. Below, Patricia talks about her experiences as a middle school ESL teacher. While she believes that she was generally well-prepared in the TESOL program, no amount of pre-service training could have fully equipped her for the difficulties she faced as a new teacher.

> The first year, I have to tell you, I was absolutely lost with nothing to grab onto. There were just things I didn't know how to do. There was so much paperwork and some things I didn't even know existed. It's not that the school didn't tell me. It's just that you can only suck up so much in the beginning. I went to the orientation and received these huge binders—one for my school, one for teaching in general, and one for ESL. And I'm like, this is too much. (Patricia)

The challenges of beginning teaching are well-documented in the literature on teacher development (Johnson, 2004). A common concern among new teachers is lack of guidance and resources for lesson and unit planning (Goodwin, 2012). Producing a curriculum and gathering instructional materials require massive amounts of mental energy and are highly labor intensive. Studies have observed novice teachers spending 10–12 hours a day juggling lesson planning, grading and the myriad demands of paperwork, committees and non-instructional duties outside of the classroom (Fry, 2007). It is difficult to maintain this kind of grueling schedule for an extended period of time, and 15% of new teachers leave the profession and another 14% change schools after their first year, often as the result of feeling overwhelmed and ineffective (Ingersoll & Smith, 2003; Smith & Ingersoll, 2004).

Another significant challenge is lack of support from colleagues. The early years of teaching are unquestionably a period of steep learning, and they are often a time of intense loneliness (Feiman-Nemser, 2012). Many new teachers feel lonely, because schools are not organized to support teachers learning from other teachers. Even though a teacher's first year is the most demanding, beginning teachers are rarely given a break – for example, reduced workloads for new teachers are virtually non-existent (Shields et al., 2003). Instead, novice teachers are more likely to get larger classes, more students with special needs or behavioral problems, more extracurricular duties and classrooms with fewer textbooks and equipment (Feiman-Nemser, 2012). New teachers often report difficult interactions with colleagues, ranging from neglect of administrators to lack of cooperation or even hostility from veteran teachers (Fry, 2007). One's success as an educator is often perceived to be dependent entirely on one's own efforts, and many new teachers feel that they are left to 'sink or swim' (Goodwin, 2012).

It is commonly assumed that as teachers gain classroom experience, they can function on their own. However, research shows that experience alone – especially private, unreflective experience – does not automatically produce growth (Feiman-Nemser, 2012). What teachers need are structured opportunities to learn from other teachers, especially those who are more experienced and doing a good job. Research shows that beginning teachers who receive some type of induction and mentoring have higher levels of job satisfaction and commitment as well as larger student achievement gains (Fletcher & Strong, 2009; Grossman & Davis, 2012).

Teacher induction and mentoring programs have multiplied in recent years in response to concerns about new teachers' struggles and high turnover rates (Strong, 2009). While the terms 'induction' and 'mentoring' are often used interchangeably, induction programs tend to include one-to-one mentoring of new teachers alongside other supports, such as classroom management seminars and peer observation sessions (Johnson *et al.*, 2005). While mentoring and induction have been shown to contribute considerably to teacher retention (Ingersoll & Kralik, 2004), the mere presence of mentors does not automatically ensure that beginning teachers will get the help they need. When mentoring consists of little more than occasional check-ins or informal chats without clear goals and expectations, it is not likely to be effective. Poorly designed mentoring has actually been shown to exacerbate new teachers' feelings of discouragement and isolation (Johnson, 2004). Moreover, while teacher retention is a high priority for many school districts, students are not served well when a district retains teachers without regard to quality. Instead, schools should seek to retain teachers who demonstrate effectiveness in the classroom and are committed to student learning.

What does an effective mentoring program look like? According to Grossman and Davis (2012), effective mentoring consists of three elements: (1) highly trained mentors, (2) a focus on content and (3) allocated time for mentoring. First, mentors need training and ongoing support to develop specific skills in assisting new teachers. It is not enough for mentors to simply be good teachers of students. Rather, mentors should be trained specifically to assess the strengths and needs of new teachers, help them set meaningful goals and provide constructive feedback on instruction. Second, mentoring should be focused on content. Grossman and Davis point out that while mentors tend to concentrate on providing emotional support to beginning teachers, they should also focus on helping novice teachers improve their pedagogical skills. It is recommended that, whenever possible, new teachers are matched with trained mentors who are knowledgeable about their subject matter so that content-specific guidance can be provided. Finally, quality time spent with a mentor is crucial, and frequent meetings between mentors and new teachers should be built into the teaching schedule.

Aside from providing beginning teachers with mentoring, a growing number of educators advocate creating collaborative professional learning communities in schools (Bieler, 2012). Professional learning communities promote partnerships among teachers that benefit novice and veteran teachers alike. They involve a fundamental shift in how teaching is viewed – not as an independent activity done behind closed doors but rather as a collaborative enterprise whose success rests on everyone working and learning together (Feiman-Nemser, 2012). Professional learning communities provide opportunities for teachers to exchange ideas and instructional resources, evaluate student work together and reflect jointly on how to improve teaching and learning. Teachers are encouraged to informally observe other teachers' teaching and share classroom strategies that work well. Incorporating new teachers into professional learning communities not only reduces teacher isolation, but it also promotes teacher effectiveness and a sense of collective responsibility for all students in the school (Bieler, 2012).

Professional learning communities are in fact what many beginning teachers want in a new job. Martha, one of the participants in this study, recently received two job offers as an elementary ESL teacher. When I asked her how she went about deciding which offer to accept, she explained that even though she was presented with numerous incentives at one of the schools, that school did not provide opportunities for teachers to work in teams. Teachers worked mostly alone in their own classrooms and rarely consulted one another. In contrast, the position she accepted was in a school that had co-planning and co-teaching built right into the teachers' schedules. Martha explains:

> Both schools invited me for a second interview to meet with the school staff and take a tour of the school. That really helped me to see that they were different. [School A] had a strong principal who had a lot of hopes for her ESL program. But all of her ESL teachers worked independently and did not really collaborate. They taught different grades and did their thing. So I realized immediately that it might be a little bit hard for me to work in that environment. The teachers at [School B], on the other hand, collaborated a lot. When the school designed their new building four years ago, they created an ESL wing. All four ESL classrooms are in that wing, facing each other, two on one side of the hall and two on the other. They have windows, so at a moment's notice, the teachers can wave at each other, talk to each other, and give materials to each other. The teachers meet on a regular basis to talk and share. And they do all

their testing and planning together. So that seemed like a good place for me. If I need help, they're just one door away. I feel like I'll be able to learn a lot from the other teachers. (Martha)

Professional learning communities are relevant in schools, because today's new faculty recruits come with more varied levels of preparation and career aspirations than those in the past (Johnson *et al.*, 2005). In her study of 50 new teachers in Massachusetts, Johnson (2004) found that almost none of the teachers expected to remain only in the classroom for their entire career. Indeed, nearly all of the teachers who considered a long-term career in education expressed a desire to assume new responsibilities after a few years in the classroom. As one respondent stated, 'I think after four or five years of it, I'd be bored. I wouldn't be challenged.... You need variety or a new challenge' (Johnson, 2004: 233). The work of teachers can be repetitive and exhausting, and as teachers gain experience, they will need fresh opportunities to maintain their engagement with students.

While turnover levels are highest in the early and late years of a teaching career, there is a growing interest in the turnover of mid-career educators (Johnson *et al.*, 2005). In a study of 160 secondary school teachers, Huberman (1993) outlined phases in the professional life cycle of educators and identified several potentially difficult periods. He found that some teachers with 5–10 years of experience struggled with 'a sense of routine, [and] the lowering of energy and interest' (Huberman, 1993: 38). Some of the teachers with 7–15 years of experience were in a 'danger zone' in which they were most likely to consider leaving teaching (Huberman, 1993: 138). 'Fatigue, routine, frustration, [and] nervous tension' were cited by 43% as reasons they might quit teaching (Huberman, 1993: 145). These results point to the need for schools to provide experienced teachers with opportunities for renewal and continuous development.

Research suggests that differentiated roles may satisfy experienced teachers' needs for new challenges and variety. Differentiated roles may include positions such as department head, grade-level team leader, mentor teacher or instructional coach. According to Johnson *et al.* (2005), these roles may encourage teacher retention in at least two ways. First, those who are less experienced may perceive the roles as a promising future opportunity and thus decide to remain in schools and the profession. Second, teachers who perform the roles may experience greater job satisfaction and renewal. Differentiated roles within healthy professional learning communities can provide teachers across all levels of experience with opportunities to learn from one another and improve their practice. Community is central to novice and veteran teachers alike, and schools that promote a culture of collaboration among teachers can reap much benefit.

Focusing on Progress and Not on Perfection

In my work as a teacher educator, I sometimes hear teachers tell me how frustrated they get when their ESL students keep making the same language mistakes in speech and writing. They wonder why their students are not internalizing the concepts they have reviewed multiple times in class and question whether their instruction is making any difference. I remind them as a matter of course that learning a second language is a developmental process and that students' language will sometimes seem to regress before showing signs of improvement. Yet, I know how easy it is for teachers to be discouraged with apparent lack of progress, especially when there is a lot of pressure to help students perform well on high-stakes tests.

High-stakes testing has taken a toll on classrooms and eroded job satisfaction among teachers. According to a recent National Education Association (NEA) survey, a majority of teachers (72%) reported feeling considerable pressure from both school and district administrators to improve test scores (Walker, 2014). Of the surveyed teachers, 42% reported that the emphasis on improving standardized test scores had a negative impact on their classes, while only 15% said the impact was positive. For ESL teachers, the pressure to improve test scores typically translates to teaching students as much English as possible, as rapidly as possible.

When educators are expected to deliver quick results or face negative consequences, they are less likely to allow students the opportunity to explore the concepts and engage in critical thinking – classroom instruction naturally becomes more teacher-driven and less student-oriented (Amrein & Berliner, 2003). As Sacks (1999: 256–257) writes, 'Test-driven classrooms exacerbate boredom, fear, and lethargy, promoting all manner of mechanical behaviors on the part of teachers, students, and schools, and bleed schoolchildren of their natural love of learning'. Because test preparation and administration typically take up large portions of instructional time, the needs of individual learners are less likely to be addressed adequately.

In an educational environment that is increasingly driven by accountability and pressure to perform, career-change teachers with life and work experiences have the potential to infuse a broader perspective into the learning and teaching process. In particular, they can cultivate relationships that motivate students to focus on the real purpose of learning. Below, Tom recounts his experience of teaching ESL in community colleges and how he wishes that the courses lasted longer so he could get to know his students better.

> I loved teaching in community colleges. If I had to say anything negative about it, it would be that the courses were too short. I mean the time you got to interact with the students was too short. I never wanted the courses to end, because I always felt like I was really just getting to

know the students not just academically but personally. You begin to get a good feel for what you can do better to help each person. To me, that was fun. (Tom)

Freedman (1999) points out that a defining capacity of older adults exists in the realm of time – not only in having time to do important work but to do that work in a particular way that can be characterized as patient and slow. 'These individuals have an understanding that some things in life—ranging from mentoring to medicine—are best done slowly, and that efficiency, expediency, and productivity have a way of undermining these endeavors', Freedman explains. 'There is an appreciation, particularly, of how slowness can nurture and deepen relationships' (Freedman, 1999: 233).

The desire to have more time to work with individual students was echoed in Elizabeth's experience with teaching adults in an intensive English program. She believes that the curriculum packs in too much material and does not allocate adequate time for students to learn the content.

In my current program, there is never enough time to work with individuals as much as I would like. I know I could do so much more if the program was not so intensive. Right now, the program is nine weeks, and I get my ESL course participants for six days before everyone else arrives. After that, I see them only a few times each week, just to help them keep up with the lectures. So I can't really help them too much. Nevertheless, the feedback I get from my students and from the other faculty who work with them gives me the energy to keep on, and I remind my students that they just need progress, not perfection. (Elizabeth)

What is noteworthy about Elizabeth's comment is that even though she is working in a less than ideal setting with little control over the curriculum, she is able to focus on the positive feedback from her students to maintain her enthusiasm about teaching. She celebrates improvements, no matter how small, and uses them to motivate students. Rather than expect her students to produce error-free English in a short period of time, she helps them set more realistic goals. What inspires her students to keep learning when the lessons become difficult is her emphasis on progress, not perfection.

Similarly, Martha demonstrates a great deal of patience in working with young children. In one of her kindergarten ESL classes, she had a student with attention deficit hyperactivity disorder (ADHD), who was particularly challenging to teach. Below, Martha explains how she helped him to pay attention in class.

Jonny just couldn't sit still. He would stand up, run around, and sometimes scream. I tried a lot of different things to calm him down but nothing worked. So out of desperation, I said to him, 'Listen, Jonny,

I got this new timer. I'm going to push this button for one minute, and I'm going to give my instruction in that one minute so you don't have to listen to me for any more than that. Do you think you can do it?' And he said, 'Yes'. So I said, 'I want your bottom on your seat, I want you facing me, and I want your attention for that one minute. Let's see if you can do it'. And he did it. I said, 'I'm going to give you a sticker because that was amazing'. So every day that was our goal. Can you pay attention for one minute? (Martha)

Martha explained that after Jonny paid attention for one minute, he was allowed to squirm, fidget and move around the room in his usual way until several minutes later, he would be asked to sit and pay attention for another minute. She knew it was not realistic for him to focus all the time. Instead, she helped him set small, attainable goals and celebrated his success each time. Because she realized that having frequent movement helped other children in the class to focus better on tasks, she modified her 30-minute lessons to allow everyone in class to do a variety of activities in different parts of the room.

Every time Jonny got a sticker, the other kids were like, 'Oh, we don't have a sticker'. So I said, 'You know what? This is a great celebration. We should all get a sticker'. They were all focusing, so they should all get a sticker. So every time he got a sticker, they all got a sticker. And the kids were just as happy as happy can be. Most kids in other classes get maybe one sticker the whole day. But my kids were getting like five stickers in one day. And Jonny said, 'I think I can do five minutes'. I said, 'Well, let's not jump to five. Let's try two'. So we went from one to two, two to three, and then we skipped to five. Then he wanted to do eight minutes. I can't remember if it took four or six weeks, but he was consistently paying attention for eleven minutes. Imagine all the celebration we had to have to go from zero to eleven. But he was so excited every time he reached a goal. (Martha)

Rather than try to fit Jonny into an instructional mold designed for other students, Martha tried to view her lessons from his perspective. She divided classroom tasks into manageable chunks, helped Jonny focus on mastering small portions of them and celebrated his successes in a visible and open way. What is marvelous about Martha's strategy is that her way of accommodating a special needs student helped her instruction of all the other students in her class. Every child in her class benefited from having more movement incorporated in each lesson, and their enthusiasm in turn encouraged Jonny to set higher goals. Learning became more fun and purposeful for everyone. But now, as the children were getting used to receiving so many stickers, Martha needed a different strategy to motivate them. She got the following idea from another kindergarten teacher.

> When they get three stickers in a thirty-minute lesson, I give them a 'smell'. I have ChapStick lip balm in different flavors—strawberry, green watermelon, and berries. I just rub it on the inside of the children's wrists, and they just smell it and love it. (Martha)

When I told Martha how impressed I was with the way she helped Jonny, she was quick to point out that her strategy was not successful all the time.

> I wish I can say my strategy was successful every day, but it wasn't. It was successful one day, not successful the next day, successful one day, not successful the next. Sometimes he just had bad days. But when he didn't get three stickers, I didn't make it personal. I just said, 'Today's not your best day. But it's okay. Tomorrow we're going to start again. But you know I can't give you a smell for that, right?' And he knew. So I didn't have to persuade him, and he didn't have to fuss. The beauty of it is, in thirty minutes, you can try five or six times. It's not all or nothing. In the beginning the successes were not very many, but they became more frequent as time went on. I think it's important to have patience and not expect success from students all the time. I try to find a way to make the goal attainable, so they can succeed multiple times. (Martha)

Martha believes that academic standards have risen significantly over the years, and today's students are expected to show mastery of more advanced material at an earlier age. With ever more rigorous grade-level standards and curricular benchmarks in place and teachers trying frantically to bring every student up to speed (or face sanctions), many children end up feeling dumb and incapable of achieving success. This is why Martha helps her students to focus on what they can do rather than what they can't do. She knows that demanding perfection from them will only turn them off to learning. Instead, she helps them to build confidence through well-placed activities that give them frequent opportunities for accomplishment.

Teachers' efforts to build students' confidence do not always materialize while classes are in session, however. Language learning is a long-term process, and teachers may not see the fruits of their labor within the time they get to interact with their students. While this slowness could be disheartening to some people, older teachers, many of whom appreciate the value of sustained conscious effort, seem to exhibit more immunity to potential disappointments. These individuals have come to realize that acquiring a language, like many things in life, takes time, and that demanding speed and expediency may actually undermine student learning. This understanding in turn enables them to press on with their work even when the challenges faced by their students seem insurmountable. Below, Marianne describes what it was like for her to witness one of her former adult basic ESL students transform into a proficient English speaker. Like almost everyone in the Basic II ESL class that she taught a few years ago, this student had struggled with English quite a bit.

> This year, we were testing for the new class, and one of my Basic II students came in. She had passed her test at [community college x] and was going to become a certified nursing assistant. And her English had improved! I call that the magic moment. It's when they decide that they're not afraid to talk anymore. When that happens, their English, their vocabulary, and their confidence just go through the roof. It's that moment when they become confident enough to start talking to Americans, practicing and using English, and not being afraid. It's just amazing. When you see them again and all these words just come out of their mouths, you know that that moment has happened. It's like, all of a sudden, they decide they know enough, that they're not going to make complete fools of themselves, and their spoken English explodes. (Marianne)

Described as 'the magic moment,' the sudden increase in these students' confidence to produce grammatical utterances in English is likened to a toddler's language development taking off like a rocket. Because she has seen some of her students go from being very hesitant speakers to 'not being afraid' and 'confident enough to start talking to Americans', Marianne can have faith that her work is making a difference in her students' lives even if she does not see its effects immediately. In the long run, this self-assurance contributes to her ability to remain and thrive in the education profession.

Conclusion

Thanks to the gift of longevity in the modern world, more and more people are staying healthy and active in later life than ever before. Adult lives now frequently last longer than their initial occupations, and switching to a different career in one's forties, fifties or sixties happens more commonly than in the past. What is especially significant about this development is that many men and women show an interest in entering careers of service that will help improve the quality of life in their communities. People are eager to gain new skills and credentials to transition into a new phase of work that will make a difference in the world around them, and they are looking for help. Given this reality, I discussed in this chapter some of the ways in which adults at various stages of life can be supported to return to school to be prepared for a new career. I considered a number of strategies for reducing barriers to integrating learning with life and work and the roles that governments, organizations and institutions of higher education can play in this process.

I made a case for creating a shared vision for lifelong learning that taps into the human potential in later life. Rethinking retirement and aging takes innovative ideas, and we need, as the title of Peter Laslett's (1991) book suggests, 'a fresh map of life', which can help us navigate the new terrains afforded by an increased life span in ways that are personally meaningful and useful to others. I argued that we need to think about aging not as a problem but as an opportunity for growth and social contribution. We also need to look for ways to combat age stereotypes and instill positive views about aging in young and older people alike. The truth is that everyone is aging. Today's young people will be tomorrow's senior citizens, and they need a framework to think about how they might want to develop across the life span. As Lawrence-Lightfoot (2009: 240) explains, 'Children preparing to live as citizens in an increasingly complex, diverse global reality need to be offered opportunities for apprenticeships and service... and people in their Third Chapters must be seen as valued mentors who bring with them not only the accumulated knowledge of their work and careers but also their wisdom, experience, and sense of perspective'. The result of this cross-generational interaction is 'a respectful reciprocity—a dynamic pedagogy in which the old and the young are both teachers and learners' (Lawrence-Lightfoot, 2009: 240).

It is important that lifelong learning be supported not just by our institutions, programs and financial assistance, but also with compassion and empathy. In her book, *Willing to Learn*, Bateson (2004) observes that new learning in later life requires a sense of adventure, risk-taking and courage and can be made possible if people are surrounded by a caring society.

> One of the things we know about the human capacity to keep on learning, to remain young at heart and willing to learn, is that it needs to be supported by cherishing. We needed to be cherished as infants, and as adults we need to cherish our children. But if we want a society of people willing and open and ready to learn, it has to be a kinder, gentler society, because we need a lot of mutual support to face change, to give up things we've always believed in. (Bateson, 2004: 87)

Bateson believes that without this culture of compassion and openness, people's capacity for new learning will diminish, and our society will be deprived of the creative contributions of older adults. For people to continue learning across the life span, they need to be provided with care and cherished.

As an ESL teacher educator, I have personally benefited from the collective wisdom of the participants in the study. My interviews have revealed things about the 30 individuals that I would have never known otherwise, and their stories have prompted me to imagine the kind of life I would like to live. Their ways of seeing and engaging with the world have inspired me to think with greater flexibility and compassion, and the differences they make in the lives of their students have renewed my resolve to serve others. I see tremendous potential in these individuals to address the need for well-trained ESL teachers in our country. Their enthusiasm for new learning and their desire to benefit others motivate me in my work as a teacher educator, and their experiences of crossing disciplinary boundaries have prompted me to rethink how I might present TESOL materials in class to engage people who are coming from different communities of practice. For one, I have resolved to value my students' skills and experiences much more explicitly than I have in the past and to help them build on that knowledge base.

I am deeply touched by the civic-mindedness of the study participants and their advocacy for immigrants. Their desire to make a positive difference in their communities and find purpose and fulfillment in improving other people's lives is deserving of praise, and I believe it is important to provide them with opportunities to express their passion for service and put their wisdom and training to good use. These individuals are at the leading edge of society, charting a productive path for our future. Through their work as ESL teachers, they help to bridge the cultural and generational gaps that exist between immigrants and US-born residents. By focusing their energies on one lesson at a time, one student at a time, they chip away at what appears to be an insuperable problem.

In the end, what impresses me most about these individuals is that they love what they do. All of them came to TESOL because, above all else, they find it fun. The following excerpt from my interview with Marianne captures her joy in teaching ESL.

One of the most interesting things that I ever saw.... I once drove through Iowa through the windmill farms, where there are like 20 or 30 windmills that generate electricity. I watched the birds playing, thousands of birds flying in and out of the blades of the windmill, going round and round. They were having a blast. They were just having so much fun. And they were choosing to do it. Well, here you have this little animal, right? Just playing around, doing something for no reason, with no care in the world. Who knew birds had fun? I feel that kind of joy. I feel like I'm able to do that, more or less. More money would be nice, but yeah, I'm pretty much living the life I want. (Marianne)

It's this kind of happiness and delight that encourages me to continue my work as a teacher educator. I am grateful for the privilege of being able to witness the growth of these extraordinary professionals.

References

AARP (2014) Staying ahead of the curve 2013: The AARP work and career study. Older workers in an uneasy job market. See http://www.aarp.org/content/dam/aarp/research/surveys_statistics/general/2014/Staying-Ahead-of-the-Curve-2013-The-Work-and-Career-Study-AARP-res-gen.pdf (accessed 3 March 2014).

Advisory Committee on Student Financial Assistance (2012) Pathways to Success: Integrating Learning with Life and Work to Increase National College Completion. Washington, DC: Author. See http://files.eric.ed.gov/fulltext/ED529485.pdf (accessed 25 April 2015).

Allen, M.B. (2005) Eight questions on teacher recruitment and retention: What does the research say? Denver, CO: Education Commission of the States. See http://files.eric.ed.gov/fulltext/ED489332.pdf (accessed 6 December 2014).

American Association of Community Colleges (2015) Plus 50 Programs in Practice: How AACC's Plus 50 Initiative is Helping Community Colleges Transform Programs and Services for Adults Age 50 and Over. Washington, DC: Author. See http://plus50.aacc.nche.edu/Documents/Plus50_Programs_in_Practice_2015.pdf (accessed 24 April 2015).

Amos, J. (2008) *Dropouts, Diplomas, and Dollars: U.S. High Schools and the Nation's Economy.* Washington, DC: Alliance for Excellent Education.

Amrein, A.L. and Berliner, D.C. (2003) The effects of high-stakes testing on student motivation and learning. *Educational Leadership* 60 (5), 32–38.

Antonek, J., McCormick, D. and Donato, R. (1997) The student teacher portfolio as autobiography: Developing a professional identity. *The Modern Language Journal* 81 (1), 15–27.

Arias, E. (2014) 'United States Life Tables, 2009'. *National Vital Statistics Reports* 62 (7). Hyattsville, MD: National Center for Health Statistics. See http://www.cdc.gov/nchs/data/nvsr/nvsr62/nvsr62_07.pdf (accessed 31 January 2014).

Ariza, E.N.W. (2006) *Not for ESOL Teachers: What Every Classroom Teacher Needs to Know About the Linguistically, Culturally, and Ethnically Diverse Student.* Boston, MA: Pearson.

Aud, S., Wilkinson-Flicker, S., Kristapovich, P., Rathbun, A., Wang, X. and Zhang, J. (2013) The Condition of Education 2013 (NCES 2013-037). US Department of Education, National Center for Education Statistics. Washington, DC. See http://nces.ed.gov/pubs2013/2013037.pdf (accessed 3 March 2014).

August, D. and Shanahan, T. (eds) (2006) *Developing Literacy in Second-language Learners: Report of the National Literacy Panel on Language-Minority Children and Youth.* Mahwah, NJ: Lawrence Erlbaum.

Austin, J.L. (1962) *How to Do Things with Words.* Oxford: Clarendon Press.

Barkley, E.F., Cross, K.P. and Major, C.H. (2005) *Collaborative Learning Techniques: A Handbook for College Faculty.* San Francisco, CA: Jossey-Bass.

Barnes, L.L., Mendes de Leon, C.F., Wilson, R.S., Bienias, J.L. and Evans, D.A. (2004) Social resources and cognitive decline in a population of older African Americans and whites. *Neurology* 63 (12), 2322–2326.

Barney, D. and Pilmer, D. (2012) What teachers can learn from actors. *Journal of Multidisciplinary Research* 4 (1), 79–89.

Bartlett, L. and García, O. (2011) *Additive Schooling in Subtractive Times: Bilingual Education and Dominican Immigrant Youth in the Heights*. Nashville, TN: Vanderbilt University Press.

Bateson, M.C. (2004) *Willing to Learn: Passages of Personal Discovery*. Hanover, NH: Steerforth Press.

Bateson, M.C. (2010) *Composing a Further Life: The Age of Active Wisdom*. New York: Knopf Doubleday Publishing Group.

Beaman, R. and Wheldall, K. (2000) Teachers' use of approval and disapproval in the classroom. *Educational Psychology: An International Journal of Experimental Educational Psychology* 20 (4), 431–446.

Berkman, L.F., Glass, T., Brissette, I. and Seeman, T.E. (2000) From social integration to health: Durkheim in the new millennium. *Social Science and Medicine* 51 (6), 843–857.

Bezzola, L., Mérillat, S., Gaser, C. and Jäncke, L. (2011) Training-induced neural plasticity in golf novices. *The Journal of Neuroscience* 31 (35), 12444–12448.

Bieler, D. (2012) What new teachers want from colleagues. *Educational Leadership* 69 (8), 46–49.

Bland, S.M. (2003) Advising adults: Telling or coaching? *Adult Learning* 14 (2), 6–9.

Blascovich, J., Spencer, S.J., Quinn, D. and Steele, C. (2001) African Americans and high blood pressure: The role of stereotype threat. *Psychological Science* 12 (3), 225–229.

Blazer, D.G. (2003) Depression in late life: Review and commentary. *Journal of Gerontology: Medical Sciences* 58A (3), 249–265.

Braine, G. (ed.) (1999) *Non-Native Educators in English Language Teaching*. Mahwah, NJ: Lawrence Erlbaum.

Brandon, E. (2009) Forget tuition: How retirees can attend college for free. *U.S. News & World Report*, 20 April. See http://money.usnews.com/money/articles/2009/04/20/forget-tuition-how-retirees-can-attend-college-for-free (accessed 25 April 2015).

Brandon, P. (2004) The child care arrangements of preschool-age children in immigrant families in the United States. *International Migration* 42 (1), 65–87.

Bromfield, C. (2006) PGCE secondary trainee teachers and effective behaviour management: An evaluation and commentary. *Support for Learning* 21 (4), 188–193.

Brophy, J. (2006) History of research on classroom management. In C.M. Evertson and C.S. Weinstein (eds) *Handbook on Classroom Management: Research, Practice, and Contemporary Issues* (pp. 17–43). Mahwah, NJ: Lawrence Erlbaum.

Brownstein, R. (2010) The gray and the brown: The generational mismatch. *National Journal*, 24 July. See http://www.nationaljournal.com/magazine/the-gray-and-the-brown-the-generational-mismatch-20100724 (accessed 27 August 2013).

Burden, P.R. (2003) *Classroom Management: Creating a Successful Learning Community*. Hoboken, NJ: Wiley/Jossey-Bass Education.

Bureau of Labor Statistics (2015a) Occupational Outlook Handbook, 2014–2015 Edition, Kindergarten and Elementary School Teachers, US Department of Labor. See http://www.bls.gov/ooh/education-training-and-library/kindergarten-and-elementary-school-teachers.htm (accessed 1 January 2015).

Bureau of Labor Statistics (2015b) Occupational Outlook Handbook, 2014–2015 Edition, High School Teachers, US Department of Labor. See http://www.bls.gov/ooh/education-training-and-library/high-school-teachers.htm (accessed 1 January 2015).

Bureau of Labor Statistics (2015c) Occupational Outlook Handbook, 2014–2015 Edition, Adult Literacy and High School Equivalency Diploma Teachers, US Department of Labor. See http://www.bls.gov/ooh/education-training-and-library/adult-literacy-and-ged-teachers.htm (accessed 1 January 2015).

Calderón, M., Slavin, R. and Sánchez, M. (2011) Effective instruction for English learners. *The Future of Children* 21 (1), 103–127.

Camarota, S.A. and Ziegler, K. (2015) *One in Five U.S. Residents Speaks Foreign Language at Home*. Washington, DC: Center for Immigration Studies. See http://cis.org/sites/cis.org/files/camarota-language-15.pdf (accessed 22 December 2015).

Carson, S. (2009) Creativity and the aging brain. *Psychology Today*, 30 March. See http://www.psychologytoday.com/blog/life-art/200903/creativity-and-the-aging-brain (accessed 27 April 2014).

Carstensen, L.L., Pasupathi, M., Mayr, U. and Nesselroade, J.R. (2000) Emotional experience in everyday life across the adult life span. *Journal of Personality and Social Psychology* 79 (4), 644–655.

Carstensen, L.L., Turan, B., Scheibe, S., Ram, N., Ersner-Hershfield, H., Samanez-Larkin, G.R., Brooks, K.P. and Nesselroade, J.R. (2011) Emotional experience improves with age: Evidence based on over 10 years of experience sampling. *Psychology and Aging* 26 (1), 21–33.

Caruso, H.M. and Woolley, A.W. (2008) Harnessing the power of emergent interdependence to promote diverse team collaboration. *Diversity and Groups* 11, 245–266.

Cave, D. (2010) A generation gap over immigration. *New York Times*, 17 May. See http://www.nytimes.com/2010/05/18/us/18divide.html?pagewanted=all (accessed 28 February 2014).

Center for Applied Linguistics (2010) *Education for Adult English Language Learners in the United States: Trends, Research, and Promising Practices*. Washington, DC: Author.

Charles, S.T., Reynolds, C.A. and Gatz, M. (2001) Age-related differences and change in positive and negative affect over 23 years. *Journal of Personality and Social Psychology* 80 (1), 136–151.

Charles, S.T. and Almeida, D.M. (2007) Genetic and environmental effects on daily life stressors: More evidence for greater variation in later life. *Psychology and Aging* 22 (2), 331–340.

Charles, S.T. and Carstensen, L.L. (2008) Unpleasant situations elicit different emotional responses in younger and older adults. *Psychology and Aging* 23 (3), 495–504.

Charles, C.M. and Senter, G.W. (2008) *Elementary Classroom Management* (5th edn). Boston, MA: Pearson.

Charles, S.T. and Carstensen, L.L. (2009) Social and emotional aging. *Annual Review of Psychology* 61, 383–409.

Chrisman F.P. and Crandall, J. (2007) *Passing the Torch: Strategies for Innovation in Community College ESL*. New York: Council for Advancement of Adult Literacy.

Cohen, G.D. (2000) *The Creative Age: Awakening Human Potential in the Second Half of Life*. New York: Avon Books.

Cohen, G.D. (2005) *The Mature Mind: The Positive Power of the Aging Brain*. New York: Basic Books.

Cohen, G.D. (2006) Research on creativity and aging: The positive impact of the arts on health and illness. *Generations* 30 (1), 7–15.

Coleman, D. (2015) The impact of immigration on the populations of the developed world and their ethnic composition. *Global Trends 2030*. See http://gt2030.com/tag/population-aging/ (accessed 23 December 2015).

Coll, C.G. and Szalacha, L.A. (2004) The multiple contexts of middle childhood. *The Future of Children* 14 (2), 81–97.

Corbin, J. and Strauss, A. (2008) *Basics of Qualitative Research: Techniques and Procedures for Developing Grounded Theory* (3rd edn). Thousand Oaks, CA: Sage.

Corporation for National and Community Service (2007) Baby boomers and volunteering: Findings from corporation research. March, 2007. See http://www.nationalservice.gov/sites/default/files/documents/boomer_research.pdf (accessed 3 March 2014).

Council for Adult & Experiential Learning (2011) Lifelong Learning Accounts: Helping to Build a More Competitive Workforce. See http://www.cael.org/all-resources (accessed 25 April 2015).

Council for Basic Education (2004) *Academic Atrophy: The Condition of the Liberal Arts in America's Public Schools*. Washington, DC: Author.

Crandall, J., Ingersoll, G. and Lopez, J. (2008) Adult ESL teacher credentialing and certification. Center for Adult English Language Acquisition. See http://www.cal.org/caela/esl_resources/briefs/tchrcred.html (accessed 1 January 2015).

Crow, G., Levine, L. and Nager, N. (1990) No more business as usual: Career changers who become teachers. *American Journal of Education* 98 (3), 197–223.

Csikszentmihalyi, M. (2013) *Creativity: The Psychology of Discovery and Invention*. New York: Harper Perennial.

Cummins, J. (2000) *Language, Power and Pedagogy: Bilingual Children in the Crossfire*. Clevedon: Multilingual Matters.

Danielson, C. (1996) *Enhancing Professional Practice: A Framework for Teaching*. Alexandria, VA: Association for Supervision and Curriculum Development.

Darling-Hammond, L. (2007) Race, inequality and educational accountability: The irony of 'No Child Left Behind'. *Race Ethnicity and Education* 10 (3), 245–260.

Dee, T.S. and Jacob, B.A. (2010) The impact of No Child Left Behind on students, teachers, and schools. *Brookings Papers on Economic Activity* Fall, 149–207.

Diaz, Z. and Mahadevan, L. (2011) Satisfying the demand for teachers. *Language Magazine*. See http://languagemagazine.com/?page_id=2106 (accessed 13 January 2015).

Dillenbourg, P. (1999) *Collaborative Learning: Cognitive and Computational Approaches*. New York: Elsevier Science.

Doerr, N.M. (ed.) (2009) *The Native Speaker Concept: Ethnographic Investigations of Native Speaker Effects*. Berlin: Walter de Gruyter.

Duff, P.A. and Uchida, Y. (1997) The negotiation of teachers' sociocultural identities and practices in postsecondary EFL classrooms. *TESOL Quarterly* 31, 451–486.

Edelman, M.W. and Jones, J.M. (2004) Separate and unequal: America's children, race, and poverty. *The Future of Children* 14 (2), 134–137.

Eisenberg, R. (2015) Colleges are failing America's midlife population. *Forbes*, 20 February. See http://www.forbes.com/sites/nextavenue/2015/02/20/colleges-are-failing-americas-midlife-population/ (accessed 21 April 2015).

Emmer, E.T. and Stough, L.M. (2001) Classroom management: A critical part of educational psychology, with implications for teacher education. *Educational Psychologist* 36 (2), 103–112.

Enayati, A. (2012) The aging brain: Why getting older just might be awesome. *CNN Health*. See http://www.cnn.com/2012/06/19/health/enayati-aging-brain-innovation/ (accessed 27 April 2014).

Erikson, E.H. (1963) *Childhood and Society* (2nd edn). New York: W.W. Norton.

Evertson, C.M. and Weinstein, C.S. (eds) (2006) *Handbook of Classroom Management: Research, Practice, and Contemporary Issues*. Mahwah, NJ: Lawrence Erlbaum.

Ewing, W.A. (2012) The future of a generation: How New Americans will help support retiring baby boomers. Immigration Policy Center, American Immigration Council. See http://www.immigrationpolicy.org/sites/default/files/docs/Future_of_a_Generation_021412.pdf (accessed 20 February 2014).

Feiman-Nemser, S. (2012) Beyond solo teaching. *Educational Leadership* 69 (8), 10–16.

FinAid.org (2015) Financial aid for older and nontraditional students. See http://www.finaid.org/otheraid/nontraditional.phtml (accessed 25 April 2015).

Fisher, C. (2012) Effective classroom management for new teachers. *ASCD Conference Daily*. See http://www.ascd.org/about-ascd.aspx (accessed 4 December 2014).

Fletcher, S.H. and Strong, M. (2009) Full-release and site-based mentoring of elementary grade new teachers: An analysis of changes in student achievement. *New Educator* 5, 329–341.

Flood, M. and Phillips, K.D. (2007) Creativity in older adults: A plethora of possibilities. *Issues in Mental Health Nursing* 28, 389–411.

Fratiglioni, L., Wang, H.X., Ericsson, K., Maytan, M. and Winblad, B. (2000) Influence of social network on occurrence of dementia: A community-based longitudinal study. *Lancet* 355, 1315–1319.

Freedman, M. (1999) *Prime Time: How Baby Boomers Will Revolutionize Retirement and Transform America*. New York: Public Affairs.

Freedman, M. (2007) *Encore: Finding Work that Matters in the Second Half of Life*. New York: Public Affairs.

Freedman, M. (2011) *The Big Shift: Navigating the New Stage Beyond Midlife*. New York: Public Affairs.

Freeman, D. and Richards, J.C. (eds) (1996) *Teacher Learning in Language Teaching*. Cambridge: Cambridge University Press.

Freeman, D. and Johnson, K.E. (1998) Reconceptualizing the knowledge-base of language teacher education. *TESOL Quarterly* 32 (3), 397–417.

Frey, W.H. (2011a) America's diverse future: Initial glimpses at the U.S. child population from the 2010 Census. Washington, DC: Metropolitan Policy Program, The Brookings Institution. See http://leavinsamericandemographics.wikispaces.com/file/view/America's%20Diverse%20Future%20by%20William%20Frey,%20short%20article.pdf/408933422/America's%20Diverse%20Future%20by%20William%20Frey,%20short%20article.pdf (accessed 6 September 2013).

Frey, W.H. (2011b) The new metro minority map: Regional shifts in Hispanics, Asians, and Blacks from Census 2010. Metropolitan Policy Program, The Brookings Institution. See https://www.brookings.edu/wp-content/uploads/2016/06/0831_census_race_frey.pdf (accessed 19 February 2014).

Frey, W.H. (2012a) Census projects new 'majority minority' tipping points. The Brookings Institution. See http://www.brookings.edu/research/opinions/2012/12/13-census-race-projections-frey (accessed 15 February 2014).

Frey, W.H. (2012b) Baby boomers had better embrace change. *The Washington Post*, 8 June. See http://www.washingtonpost.com/opinions/baby-boomers-had-better-embrace-change/2012/06/08/gJQAwe5jOV_story.html (accessed 30 August 2013).

Frey, W.H., Berube, A., Singer, A. and Wilson, J. (2011) Five Things the Census Revealed About America in 2011. The Brookings Institution. See http://www.brookings.edu/research/opinions/2011/12/20-census-demographics#3 (accessed 28 August 2013).

Frum, D. (2012) How we need to learn to say no to the elderly. *Newsweek*, 19 July. See http://www.newsweek.com/david-frum-how-we-need-learn-say-no-elderly-65093 (accessed 17 March 2014).

Fry, R. (2008) *The Role of Schools in the English Language Learner Achievement Gap*. Washington, DC: Pew Hispanic Center.

Fry, S.W. (2007) First-year teachers and induction support: Ups, downs, and in-betweens. *The Qualitative Report* 12 (2), 216–237.

Furlong, M., Morrison, G., and Pavelski, R. (2000) Trends in school psychology for the 21st century: Influences of school violence on professional change. *Psychology in the Schools* 37, 81–90.

Gándara, P. and Hopkins, M. (eds) (2010) *Forbidden Language: English Learners and Restrictive Language Policies*. New York: Teachers College Press.

Gardner, H. (1983) *Frames of Mind: The Theory of Multiple Intelligences*. New York: Basic Books.

Gardner, H. (1993) *Creating minds: An Anatomy of Creativity Seen Through the Lives of Freud, Einstein, Picasso, Stravinsky, Eliot, Graham, and Gandhi*. New York: Basic Books.

Gee, J.P. (1996) *Social Linguistics and Literacies: Ideology in Discourses* (2nd edn). London: Taylor & Francis.

Gladwell, M. (2008) *Outliers: The Story of Success*. New York: Little, Brown and Company.

Glaser, B.G. (2002) Conceptualization: On theory and theorizing using grounded theory. *International Journal of Qualitative Methods* 1 (2), 23–38.

Glei, D.A., Landau, D.A., Goldman, N., Chuang, Y.-L., Rodríguez, G. and Weinstein, M. (2005) Participating in social activities helps preserve cognitive function: An analysis of a longitudinal, population-based study of the elderly. *International Journal of Epidemiology* 34, 864–871.

Glymour, M.M., Weuve, J., Fay, M.E., Glass, T. and Berkman, L.F. (2008) Social ties and cognitive recovery after stroke: Does social integration promote cognitive resilience? *Neuroepidemiology* 31 (1), 10–20.

Golombek, P.R. (1998) A study of language teachers' personal practical knowledge. *TESOL Quarterly* 32, 447–464.

González, N., Moll, L. and Amanti, C. (2005) *Funds of Knowledge: Theorizing Practices in Households, Communities, and Classrooms*. Mahwah, NH: Lawrence Erlbaum.

Goodson, I.F. (1992) Sponsoring the teacher's voice: Teachers' lives and teacher development. In A. Hargreaves and M.G. Fullan (eds) *Understanding Teacher Development* (pp. 110–121). New York: Teachers College Press.

Goodson, I.F. and Walker, R. (1991) *Biography, Identity and Schooling: Episodes in Educational Research*. London: The Falmer Press.

Goodwin, B. (2012) Research says new teachers face three common challenges. *Educational Leadership* 69 (8), 84–85.

Gregory, M. (2006) From Shakespeare on the page to Shakespeare on the stage: What I learned about teaching in acting class. *Pedagogy: Critical Approaches to Teaching Literature, Language, Composition, and Culture* 6 (2), 309–325.

Grossman, P.L. (1992) Why models matter: An alternate view of professional growth in teaching. *Review of Educational Research* 62 (2), 171–179.

Grossman, P. and Davis, E. (2012) Mentoring that fits. *Educational Leadership* 69 (8), 54–57.

Hanna, G. (2006) Focus on creativity and aging in the United States. *Generations* 30 (1), 47–49.

Hannaway, J. and Hamilton, L. (2008) Performance-based accountability policies: Implications for school and classroom practices. Washington, DC: The Urban Institute. See http://www.urban.org/sites/default/files/alfresco/publication-pdfs/411779-Accountability-Policies.PDF (accessed 19 January 2015).

Heller, M. (2003) Globalization, the new economy, and the commodification of language and identity. *Journal of Sociolinguistics* 7 (4), 473–492.

Hellmich, N. (2010) Baby boomers by the numbers: Census reveals trends. *USA Today*, 3 March. See http://usatoday30.usatoday.com/news/nation/census/2009-11-10-topblline10_ST_N.htm (accessed 27 February 2014).

Hernandez, D.J. (2004) Demographic change and the life circumstances of immigrant families. *The Future of Children* 14 (2), 17–47.

Holmes Group. (1986) *Tomorrow's Teachers: A Report of the Holmes Group*. East Lansing, MI: Author.

Huberman, M. (1993) *The Lives of Teachers*. New York: Teachers College Press.

Humes, K.R., Jones, N.A. and Ramirez, R.R. (2011) Overview of race and Hispanic origin: 2010. 2010 Census Briefs. US Census. See http://www.census.gov/prod/cen2010/briefs/c2010br-02.pdf (accessed 15 February 2014).

Ingersoll, R. and Kralik, J.M. (2004) *The Impact of Mentoring on Teacher Retention: What the Research Says*. Denver, CO: Education Commission of the States.

Ingersoll, R.M. and Smith, T.M. (2003) The wrong solution to the teacher shortage. *Educational Leadership* 60 (8), 30–33.

Isaacowitz, D.M., Wadlinger, H.A., Goren, D. and Wilson, H.R. (2006) Is there an age-related positivity effect in visual attention? A comparison of two methodologies. *Emotion* 6 (3) 511–516.

Isaacs, J.B. (2009) Spending on children and the elderly. An Issue Brief, The Brookings Institution. See https://www.brookings.edu/wp-content/uploads/2016/06/1105_children_elderly_isaacs.pdf (accessed 27 February 2014).

Jacobsen, L.A., Kent, M., Lee, M. and Mather, M. (2011) 'America's Aging Population'. *Population Bulletin* 66 (1). See http://www.prb.org/pdf11/aging-in-america.pdf (accessed 13 February 2014).

Jaminet, P. and Jaminet, S.C. (2012) The rise—and fall?—of American health. *Psychology Today*, 13 November. See http://www.psychologytoday.com/blog/perfect-health-diet/201211/the-rise-and-fall-american-health (accessed 9 February 2014).

Johnson, K.E. (1999) *Understanding Language Teaching: Reasoning in Action.* Boston, MA: Heinle & Heinle.

Johnson, K.E. (ed.) (2000) *Teacher Education.* Alexandria, VA: TESOL.

Johnson, K.E. and Golombek, P.R. (2002) Inquiry into experience: Teacher's personal and professional growth. In K.E. Johnson and P.R. Golombeck (eds) *Teachers' Narrative Inquiry as Professional Development* (pp. 1–14). Cambridge: Cambridge University Press.

Johnson, S.M. (2004) *Finders and Keepers: Helping New Teachers Survive and Thrive in Our Schools.* San Francisco, CA: Jossey-Bass.

Johnson, S.M., Berg, J.H. and Donaldson, M.L. (2005) Who stay in teaching and why: A review of the literature on teacher retention. Washington, DC: AARP. See http://assets.aarp.org/www.aarp.org_/articles/NRTA/Harvard_report.pdf (accessed 29 April 2015).

John-Steiner, V. (1997) *Notebooks of the Mind: Explorations of Thinking.* Oxford: Oxford University Press.

Kanno, Y. and Stuart, C. (2011) Learning to become a second language teacher: Identities-in-practice. *Modern Language Journal* 95, 236–252.

Karoly, L.A. and Gonzalez, G.C. (2011) Early care and education for children in immigrant families. *The Future of Children* 21 (1), 71–101.

Kersting, K. (2003) What exactly is creativity? *Monitor on Psychology* 34 (10), 40. See http://www.apa.org/monitor/nov03/creativity.aspx (accessed 26 April 2014).

Kim, S., Hasher, L. and Zacks, R.T. (2007) Aging and a benefit of distractibility. *Psychonomic Bulletin & Review* 14 (2), 301–305.

Lane, M. (2005) Creativity and spirituality in nursing. *Holistic Nursing Practice* 19 (3), 122–125.

Larotta, C. (2009) Final thoughts on community in adult ESL. *New Directions for Adult and Continuing Education* 121, 75–77.

Laslett, P. (1991) *A Fresh Map of Life: The Emergence of the Third Age.* Cambridge, MA: Harvard University Press.

Lave, J. (1996) Teaching, as learning, in practice. *Mind, Culture, and Activity* 3, 149–164.

Lave, J. and Wenger, E. (1991) *Situated Learning: Legitimate Peripheral Participation.* Cambridge: Cambridge University Press.

Lawrence-Lightfoot, S. (2009) *The Third Chapter: Passion, Risk, and Adventure in the 25 Years After 50.* New York: Farrar, Straus and Giroux.

Leung, A.K., Maddux, W.W., Galinsky, A.D. and Chiu, C. (2008) Multicultural experience enhances creativity: The when and how. *American Psychologist* 63, 169–181.

Leung, A.K. and Chiu, C. (2010) Multicultural experience, idea receptiveness, and creativity. *Journal of Cross-Cultural Psychology* 41, 723–741.

Leung, C., Harris, R. and Rampton, B. (1997) The idealized native speaker, reified ethnicities, and classroom realities. *TESOL Quarterly* 31 (3), 543–560.

Levy, B.R. (2003) Mind matters: Cognitive and physical effects of aging self-stereotypes. *Journals of Gerontology, Series B: Psychological Sciences and Social Sciences* 58, 203–211.

Levy, B. (2009) Stereotype embodiment: A psychosocial approach to aging. *Current Directions in Psychological Science* 18 (6), 332–336.

Levy, B.R., Slade, M.D., Kunkel, S.R. and Kasl, S.V. (2002) Longevity increased by positive self-perceptions of aging. *Journal of Personality and Social Psychology* 83, 261–270.

Levy, B.R. and Leifheit-Limson, E. (2009) The stereotype matching effect: Greater influence on functioning when age stereotypes correspond to outcomes. *Psychology and Aging* 24, 230–233.

Levy, B.R., Zonderman, A.B., Slade, M.D. and Ferrucci, L. (2009) Age stereotypes held earlier in life predict cardiovascular events in later life. *Psychological Science* 20 (3), 296–298.

Levy, B.R., Slade, M.D., Murphy, T.E. and Gill, T.M. (2012) Association between positive age stereotypes and recovery from disability in older persons. *Journal of American Medical Association* 308 (19), 1972–1973.

Liew, W.M. (2013) Effects beyond effectiveness: Teaching as a performative act. *Curriculum Inquiry* 43 (2), 261–288.

Lopez, M.H. and Velasco, G. (2011) Childhood poverty among Hispanics sets record, leads nation. Pew Hispanic Center. See http://www.pewhispanic.org/files/2011/10/147. pdf (accessed 6 September 2013).

Lustig, C., Shah, P., Seidler, R. and Reuter-Lorenz, P.A. (2009) Aging, training, and the brain: A review and future directions. *Neuropsychological Review* 19, 504–522.

Maddux, W.W. and Galinsky, A.D. (2009) Cultural borders and mental barriers: The relationship between living abroad and creativity. *Journal of Personality and Social Psychology* 96 (5), 1047–1061.

Mannix, E. and Neale, M.A. (2005) What differences make a differences?: The promise and reality of diverse teams in organizations. *Psychological Science in the Public Interest* 6 (2), 31–55.

Marzano, R.J. and Marzano, J.S. (2003) The key to classroom management. *Educational Leadership* 61, 6–13.

Mather, M. and Carstensen, L.L. (2003) Aging and attentional biases for emotional faces. *Psychological Science* 14 (5), 409–415.

Mather, M., Canli, T., English, T., Whitfield, S., Wais, P., Ochsner, K., Gabrieli, J.D.E. and Carstensen, L.L. (2004) Amygdala responses to emotionally valenced stimuli in older and younger adults. *Psychological Science* 15 (4), 259–263.

Mayotte, G. (2003) Stepping stones to success: Previously developed career competencies and their benefits to career switchers transitioning to teaching. *Teaching and Teacher Education* 19, 681–695.

McDonald, M. (2014) Small U.S. colleges battle death spiral as enrollment drops. *Bloomberg Business*, 14 April. See http://www.bloomberg.com/news/articles/2014-04-14/small-u-s-colleges-battle-death-spiral-as-enrollment-drops (accessed 27 April 2015).

McHugh, M., Gelatt, J. and Fix, M. (2007) Adult English language instruction in the United States: Determining need and investing wisely. Washington, DC: Migration Policy Institute. See www.migrationpolicy.org/pubs/NCIIP_English_Instruction073107.pdf (accessed 12 January 2015).

Meier, D. and Wood, G. (eds) (2004) *Many Children Left Behind: How the No Child Left Behind Act is Damaging our Children and our Schools*. Boston, MA: Beacon Press.

Mensah, G.A. and Brown, D.W. (2007) An overview of cardiovascular disease burden in the United States. *Health Affairs* 26 (1), 38–48. See http://content.healthaffairs.org/content/26/1/38.full.pdf+html (accessed 9 February 2014).

MetLife Foundation/Civic Ventures (2005) New face of work survey. Author. See http://www.issuelab.org/resources/10398/10398.pdf (accessed 8 June 2015).

Morse, A. (2014) Instate tuition and unauthorized immigrant students. Washington, DC: National Conference of State Legislatures. See http://www.ncsl.org/research/immigration/in-state-tuition-and-unauthorized-immigrants.aspx (See March 8 2014).

Myers, D. (2007) *Immigrants and Boomers: Forging a New Social Contract for the Future of America.* New York: Russell Sage Foundation.

National Association of State Boards of Education (2003) The complete curriculum: Ensuring a place for the arts and foreign languages in America's schools. Alexandria, VA: Author.

National Commission on Teaching and America's Future (2011) Nation's schools facing largest teacher retirement in history. See http://nctaf.org/announcements/nations-schools-facing-largest-teacher-retirement-wave-in-history/ (accessed 13 January 2015).

National Education Association (n.d.) Research Spotlight on Recruiting & Retaining Highly Qualified Teachers: Recruiting & Retaining a Highly Qualified, Diverse Teaching Workforce. See http://www.nea.org/tools/17054.htm (accessed 4 December 2014).

National Research Council (2012) *Aging and the Macroeconomy: Long-Term Implications of an Older Population.* Committee on the Long-Run Macroeconomic Effects of the Aging US Population. Board on Mathematical Sciences and their Applications, Division on Engineering and Physical Sciences and Committee on Population, Division of Behavioral and Social Sciences and Education. Washington, DC: The National Academies Press.

Neugarten, D. (1996) *The Meanings of Age: Selected Papers of Bernice L. Neugarten.* Chicago, IL: University of Chicago Press.

Nicol, D. (2010) From monologue to dialogue: Improving written feedback processes in mass higher education. *Assessment & Evaluation in Higher Education* 35 (5), 501–517.

Nieto, S. and Bode, P. (2011) *Affirming Diversity: The Sociopolitical Context of Multicultural Education* (6th edn). New York: Allyn & Bacon.

Nightingale, D.S. and Fix, M. (2004) Economic and labor market trends. *The Future of Children* 14 (2), 49–59.

Norton, B. (1997) Language, identity, and the ownership of English. *TESOL Quarterly* 31 (3), 409–429.

Novelli, W.D. and Goyer, A. (2004) Commentary 4. *The Future of Children* 14 (2), 155–159.

Orgeta, V. (2009) Specificity of age differences in emotion regulation. *Aging & Mental Health* 13 (6), 818–826.

Passel, J. (2007) *Growing Share of Immigrants Choosing Naturalization.* Washington, DC: Pew Hispanic Center.

Pavlenko, A. and Blackledge, A. (eds) (2004) *Negotiation of Identities in Multilingual Contexts.* Clevedon: Multilingual Matters.

Peace Corps (2010) Peace Corps reaches 40-year high in number of volunteers. See https://www.latintrends.com/peace-corps-reaches-40-year-high-in-number-of-volunteers/ (accessed 21 April 2015).

Peregoy, S.F. and Boyle, O.F. (2005) *Reading, Writing, and Learning in ESL: A Resource Book for K-12 Teachers* (4th edn). Boston, MA: Pearson.

Perlstein, S. (2006) Creative expression and quality of life: A vital relationship for elders. *Generations* 30 (1), 5–6.

Peterson, S.S. (2008) *Writing Across the Curriculum: All Teachers Teach Writing.* Winnipeg: Portage & Main Press.

Pew Hispanic Center (2013) A nation of immigrants. See http://www.pewhispanic.org/files/2013/01/statistical_portrait_final_jan_29.pdf (accessed 30 August 2013).

Pew Research Center (2011) The generation gap and the 2012 election. See http://www.people-press.org/files/legacy-pdf/11-3-11%20Generations%20Release.pdf (accessed 6 September 2013).

Pifer, A. and Bronte, L. (eds) (1986) *Our Ageing Society: Paradox and Promise.* New York: Carnegie Corporation of New York.

Pineau, E.L. (1994) Teaching is performance: Reconceptualizing a problematic metaphor. *American Educational Research Journal* 31 (1), 3–25.

Priyadharshini, E. and Robinson-Pant, A. (2003) The attractions of teaching: An investigation of why people change careers to teach. *Journal of Education for Teaching* 29, 95–112.

Rajadurai, J. (2010) 'Malays are expected to speak Malay': Community ideologies, language use and the negotiation of identities. *Journal of Language, Identity, and Education* 9, 91–106.

Ramscar, M., Hendrix, P., Shaoul, C., Milin, P. and Baayen, H. (2014) The myth of cognitive decline: Non-linear dynamics of lifelong learning. *Topics in Cognitive Science* 6, 5–42.

Reupert, A. and Woodcock, S. (2010) Success and near misses: Pre-service teachers' use, confidence and success in various classroom management strategies. *Teaching and Teacher Education* 26, 1261–1268.

Richards, J.C. (2008) Second language teacher education today. *RELC Journal* 39, 158–177.

Ryff, C.D. and Singer, B.H. (2001) Integrating emotions into the study of social relationships and health. In C.D. Ryff and B.H. Singer (eds) *Emotion, Social Relationships, and Health* (pp. 3–22). Oxford: Oxford University Press.

Saad, L. (2012) No Child Left Behind rated more negatively than positively. *Gallup,* 20 August. See http://www.gallup.com/poll/156800/no-child-left-behind-rated-negatively-positively.aspx (accessed 16 July 2015).

Sacks, P. (1999) *Standardized Minds: The High Price of America's Testing Culture and What We Can Do to Change it.* Cambridge, MA: Perseus Books.

Salthouse, T. (2010) *Major Issues in Cognitive Aging.* Oxford: Oxford University Press.

Santos, F. (2007) Demand for English lessons outstrips supply. *New York Times,* 27 February. See http://www.nytimes.com/2007/02/27/education/27esl.html?pagewanted=1 (accessed 16 February 2011).

Saunders, W. and Goldenberg, C. (2010) Research to guide English language development instruction. In California Department of Education (ed.) *Improving Education for English Learners: Research-Based Approaches* (pp. 21–81). Sacramento, CA: California Department of Education.

Scarcella, R.C. (2002) Some key factors affecting English learners' development of advanced literacy. In M.J. Schleppegrell and M.C. Colombi (eds) *Developing Advanced Literacy in First and Second Languages: Meaning with Power* (pp. 209–226). Mahwah, NJ: Lawrence Erlbaum.

Schaetzel, K., Peyton, J.K. and Burt, M. (2007) Professional Development for Adult ESL Practitioners: Building Capacity. The Center for Adult English Language Acquisition. See http://www.cal.org/caela/esl_resources/briefs/profdev.html (accessed 31 December 2014)

Schecter, S.R. and Bayley, R. (1997) Language socialization practices and cultural identity: Case studies of Mexican-descent families in California and Texas. *TESOL Quarterly* 31 (3), 513–541.

Schmidt, P.B. (2006) Creativity and coping in later life. *Generations* 30 (1), 27–31.

Schwartz, A. (1982) Meaningful work. *Ethics* 92 (4), 634–646.

Searle, J.R. (1969) *Speech Acts: An Essay in the Philosophy of Language.* Cambridge: Cambridge University Press.

Selim, L. (2014) Colleges are failing their biggest group of students. *The Atlantic,* 29 January. See http://www.theatlantic.com/education/archive/2014/01/colleges-are-failing-their-biggest-group-of-students/283435/ (accessed 24 April 2015).

Sheehy, G. (1995) *New Passages: Mapping Your Life Across Time*. New York: Ballantine Books.

Sherman, A. (2006) Toward a creative culture: Lifelong learning through the arts. *Generations* 30 (1), 42–46.

Shields, P., Esch, C., Humphrey, D., Wechsler, M., Chang-Ross, C. and Gallagher, A. (2003) *The Status of the Teaching Profession 2003: Research Findings and Policy Recommendations*. Santa Cruz, CA: Center for the Future of Teaching and Learning.

Shields, M.K. and Behrman, R.E. (2004) Children of immigrant families: Analysis and recommendations. *The Future of Children* 14 (2), 4–15.

Shih, M., Pittinsky, T.L. and Ambady, N. (1999) Stereotype susceptibility: Identity salience and shifts in quantitative performance. *Psychological Science* 10, 80–83.

Shin, S.J. (2005) *Developing in Two Languages: Korean Children in America*. Clevedon: Multilingual Matters.

Shin, S.J. (2006) Learning to teach writing through tutoring and journal writing. *Teachers and Teaching: Theory and Practice* 12 (3), 325–345.

Shin, S.J. (2013) *Bilingualism in Schools and Society: Language, Identity, and Policy*. New York/London: Routledge.

Simonton, D.K. (2010) Creativity in highly eminent individuals. In J.C. Kaufman and R.J. Sternberg (eds) *The Cambridge Handbook on Creativity* (pp. 174–188). Cambridge: Cambridge University Press.

Singh-Manoux, A., Richards, M. and Marmot, M. (2003) Leisure activities and cognitive function in middle age: Evidence from the Whitehall II study. *Journal of Epidemiology and Community Health* 57 (11), 907–913.

Smith, B.L. and MacGregor, J.T. (1992). *Collaborative Learning: A Source Book for Higher Education*. University Park, PA: National Center on Postsecondary Teaching, Learning, and Assessment.

Smith, G.E., Housen, P., Yaffe, K., Ruff, R., Kennison, R.F., Mahncke, H.W. and Zelinski, E.M. (2009) A cognitive training program based on principles of brain plasticity: Results from the Improvement in Memory with Plasticity-based Adaptive Cognitive Training (IMPACT) Study. *Journal of American Geriatrics Society* 57, 594–603.

Smith, T.M. and Ingersoll, R.M. (2004) What are the effects of induction and mentoring on beginning teacher turnover? *American Educational Research Journal* 41 (3), 681–714.

Steele, C.M. (2010) *Whistling Vivaldi: How Stereotypes Affect Us and What We Can Do*. New York: Norton.

Steele, C.M. and Aronson, J. (1995) Stereotype threat and the intellectual test performance of African Americans. *Journal of Personality and Social Psychology* 69, 797–811.

Stoughton, E.H. (2007) 'How will I get them to behave?': Preservice teachers reflect on classroom management. *Teaching and Teacher Education* 23 (7), 1024–1037.

Strong, M. (2009) *Effective Teacher Induction and Mentoring: Assessing the Evidence*. New York: Teachers College Press.

Tannen, B. (1994) *Talking from 9 to 5: Women and Men at Work*. New York: Quill.

Taylor, J. and Lamoreaux, A. (2008) Teaching with the brain in mind. *New Directions for Continuing and Adult Education* 119, 49–59.

Teranishi, R.T., Suárez-Orosco, C. and Suárez-Orosco, M. (2011) Immigrants in community colleges. *The Future of Children* 21 (1), 153–169.

Terkel, S. (1974) *Working: People Talk About What They Do All Day and How They Feel About What They Do*. New York: Ballantine Books.

Terrazas, A. and Fix, M (2009) *The Binational Option: Meeting the Instructional Needs of Limited English Proficient Students*. Washington, DC: Migration Policy Institute.

Tienda, M. and Haskins, R. (2011) Immigrant children: Introducing the issue. *The Future of Children*, 21 (1), 3–18.

Tsang, W.K. (2004) Teachers' personal practical knowledge and interactive decisions. *Language Teaching Research* 8 (2), 163–198.

United Nations Population Fund (2012) Ageing in the Twenty-First Century: A celebration and a challenge. Executive Summary. United Nations Population Fund.

US Census Bureau (2012a) US Census Bureau Projections Show a Slower Growing, Older, More Diverse Nation a Half Century from Now. See http://www.census.gov/newsroom/releases/archives/population/cb12-243.html (accessed 30 August 2013).

US Census Bureau (2012b) Most Children Younger Than Age 1 are Minorities, Census Bureau Reports. See https://www.census.gov/newsroom/releases/archives/population/cb12-90.html (accessed 19 February 2014).

US Department of Education (2015) Teacher shortage areas: Nationwide Listing 1990–1991 through 2015–2016. US Department of Education, Office of Postsecondary Education. See http://www2.ed.gov/about/offices/list/ope/pol/tsa.doc (accessed 1 January 2015).

US Department of Education, National Center for Education Statistics (2011) The Condition of Education 2011 (NCES 2011-033), Table A-20-1. See https://nces.ed.gov/pubs2011/2011033.pdf (accessed 4 May 2012).

US Department of Education, National Clearinghouse for English Language Acquisition and Language Instruction Educational Programs (NCELA) (2011) The growing numbers of English learner students. See http://www.ncela.us/files/uploads/9/growingLEP_0809.pdf (accessed 19 October 2011).

US Department of Education, Office of Vocational and Adult Education (2011) National Reporting System. See from: http://wdcrobcolp01.ed.gov/CFAPPS/OVAE/NRS/reports/index.cfm (accessed 16 February 2011).

Vacarr, B. (2014) An aging America: Higher education's new frontier. *The Chronicle of Higher Education*, 8 December. See http://chronicle.com/article/An-Aging-America-Higher/150425/ (accessed 24 April 2015).

Valdés, G. (2001) *Learning and Not Learning English: Latino Students in American Schools*. New York: Teachers College Press.

Van de Water, P.N. (2008) Immigration and Social Security. Center on Budget and Policy Priorities. See http://www.cbpp.org/files/11-20-08socsec.pdf (accessed 23 February 2014).

Van Der Werf, M. and Sabatier, G. (2009) The College of 2020: Students. Washington, DC: Chronicle Research Services. See http://www.uwec.edu/CETL/bundles/upload/college2020-dl.pdf (accessed 24 April 2015).

Varghese, M., Morgan, B., Johnston, B. and Johnson, K.A. (2005) Theorizing language teacher identity: Three perspectives and beyond. *Journal of Language, Identity, and Education* 4 (1), 21–44.

Vygotsky, L.S. (1978) *Mind in Society*. Cambridge, MA: Harvard University Press.

Walker, T. (2014) NEA Survey: Nearly half of teachers consider leaving profession due to standardized testing. *NEA Today*. See http://neatoday.org/2014/11/02/nea-survey-nearly-half-of-teachers-consider-leaving-profession-due-to-standardized-testing-2/ (accessed 19 March 2015).

Wallace, D.B. and Gruber, H.E. (eds) (1989) *Creative People at Work: Twelve Cognitive Case Studies*. Oxford: Oxford University Press.

Wallace, K.R. (2001) *Relative/Outsider: The Art and Politics of Identity Among Mixed Heritage Students*. Westport, CT: Ablex.

Weintraub, A. (2010) *Selling the Fountain of Youth: How the Anti-Aging Industry Made a Disease Out of Getting Old – and Made Billions*. New York: Basic Books.

Wenger, E. (1998) *Communities of Practice: Learning, Meaning, and Identity*. Cambridge: Cambridge University Press.

Williams, J. (2010) Constructing a new professional identity: Career change into teaching. *Teaching and Teacher Education* 26, 639–647.

Wong, A. (2015) Life after No Child Left Behind. *The Atlantic*, 8 July. See http://www.theatlantic.com/education/archive/2015/07/life-after-no-child-left-behind/397937/?google_editors_picks=true (accessed 16 July 2015).

Wrigley, H.S., Chen, J., White, S. and Soroui, J. (2009) Assessing the literacy skills of adult immigrants and adult English language learners. *New Directions for Adult and Continuing Education* 121, 5–24.

Zarate, M. and Pachon, H. (2006) *Perceptions of College Financial Aid among California Latino Youth.* Los Angeles, CA: Tomás Rivera Policy Institute.

Zehr, M.A. (2008) Research on push-in vs. pull-out. *Education Week*, 24 June. See http://blogs.edweek.org/edweek/learning-the-language/2008/06/research_on_pushin_versus_push.html (accessed 19 January 2015).

Zeichner, K.M. (2003) The adequacies and inadequacies of three current strategies to recruit, prepare, and retain the best teachers for all students. *Teachers College Record* 105 (3), 490–519.

Zeichner, K. and Gore, J. (1990) Teacher socialization. In W.R. Houston (ed.) *Handbook of Research on Teacher Education* (pp. 329–348). New York: Macmillan.

Author Index

Subject Index